Routledge Revivals

Form and Spirit

First published in 1951 *Form and Spirit* deals with two primary questions regarding religion- a) the nature of religion as a permanent need in human life, and its relation to the cults and creeds in which it has been embodied, and b) whether what is admittedly a crying need of our time can be met by the revival of religious forms which have lost their hold. An attempt is made to trace the evolution of religion, and a brief survey is given of the development of the chief world religions. The object is not to show that any of these can be accounted 'truer' than the rest but rather to see what were the reasons for the forms that they have taken, and what elements and tendencies are common to them, as throwing light both on the meaning of religion and on the needs of man's spiritual nature. This is an essential read for general readers interested in religion.

Form and Spirit

A Study in Religion

J.H. Badley

Routledge
Taylor & Francis Group

First published in 1951
by Routledge & Kegan Paul

This edition first published in 2023 by Routledge
4 Park Square, Milton Park, Abingdon, Oxon, OX14 4RN

and by Routledge
605 Third Avenue, New York, NY 10017

Routledge is an imprint of the Taylor & Francis Group, an informa business

Publisher's Note
The publisher has gone to great lengths to ensure the quality of this reprint but points out that some imperfections in the original copies may be apparent.

Disclaimer
The publisher has made every effort to trace copyright holders and welcomes correspondence from those they have been unable to contact.

A Library of Congress record exists under LCCN: 51006474

ISBN: 978-1-032-61029-0 (hbk)
ISBN: 978-1-003-46166-1 (ebk)
ISBN: 978-1-032-61032-0 (pbk)

Book DOI 10.4324/9781003461661

FORM AND SPIRIT

A STUDY IN RELIGION

by

J. H. BADLEY

FORM AND SPIRIT

First published in 1951 by Routledge and Kegan Paul, Ltd.
Reissued in 1971 by Kennikat Press by arrangement
Library of Congress Catalog Card No: 77-113347
ISBN 0-8046-1398-2

Manufactured by Taylor Publishing Company Dallas, Texas

ESSAY AND GENERAL LITERATURE INDEX REPRINT SERIES

PREFACE

In a book that treats of so vast a subject as religion, it should be made clear at the outset in what way it will be approached.

Two questions are here under discussion. One is concerned with the nature of religion as a permanent need in human life, and its relation to the cults and creeds in which it has been embodied. The other is whether what is admittedly a crying need of our time can be met by the revival of religious forms which have lost their hold.

In the first place, then, an attempt is made to trace the evolution of religion, and a brief survey is given of the development of the chief world-religions. The object is not to show that any one of these can be accounted 'truer' than the rest, but rather to see what were the reasons for the forms that they have taken, and what elements and tendencies are common to them, as throwing light both on the meaning of religion and on the needs of man's spiritual nature.

There is here a danger, which besets any comparative study of existing religions. The real essence of each can hardly be discovered by one who looks at it only from the outside, and whose attention is apt to be concentrated on the points of greatest difference which it shows from ideas and feelings to which he is himself habituated. On the other hand, it is hardly less difficult to look with objective impartiality on the one with which he is most familiar. Either he is likely to be blind to what in others he would recognise as logical or ethical weaknesses, or else reaction against its authority may lead him to dwell on such weaknesses to the exclusion of much that is not affected by them, and so to condemn what is good together with the bad.

The writer's own standpoint is therefore a material factor. In the present case, though by no means that of Dr. Thwackum ('When I mention religion I mean the Christian religion; and not only the Christian religion but the Protestant religion; and not only the Protestant religion, but the Church of England'), it is that of one who, thanks to the inherited tradition and mental make-up of Western civilisation, finds religion most fully exemplified in the spirit of Christianity; and moreover of one whose Protestant upbringing has tended to give to individual judgment and conscience a greater weight than that of tradition and authority.

The second question is that presented by the decay of religion both in our own country and in others at the present time. Few would deny that, in the forms of doctrine and observance with which it has long been associated, it no longer holds the place that it held even a generation or two ago. In the Western world and wherever Western influences are predominant the decay of institutional religion is the subject of grave concern to religious leaders of all creeds and denominations. Thus in our own country a bishop,[1] writing of the historical development and present position of the Church of England, has said: 'The modern world seems to be ever more completely self-absorbed and self-satisfied. It has no use for religion in any form.' And in another passage he speaks of 'the waning tradition of Christian feeling' and 'the general abandonment of Christian principles'.

This cannot be dismissed as the judgment, possibly mistaken, of a single observer. In an account by various writers of the attitude of the men serving in the army during the war of 1914–1918 towards religion and the Christian Churches, it was said that 'about ten per cent. were in vital relation to Churches, and another ten per cent. were nominal adherents. The remaining eighty per cent. were quite outside.' And again: 'it was generally agreed that the men as a whole had little or no use for the Churches. They were regarded as effete institutions out of touch with real life, too much concerned with their own interests, and greatly hampered by their disunion.'[2]

To most people today the Church of their fathers is no longer their spiritual home. To some it stands for the memory of a prison from which they are thankful to have escaped. To others it retains, like the

[1] Dr. H. Hensley Henson, in *The Church of England*.

[2] Taken from an article on 'The Army and Religion', in the *Spectator* of 2nd February 1940.

buildings that were its fitting outward expression in ages when it held a great and real part in men's lives, a beauty rich with old associations of symbols and stories of noble effort and high ideals; but now is hardly more than an empty shell, with little service for human needs in its repetition of formulas that once held living truth and shook the world. To the younger generations its language is for the most part unintelligible; in its warnings and promises there is little that seems to them either real or attractive. If this is religion, they feel, then religion is a relic of an outgrown past, serving now only as hindrance to the freedom they demand.

To those who regard religion as bound up with membership of some Church this is indeed a serious state of things. To them all the evils of the time are an inevitable outcome of the abandonment of what has long been held to give its strongest sanction to morality. In the words of the Dean of St. Paul's,[1] 'The past thirty years have shown a world-wide weakening of the hold of religion on men's minds. Whatever may be the cause, civilised men everywhere have come to doubt or reject the beliefs about God which their fathers held. Can it be said that men are nobler, more just, more compassionate in their dealings? There has been a disastrous decay of the qualities of human character.' It is no wonder that the Churches should view these tendencies with the profoundest concern, and that the late Archbishop of Canterbury should have declared the greatest need of our time to be a national return to religion.

But is this—in the sense in which he was using the term—now possible? When a building no longer meets the requirements of an age very different from that in which it was designed, there comes the question whether by any alterations and additions it can be adapted to the new needs, or must be rebuilt either on the old foundations or on a new site. Those who have grown deeply attached to their old home will wish to continue living in it still in spite of all its drawbacks. But at last there comes a generation that can put up with them no longer; even if another has not yet been found to satisfy its needs, it prefers to make shift with some temporary dwelling until it can find what it requires.

So it is now with religion. As a result of changed conditions and

[1] Dr. W. R. Matthews, in his Warburton Lecture on *Morals Secular and Supernatural.*

needs that it can no longer satisfy, a structure that for some forty generations has been a centre of our national life is now fast falling into disuse. Among tendencies growing in momentum throughout the past century have been: the effect of scientific thought and method in forming a new mental background and replacing much that was held to be the infallible teaching of religion; concern with our present life and its possibilities, and with our relations with each other in the actual world, rather than with a life to come; and recognition that conclusions reached by men who lived under conditions quite different from our own, and sanctions of conduct which they found valid, cannot be accepted as equally certain for us and as giving sure guidance in meeting the problems of modern life.

But if, for reasons of this kind, the drift away from long-established forms of religion is seen as a tendency that cannot now be reversed, must we take this, as some do, to show that religion belonged only to a more childish stage of human development and, having played its part for good and ill, is now, in the maturer life of the race, to be left behind as concerned only with rules and toys of the nursery? To answer such a question we must distinguish between *religion* and *religions*—between what is a universal need of the human spirit and the forms and institutions in which from time to time the need has found embodiment. We need not assume that religion has been lost if some form in which it once took shape as a living growth has now ceased to furnish it with the means of vital expression, and if dogmas with which it has been overlaid have lost their hold, together with an ecclesiasticism which has done much to stifle its spirit. The value of religion does not lie in these. Its essential quality is to be sought rather in the spiritual attitude—the faith—that underlies and finds expression not merely in some outward form but in the whole way of life that is its outcome.

It is with this distinction that the present study is concerned. Starting with the assumption that there is a common element which gives to a particular outlook and way of life a religious character, it attempts to trace in outline certain aspects of the evolution of religion, from earlier developments of which traces have survived into historical times, to the foundation and growth of the chief world-religions, with the main trends of thought and feeling to which they give embodiment. Such a survey, partial as it must be, may at least help to make clearer the grounds for holding that religion is a permanent factor in human nature; one which, through many different modes of expression, has played a leading part in the spiritual development of mankind, and must still, under whatever form, continue to do so in the future.

This book, then, is addressed not to those to whom religion is something set forth, to their full satisfaction, in the doctrines and worship of the Churches; nor yet to those to whom it has no meaning and no place in the modern world; but rather to any who may feel that without some kind of faith and worship fulness of life is no more possible than without beauty or affection, and who see in the life of the spirit that which is of greatest moment in any age.

J. H. BADLEY.
Cholesbury

Note: It would serve no useful purpose to give a list—it would be a long one—of all the books, in addition to those named in the text or in the notes, consulted in writing the following chapters. Any readers who are interested in the comparative study of religions will welcome the series now being issued in Hutchinson's University Library under the general title of *World Religions*. The introductory volume, *The Beginnings of Religion*, written by Professor E. C. James, is at once scholarly and simple, and could hardly be bettered for its purpose.

CONTENTS

FORM AND SPIRIT

CHAPTER ONE

INTRODUCTORY

1. WHAT IS RELIGION?

WHAT is the common element which is present in all religions? Or, to put the question in another way, what is it that gives to a particular attitude to life its religious character? To find an answer to this question let us turn for our starting point not to the official exponents of this or that creed, whose statements presume acceptance of doctrines that they hold to be divinely revealed; nor yet to the philosophers, whose definitions seldom carry conviction to the plain man—being thinkers they have usually regarded the intellectual aspect of religion as its most characteristic manifestation, and the terms that they employ themselves require definition and explanation before they can become readily understood—but rather to the view of religion commonly held by the man in the street.

This is, in the first place, the performance of certain ceremonial actions, such as taking part, at set times and places, in a prescribed form of 'divine worship'. The times, places, and forms so prescribed may differ widely in different religions; but in all of them some form of worship—of actions that is, expressing a relation with a higher Power—is held to be essential.

Secondly, with this is associated the profession of certain beliefs, often embodied in set forms of words, as to the nature and action of Powers acknowledged as divine; together with the reading of passages from books that are held to be sacred in which these beliefs are to be found expressed or from which they are derived. In each of the great religions of mankind acceptance of particular doctrines associated with its founder has been felt to be of immense importance, affecting both the present and future welfare of the believer. Religion, therefore, is commonly held to imply, besides the practice of certain customary observances, profession of a creed summing (in headlines, as it were) a body of doctrines, whether these are understood or not: some kind of ceremonial worship, that is, and some kind of traditional belief.

There are, no doubt, many to whom religion means no more than this. Most of us, however, feel that in anything that is rightly to be called religion something more is involved. Creeds and forms of worship are only the externals of religion; it has little reality unless it finds expression in the conduct of life on other than merely ceremonial occasions. Not that it necessarily implies a particular manner of life, distinguished from the ordinary life of the time by any marked difference of dress or demeanour; but a religion that did not have *any* influence on the daily life of those who profess it, and on their relations with their fellows, would seem to most people not worth a moment's consideration. It may, it is true, be held of importance as affecting the future life rather than the present; but the trend of religious evolution has been towards regarding religion less as concerned with another world and more as a motive and guide to activity in the affairs of this one. Our real religion, it is increasingly realised, is not a matter of beliefs of which we make profession on particular occasions, but of those which influence our motives and show themselves in our actions at other times as well. Even if in the eyes of the unthinking the requirements of religion can be kept entirely separate from behaviour in the general concerns of life, finer spirits have always felt that its essence lies not in outward forms of ritual and creed but in the spirit that underlies them, finding its fullest expression in the life of the worshipper.

Religion, then, in common estimation, may be said to imply: (1) the holding of certain beliefs about the existence of a divine Power or Powers and about their relations with mankind; and (2) the practice of certain forms of worship in which these beliefs find expression, and their effect on the general conduct of life. Such an account of religion, rough and ready though it may be, is in accord with the facts of everyday experience and can be applied to the adherents of any creed, and also (if we do not restrict the terms 'divine Powers' and 'forms of worship' to a particular theological or ecclesiastical meaning) to many who do not belong to any of the recognised Churches.[1]

This, then, we may take as our starting-point. In any religion what we have to look for, as at once constituting its specifically religious character and distinguishing it from other religions, is, on the one hand, the nature of its beliefs and the strength of conviction with which they are held, and on the other, the kind of activity in which this conviction issues. To a superficial view, these may seem to be comprised in its creed and ceremonial observances. Looking a little deeper, we realise that a creed is an attempt to put into words some part at least of an underlying apprehension of reality; and similarly, ceremonial observances are modes of response, of a particular kind, to what is felt to be of supreme value. In this apprehension of reality and in the modes of response which it evokes—in the language of religion, *faith* and *worship*—are to be found the two essential features of religion, if by 'faith' we understand not merely intellectual assent to a given creed or body of doctrine presented for acceptance as having unquestioned authority, but acceptance involving the whole of one's being, emotional and practical as well as intellectual, of what is felt to be an ultimate reality; and if, in the same way, 'worship' is not limited to some kind of religious ritual, but is held to include all objects that are felt to be of supreme importance, and all conduct of whatever kind that is prompted by this feeling.

'Faith' is a word so closely associated with religion that it is usually assumed to denote some kind of theological belief. This, however, is to narrow unduly the application of the term. Faith of some kind, however little recognised as such and however little expressed in religious terms, we all have. Even one who appears to be or affirms

[1] If we want a succint definition of religion expressed in more philosophic terms, one that is at once fairly simple and comprehensive is that given by William James in *The Varieties of Religious Experience*—'the belief that there is an unseen order and that our supreme good lies in harmoniously adjusting ourselves thereto' —if by his 'unseen order' is understood something, whether personal or not, that is beyond and ultimately more important than the material world of which we have experience through the bodily senses, and if the process of harmonious adjustment is held to include, together with all forms of worship, the whole conduct of life.

that he is wholly indifferent to spiritual things shows, by the things with which he concerns himself, what it is that to him matters most; and this, even if it is only acceptance of the morality of the sty or jungle, may be said to be an expression of his faith. In most of us there is at least a glimmering of something that matters more than this. We find the satisfaction of a need in the things of the spirit—in duty, it may be, or in knowledge, in helpfulness or justice; some apprehension of what is felt to be greater than ourselves comes to us as a revelation of power or beauty or love.

This 'greater than ourselves' men in all ages have distinguished from our limited human powers and attainments as divine; and it is this that gives to faith a religious colouring. But even so, it need not give to our faith a specifically religious form. The vision of the divine may come in many forms. It may come in the guise of science or art or of loyalty to some cause. Religion in the wider sense—our reactions of emotion and purpose (to adapt the words of a philosopher[1] of our time) due to such intuitions as we have into the ultimate mystery of the universe—may have little in its mode of expression that would appear to be outwardly religious. To have this quality there must be faith in something—embodied, it may be, in a person or cause, or embracing a whole philosophy and way of life—so far greater than oneself that not merely is intellectual assent required, but feeling and will also are enlisted in its service. There is faith, in the religious sense, only when it gives rise to something in the nature of worship—of devoted service, that is, to the truths that we see and the values that we feel. It is this quality which differentiates faith from other kinds of belief; and it is this also which differentiates religion from the mere profession of a creed and the customary practice of observances that may have no real faith behind them.

If this be granted, it is plain that religion is not to be confined to theological questions and to ceremonial observances of a particular kind, but can—and indeed must—include any matter by which mankind, individually and in the mass, is deeply moved and impelled to action that has for object something beyond the satisfaction of its immediate needs. But in all ages there have been certain objects of thought and feeling which have been the main preoccupation, as centres of faith, to those in whom mankind has come to see the

[1] Professor A. N. Whitehead in *Adventures of Ideas.*

exemplars of religion. Beneath the widely different forms that cults and creeds have taken there is to be found a faith in the reality and supreme importance of something more than is directly revealed by the senses. This apprehension of something beyond the visible world and its happenings has always been the characteristic mark of religious belief. Beginning with the primitive sense of the uncanny and the unexpected, to be met and dealt with by some form of magic, it developed into the more fully religious feeling of what is 'numinous' (as it has been termed),[1] and—in the yet further stage to which the historical religions belong—'divine'.

In these religions it has become a faith in the existence of an unseen Power looked upon as the source of life and of its highest values. In most of them, also, there have been two other certainties of faith: the one, that in us too there is something more than the bodily life—a life of the spirit transcending its present needs and limitations and, as most have felt, or at least have hoped, continuing in some form after the bodily life is over; the other, faith in a validity beyond that merely of law and custom in the distinction between right and wrong, and in a divine sanction for motives of conduct higher than the satisfaction of immediate needs and desires.

2. THE SPHERE OF RELIGION

It is, then, in the apprehension of something beyond the evidence of the bodily senses and the satisfaction of the needs of the moment that the germ of religion is to be found. The religious sense, as we may call it, thus takes its place with other inner senses which are concerned with values. There is, however, one addition that must be made. Alone, a sense of the Unseen may be no more than apprehension of the uncanny, such as we all know in our own experience and may at times see in the behaviour of dogs. Similarly our sense of values may be no more than an individual preference for one form of enjoyment rather than another. It is when the two are combined in an

[1] This term was suggested by Dr. Rudolf Otto in his book *Das Heilige* (translated under the title *The Idea of the Holy*) to denote the sense of awe in primitive religious feeling, without the later implication of moral goodness in the word 'holy'.

apprehension of spiritual reality and of spiritual values,[1] that we have the essential element of religion.

In the realm of values there are some that are called ultimate, as being not merely relative and changeable, but seeming (like mathematical relations) to have a validity independent of individual experience; these we feel to be of a higher order than those associated with sense-gratification, and to have a claim on our allegiance at the cost, if need be, even of material well-being. One of the means of apprehending such values is religion. It will be helpful, therefore, in order to distinguish its special character, to consider briefly in what relation it stands to other spheres of activity, science, philosophy, art, morality, to which the quest of these ultimate values has given rise.

Science is concerned with the discovery of truth; but with those aspects of truth only that have to do with objective fact and with the logical connection of ideas. Its main concern is with a certain part of our total experience, the facts of sense-perception and logical consistency. These it tries to formulate in exact terms, so that the sequences they tabulate can be repeated at will and utilised for the mastery of the external world. Religion, on the other hand, is concerned with truths of spiritual perception. The inner experience with which it is preoccupied—the sense of an unseen reality beyond the material world—cannot be scientifically demonstrated but only felt. If this difference is recognised, there is no need for opposition or contradiction between science and religion, so long as neither presumes to lay down what must or must not be accepted as truth in the other's sphere of experience, and so long as each is ready to accept the validity of truth other than its own, and does not attempt to build a system based on its denial.

Science, though within its limits the most powerful of instruments for the discovery of truth, covers only a part of the total field of experience. Philosophy seeks to cover the whole and, by co-ordinating all branches of knowledge and including all kinds of experience, to

[1] The use of the term 'spiritual' must not be taken to imply that religion necessarily makes for good. There can be spiritual as well as physical harm, and the deadliest form of evil is spiritual evil. Religion can only too easily become a blind fanaticism, inspired by base motives and directed to harmful ends. Its history tells mainly of the worship of false gods. Yet it is a narrow and distorted view of history that sees in religion only a source of evil, and does not recognise in it also one of the greatest of agencies for good in the spiritual evolution of man's nature.

give an interpretation of the universe in which no aspect of truth shall be neglected. It is thus, in one respect, of wider range than religion, as including other spheres of interest as well; but in another respect it is religion that is the wider. The interpretation of the universe that philosophy seeks to give is intellectual, a rational understanding that may be content to remain merely contemplative. The interpretation that religion offers is spiritual, in which understanding is only one means of revealing and heightening a value that owes even more to the emotions than to the intellect. Not that religion is only an emotional attitude to life. It must have a philosophy, implicit at least, even if not consciously formulated; but it does not base its view of the universe so much on rational proof, such as philosophy attempts to give, as on faith, which is ignored by science (though the fundamental axioms of science are all matters of faith) and distrusted by the majority of philosophers. And whereas philosophy may be content to understand and to explain, without seeking to apply its findings to practical questions, religion, if it is genuine, cannot be satisfied with a faith that does not express itself in conduct.

In being a matter of emotional rather than intellectual apprehension, religion is more closely akin to art than to science or philosophy. Art also is an interpretation of the universe in terms of feeling, and is concerned not merely, like science, with an objective description of the external world but with its own personal attitude towards it. Art does not merely accept what is given and seek to understand it better; it is creative, in that it gives expression to values through the medium of sensible forms. In these respects, religion resembles art; there is in it a large element of wonder, awe, and love, in contemplation of the spiritual world, and of the natural world as expression and symbol of the spiritual realities that underlie it. It is concerned, no less than art, to translate these spiritual values into the realm of actual fact. But whereas art is content to objectify what it feels in some external material form, religion seeks to express itself in personal conduct and in the relations of individuals with each other. It is this concern, so characteristic of the greatest religions, with conduct and motive, that now differentiates religion from art, whereas in the primitive manifestations of religion there was often little distinction between them.

Like aesthetic sensibility, the religious sense is common in some degree to all races of mankind and is felt—by those at least in whom it is more fully developed—to be of the utmost importance for any real well-being. It may seem that individuals have or have not a religious sense just as they may or may not have a highly developed sense of beauty. In the minds of those who have either in any marked degree, the strongest of sentiments gather round it, so that it comes to colour and direct the greater part of their activities. To those, on the other hand, who are insensitive to it, such intensity of feeling in matters of the kind seems hardly intelligible. The conduct to which it leads is apt, in the eyes of more ordinary people, to be unworldly to a degree which is altogether unpractical; so that, although at times it cannot but compel admiration, at others it may awaken ridicule.

So far as it goes, this account of the religious sense corresponds to facts of common experience; but it is by no means a complete account. Religion is not only a personal concern; it has also a social aspect. In its early forms, indeed, it was mainly social in its modes of expression; and as custom grew into law and the moral sense was developed, it was in religion that the sanctions of conduct were found. While ethics remains a branch of philosophic study which seeks to find a rational basis for human conduct in its various relations, morality—the ordering of conduct in practice—has long been regarded as one of the main concerns of religion and largely dependent on religion for its authority. To religion, moral law belongs to the order of the spiritual world; breach of it is a sin against a divine law that is recognised as higher than any social code of morality. While society is satisfied if its members do the duties laid on them with no unnecessary interference from each other, religion in its higher development regards human relationships in the light not merely of duty and of refraining from what is harmful, but still more of mutual helpfulness and good-will and unstinting love.

Science, philosophy, art, morality, religion, all are ways of enlarging experience and heightening its value, both as an object of contemplation and in practical life. Each deals, in its own way and from its own point of view, with experience; but each tends to take as its centre of interest a different mode of experience and a different group of facts, and to regard the rest as of secondary importance. Those of widest range are philosophy and religion. But, as said above, philosophy, with its intellectual method of approach, is narrower in its scope than religion, in which thought, feeling, and action all have a part. Religion, indeed, in its fullest form combines the quest of truth, beauty, and moral good. It is not owing merely to the predilection of some philosopher that these have been acclaimed as ultimate values. As has been pointed out elsewhere by the present writer,[1] the recognition of them as such is imposed upon us by the very constitution of our minds, as being the goal to which our mental life, in its three main modes of activity—cognitive, emotional, and conative—is directed. These are not separate modes of experience, but different aspects, separable only by analysis in order to make them more easily intelligible, of the impulses that make up the complex activity of life. So also truth, beauty, and moral good have been seen by philosophers and poets to be different aspects of a single reality, manifestations from different points of view of what is so far beyond man's full comprehension and attainment that he has always thought of it as 'divine'. Just as the pursuit of these values has found embodiment of different kinds in science and philosophy, in the arts, and in attempts to bring the conduct of life into accord with moral laws, so too the quest of that of which these values are manifestations—the quest of God, to use the name that religion gives to its ultimate reality—has given rise to all the many forms of religious belief and practice. Looked at in this way, religion at its fullest would be nothing less than the response of the whole of our personality to the whole of experience. In its various embodiments it has, it must be admitted, except in some few of the finest and most spiritual natures, been something much less than this. In its full meaning, however, it must be regarded not merely as a matter of faith and worship in the narrow sense of creed and ritual, but rather as our whole attitude towards life, the central spring of motive and sense of values by which the intellectual and emotional sides of our nature are unified in a way of living.

It is part of man's very greatness, the price that he has to pay for his psychological advance, that the finer the powers of which he becomes possessed, the less instinctive certainty has he in their use, and the easier it is to turn them to harm or waste them in futility. In religion, every side of man's nature is involved, and in particular

[1] In *The Will to Fuller Life* (G. Allen & Unwin, 1937), Chapter III, on 'Spiritual Values'.

those higher powers of mind and spirit which are latest developed and least firmly established, as well as his crude instinctive feelings. Small wonder, then, that every weakness to which he is subject should find expression in it. Yet through all, imperfect and distorted as it may be, it is the expression of the spiritual values that he has come to feel. That is not a matter of church and creed. Our real religion—that which matters most in every age and in each individual—is whatever we feel to be most worth while in life, the dominant object of our reverence and aspiration, and the response that this provokes in the conduct of our lives.

CHAPTER TWO

THE CHILDHOOD OF RELIGION

1. ORIGINS

EVEN if we remember little of our own feelings and reactions in early childhood, we can see in the behaviour of small children certain features that seem to be normal in the gradual enlargement of experience. Of these one is resistance to what is irksome, with attempts to overcome obstacles and to exert mastery over immediate surroundings. Another is acceptance of what is familiar, showing itself in compliance with recognised authority and also in experiment and initiative in the use of whatever may serve to give pleasure and satisfy needs. Outside this gradually widening circle of familiar experience lies the unknown, usually disregarded, but when it forces itself into notice—by some loud noise, perhaps, or sudden movement, or as darkness which obliterates all familiar objects—arousing shapeless fears and bringing a sense of helplessness and need of comfort and protection. To most children anything strange, if fairly small, is an object of curiosity, to be handled and mastered; but if it is large or threatening, fear prompts avoidance and escape to where safety and love are to be found.

In various parts of the world there remain groups of human beings that are still in early stages of development. Though they have now advanced far enough along their particular lines of human evolution to have divergent forms of custom and belief, these still have enough general resemblance to show that, wherever any human race had its origin, the reactions of each to its environment were largely similar, and that an analogy with the normal development of early childhood is justifiable.

However limited the circle of his experience, within that circle, we may be sure, primitive man felt little doubt as to his ability to deal with all familiar and normal happenings, and to obtain and keep sufficient mastery of his surroundings to satisfy his immediate needs. This degree of confidence in the workings of nature and in his own powers he shared with other animals—it has been well called 'animal faith', and is the starting-point of all our intuitions and beliefs—though in him it could rise, further than with other animals, above the sub-conscious level. But, as with the child, outside this circle of familiar experience, with which he felt himself able to deal, lay an unknown from which came frequent incursions of strange happenings, unforeseeable and uncontrollable, and at times inexplicable. And with the growth of imagination and some power of reflection came the doubt whether even the normal routine of nature was sure to follow the course he needed. If the alternation of day and night was frequent and regular enough to be accepted as normal, the succession of the seasons seemed less certain; there was always the fear that the sun might lose its power and the earth fail to renew its fertility. If ordinary objects kept their form and nature sufficiently to be depended upon for providing food, drink, shelter, and various kinds of use, or as known dangers to be avoided, others were unaccountable in themselves or in their activity. At any moment an invisible force might snap the strongest tree and sweep away any but the most firmly planted objects. The sky might roar and strike with sudden arrows of flame. Drought, fire or flood might destroy life and the means of life. Food might turn to poison. Vigour might be laid low by wasting disease or destroyed by some unexpected happening. On all sides was much that was 'uncanny' in being intangible or having no known origin. The dark hid not only known dangers but those, still more dreadful, of the imagination. The dead might return in ghostly shape, and probably with no friendly purpose. 'Our life,' said the writer of the book of Esdras, 'is astonishment and fear.'

Of much in the life of primitive man, whether in the remote childhood of humanity or today, that may be said; and it was in feelings of this kind that religion had some of its deepest roots.

In a world where so much was unaccountable, arousing both his wonder and his fears, man was conscious of something stronger than himself of which no comprehension was possible except by projection of his own motive-impulses into everything by which he felt himself affected. He took for granted that things should be what they are and do what they do by virtue of an inherent power acting, as he felt himself to act, of his own volition, either from set purpose or caprice. How was such a power to be met, since, being unseen and intangible, it could not be dealt with like the things with which he was familiar?

As with the child, there were two possible reactions: either an attempt to master and make it subservient to his desires, or an attempt to escape from the dangers it seemed to threaten and to seek help and protection against them. In dealing with the unseen, mastery and refuge alike could only be symbolically represented and only attained by some means of spiritual rather than merely material efficacy. Hence the resort to magic and to some kind of ritual approach to the unseen power whose agency was to be employed or its help and protection implored.

Magic—the attainment of a desired end by unusual means known only to those who practise it—was no doubt originally the outcome of some special skill and intelligence, and of special knowledge handed on from one expert to a successor as a secret tradition. It was in part primitive but genuine science—that of the 'medicine man', for instance, with some knowledge of the helpful and harmful properties of herbs, and methods derived from experiment in the treatment of injuries and disease—and in part imagination, belief in the mysterious power of language by which knowledge of the names of persons or things gave a special hold over them, and in the power of special forms of words to exercise a spell and so bring about the end desired; or belief that like results must follow from like causes, and so imitation of a particular activity or happening would, if properly performed, bring about the making of rain, the destruction of an enemy, or whatever it might be. All depended on knowledge of the right things to say and do, and on their being said and done in the right manner, which only the possessor of the magic power could ensure.

The other mode of obtaining the help of the unseen power and escaping from dangers real or imagined had something in common with magic, but differed from it in the spirit and manner of approach. Whereas the magician sought to compel the course of events by exercise of his superior technical equipment, the worshipper approached as a suppliant admitting dependence on a power greater than his own and appealing for help and protection with reminder of the need and of ways in which it could be met—renewal of the fertility, for instance, which each year seemed in danger of being lost, or maintenance of the food supply, or defence of the community against enemies and dangers of all kinds.

For all this there was need, as in magic, of a proper ritual approach, with use of fitting words and actions that must be correctly repeated in traditional forms known to those whose duty it was to preserve them, whether the head of a family, patriarch of a tribe, king of a larger and more settled community, or a priesthood specially appointed for the purpose. In such ritual there was inevitably much similarity to magical procedure. In the earlier stages of religious evolution, indeed, although the two modes of approach to the Unseen were radically different, they tended to coalesce, and there has always been a certain amount of confusion between them. Even down to the present day there is a claim to magical powers on the part of the priest, and an admixture of magic formulas and incantations in the liturgies of all religions.[1] But the finer development of religion has been away from magical procedure and the ideas underlying it to a worship arising from a sense of dependence upon a Power not only immeasurably greater than any human knowledge but spiritually 'higher'—a worship, therefore, not of ritual only but of feeling, thought, will, and conduct in service of that 'higher' apprehended by man's spiritual nature.

2. SOME EARLY LINES OF DEVELOPMENT

It may seem strange to have begun a study of religion with consideration of ritual, and the inclusion in it of an element of magic, instead of with the ideas of which the different forms of religion and their ritual may be regarded as the expression. But this starting-point has been taken in order to follow, as closely as may be, the actual course of religious evolution, which began with the expression, in some practical form, of emotions and desires and of intuitions not

[1] E.g. in the liquefaction of the blood of St. Januarius in the annual 'miracle' at Naples; in the Holy Fire that appears at Easter in the Church of the Holy Sepulchre at Jerusalem; and, in Catholic churches, in the transubstantiation of the Mass.

yet formulated in definite ideas or clothed with myth and legend. There is much truth in Andrew Lang's assertion[1] that 'savage religion is something not so much thought out as danced out'. Primitive man did not, we may be sure, sit down to think out his beliefs until they had been in some measure shaped by his instinctive reactions to what was strange and frightening and not to be met by the normal routine of experience.

While the behaviour of small children is to some extent a guide as to similar reactions in the childhood of mankind, there is little such guidance to be found in the development of their ideas, as these have not now a free field but are mostly taken over from their elders and adopted without question until a much later stage of growth. Such transmission of ideas there must also have been in early times from one group to another; but of this we can have no knowledge. It seems, to say the least, highly improbable (though maintained by some) that mankind had its origin in one part only of the earth, and that all races and all cultures have come, by dispersion and dissemination, from a single source. It is much more probable that there were different beginnings in different regions where conditions were favourable, and that they followed lines of development similar in the main but by no means identical; and that this was the case also with ideas and customs in which there is a certain general likeness, rather than that these were acquired only by contact.

Thus in regions as far apart as Melanesia, Africa, and North America we find races all of which have a conception of an unseen power capable of entering into persons and objects and enduing them with some additional part of its energy, so that they can at times show exceptional vigour and activity. For this mysterious force English anthropologists who have studied the customs and ideas of Australasian races usually employ their name *Mana* to denote this conception. By German writers it is often denoted by *Orenda*, an Iroquois word conveying a similar conception. The power seems to be thought of as impersonal, much as 'Heaven' is to the Chinese and 'Providence' in common parlance with us, although, owing to the impossibility of imagining anything wholly different from what is familiar, its activity may seem to be endued with something like will and purpose.

[2] In *The Making of Religion* (published in 1898).

To the primitive mind (not only, that is, at some remotely early stage of human evolution but in those still at a childish stage of development) such power can seem to be attached in a special degree to objects which, for some reason—a peculiarity, perhaps, of shape or origin or some traditional association—arouse a sense of the 'numinous'. Such objects—stones, meteorites, rude images carved in wood—readily became to primitive man fetishes endowed with special power: objects therefore of worship, or a means of working magic. There are still to be found remnants of races at so low a level of culture that they have not advanced beyond this early phase of religious development—if that term can rightly be applied to belief in a power at the service of one who is possessed of a powerful fetish and who knows the ritual required to make its influence available; and even among civilised people it survives in the use of charms, amulets, mascots and the like.

It is not easy to say how far such objects are or have been thought of as possessing individual power of action, to be classed not as instruments of a larger *Mana* but as separate spiritual agencies. It was suggested by E. B. Tylor[1] that at an early stage of thought men came to the conclusion that everything in nature—everything, at least, which moved and changed—was alive, and that even inanimate objects were actuated by 'spirits', phantom-like beings such as were shown by reflections in water, just as in man himself there was evidently a spirit, which could be seen in dreams or as a ghost or, still more tenuously, in his breath on a frosty morning, and which left his body at death. This is the theory of 'animism' which was widely accepted as the first stage in the development of ideas of spiritual beings and the deities of later religions. It was, however, questioned by others as too sweeping a theory, and was amended into one of 'animatism'—the entry, that is, as a supernatural occurrence, of a spiritual agency into certain objects and activities that could not be otherwise accounted for. It may well be that something of this kind was commonly accepted before any system of belief in individual spirits and in a hierarchy of spiritual beings had been reached.

One would suppose that the first supernatural beings to whom man's imagination gave form were demons and malignant spirits whose harmful activities he sought to escape. It is easy to people the

[1] In his *Primitive Culture* (1871).

dark with shapes of terror. The fiery breath of the volcano, the dazzling javelins of the storm, the fury of the river in spate could well seem to be proofs not of merely natural forces but of beings with passions like his own. It is less easy to see such forms in the friendly workings of nature. Yet to an imaginative child any treasured possession can be as real as one of flesh and blood; and to such beings the child in primitive man could turn for comfort and help in time of danger, and offer gratitude when his hopes were realised.

Among these beings were, as many ancient customs show, spirits of the dead—for these, though no longer in visible form, were thought to have a continued existence and power to harm or help the living—and especially of those who had in their life-time been great leaders, and would still, if duly honoured, remain protectors and benefactors of the community. In many parts of the world ancestor-worship has a great place in religion—it is part of the universal tendency to think of old times and their heroes as finer than the present. The Greek philosopher Euhemerus thought that all the deities of later worship had once been human beings whose exploits and discoveries were thus commemorated and their personalities magnified in the haze of antiquity. Like the theory of animism, this is far too sweeping, but undoubtedly contains some truth. It seems certain that outstanding rulers, benefactors, and culture-heroes were thus raised to the rank of divine powers amongst the natural agencies—the sun and other heavenly bodies, mother earth, vegetation spirits and fertility powers—to which, in order to ensure their continuance and favour, worship was paid.

Amongst certain tribes we can see also another source of the personification of spiritual agencies in the honour paid to totems—an animal, or sometimes plant on which the tribe was chiefly dependent for food, and to which it held itself to be closely bound by ties of kinship and descent. To primitive man animals were, so to speak, near relations, many of them stronger, swifter, and cleverer than man himself, and therefore to be regarded with awe. It is not surprising, therefore, that when spiritual beings were represented in bodily form they should often take the forms of animals. The animal-headed gods of ancient Egypt are familiar examples. Even when deities were fully humanised, as in Classical mythology, the association of animals with them, as symbols or as assistants, was often maintained.

From some such beginnings, we may conjecture—from multifarious imaginings of demons and monsters, malicious and kindly spirits, animal and human, ancestors and nature-powers—grew more coherent systems of belief in deities with special attributes and powers. Such systems of belief belong to the myth-making stage of mental development. Human evolution must have been far advanced before man had sufficient mastery over his environment to have time and thought to spare for reflection on experience and for wondering about the reasons for what in it was strange, and still more for what was familiar. There came a time, however, when he wanted to know how the things around him—including his own community and its customs—had come about: surely they must originally have been made and set in order by someone. Australian tribes, the most primitive human communities now surviving, have legends of the creation of the world as known to them out of some previously existing chaos—a supposition that we find in all creation myths. This creation of the existing world and of living beings they look upon as the work of some shadowy All-father, who is still interested in due observance of the initiation ceremonies necessary before full entry into community life and knowledge of its religions and other requirements and customs, but who is otherwise too remote to be concerned, like nearer and more accessible powers, with its everyday affairs.

When the power of spiritual beings was established and elaborated in myths, as the only imaginable way in which animals and inanimate objects were brought into existence and sustained in their activities, there was necessarily one among such beings—whether regarded as a first ancestor or further back still as Creator—who was looked upon as guardian spirit of the community, giver of its laws and customs. To this Power worship must be paid with the due ceremonial handed on from generation to generation by the official guardians of religion, since on such worship depended the welfare of the community and of all who belonged to it. It will be seen later how the status of such a Being amongst others to whom worship was also paid was affected by the social and political development of the community.

It has already been insisted that any such growth of religious ideas did not precede the establishment of ritual worship, but rather was a way of accounting for an instinctive expression of emotions aroused in the presence of what was first vaguely felt to be 'numinous'—uncanny, that is, and mysterious—then more definitely as 'sacred'—not to be approached without protection of the proper rites—and finally as 'holy', implying an awe so great as to preclude any response other than complete submissiveness.[1] At this level of development, with the conception of beings not merely possessed of superhuman power but actuated by feelings and impulses resembling, though with greater scope and intensity, those of mankind, and invested with a holiness in presence of which fear was transformed into reverence, religion was no longer a matter mainly of magic and ritual for averting harm and ensuring communal security, but had begun to take on a more personal character of self-surrender in presence of the Unseen, and an inner worship of obedience to divine law.

Originating in emotions aroused by contacts with a world in which much was unknown and mysterious and in which on all sides were real and imagined dangers, religious evolution is the story first of practices and then of ideas and beliefs in which these emotions found embodiment both good and bad. Through its texture has always run the dark thread of fear. Like our other instinctive reactions, fear has had its uses as a means of survival and of promoting the development of our powers. It has done much to sharpen senses and wits in order to detect the presence of danger and to find some means of escape. But in proportion as fear has acquired an imaginative content—when it was no longer, that is, merely the momentary instinctive response of the animal, passing with the need that called it forth, but could fill the mind with dread of danger remembered or anticipated—the greater has become its power for harm. When intensely aroused it inhibits finer feelings and prompts, as we see in time of panic, actions which, however ill-advised and however inhuman, seem to give hope of self-preservation.

So it has been in religion. The greater the element of fear the more

[1] When Schleiermacher insisted that a feeling of absolute dependence was the chief mark of religion, Hegel retorted that in that case his dog was more pious than its master. The retort contained more truth than was intended; there could hardly be a better example of a feeling that may be called religious *at the instinctive level* than a dog's worship of its master, made up of dependence upon one possessed of super-canine power, submission to his will, and readiness to do anything for him.

abject the resulting submissiveness, in which sense of the immeasurable distance between worshipper and an overwhelming Power heightens the dread of displeasure incurred by any shortcoming in the service demanded. Under the influence of fear worship was often little more than the offering of gifts by which to win favour or to appease anger. Imagined devils, monsters worshipped with cruel rites, human sacrifice, self-mutilation[1] and every kind of neglect or maltreatment of the body, there is no end to the inhumanities and aberrations to which fear has led, in the name of religion as in other aspects of human life; and in fear of ills here and of what may await us hereafter every cult has found one of the strongest of motives to which to appeal in order to win and retain adherents.

But though so strongly patterned by fear, through the texture of religion have run other threads as well. The stimulation of hope and courage, both by its promises and through the psychological effect of common modes of worship, has always been one of its main functions. From the first the sympathy that binds man to his fellows has played a large part in its development. This first came into consciousness as a tie of blood-relationship between members of a family, and later between those of a tribe, in which the bond was held to be one of actual kinship. In the loyalties and affections engendered by the various relationships entered into by members of a community is to be found the source of one of the strongest and one of the finest elements in religion, the feeling of fellowship that it does so much to deepen. This sense of unity was capable of expansion in ever-widening circles. It could extend to the dead, whom primitive man regarded as being still members of the community, able to exercise a helpful or harmful influence according to the respect or neglect shown to them by the living. It could also take in those who belonged to the group not by blood-relationship but by adoption or common interest, and could even extend to a feeling of continuity with the life believed by the child-mind to animate natural objects. And beyond this underlying feeling of unity with other human beings and with nature is the sense of communion with the divine which has been the crowning

[1] It is noteworthy how widespread, as we learn from imprints on the walls of caves, was the practice of cutting off finger joints on various occasions: largely, it would seem, as a propitiatory offering to avert some evil. See Sollas: *Ancient Hunters*, ch. VIII.

experience, in the higher forms of religion, of its prophets and saints. Thus, slowly and hesitatingly, man has won beyond his fears to a religion of trust and love.

3. THE INFLUENCE OF ENVIRONMENT

Although springing from instinctive feelings that are universal in human nature, it was not possible for religion, any more than for language or art, to develop everywhere along similar lines. Life in a sub-tropical or a temperate climate, in the desert or in fertile surroundings, offers different problems. The shepherd and the tiller ofthe soil, the soldier and the trader, the peasant and the townsman, look at things with very different eyes. Those who are still in the tribal stage of development have a different outlook from those who are members of a large and settled community; still more from those who come into close contact, whether by conquest or commerce, with other kinds of civilisation than their own.

Religions, like other racial differences, have been shaped by the conditions of environment, manner of life, and social organisation, in those regions in which they have grown up. It is easy to see how much in Confucianism for instance, or in Hinduism or Islam, is due to the geographical and social conditions of their respective countries of origin. The development of Christianity bears no less clearly the stamp of its connection with the Roman Empire. There is thus little cause for wonder that 'what we have in the world is not religion but religions'.[1]

Of such environmental influences, one of the strongest and most far-reaching was that exerted by the change of habit and occupation when the life of hunter and food-gatherer was exchanged for that of herdsman and grower of grain. Any high degree of civilisation has only been possible since men have lived in settled communities and were no longer dependent on hunting for food and the necessaries of

[1] These are the opening words of *Living Religions and a World Faith*, by Professor W. E. Hocking. It is noteworthy that one result of the drawing together of all parts of the world through the spread of commerce and the applications of science is the gradual extension of a civilisation that is no longer wholly dependent on local conditions; and, with this, a growing recognition that religion is something more universal and more permanent than existing religions.

life. The domestication of animals, and still more the practice of agriculture which made a settled community-life possible, mark a new starting-point in human evolution; in that of religion no less than in other lines of advance.

A nomad pastoral existence has usually been supposed to represent an earlier stage of development than a settled agricultural life. It seems likely, however, that the first beginnings of agriculture go back to the primitive food-gathering existence in which hunting was supplemented by the gathering of roots, berries, and succulent leaves. Some primitive garden-culture may even have helped to bring about the domestication of animals by providing a reserve of food for the herd as well as for its masters; and such garden-culture is not incompatible with a wandering life, provided there was a stay in one place long enough to grow some sort of crop. However this may be, special conditions of environment brought about two divergent lines of development, pastoral and agricultural, rivalry between which, exemplified in the story of Cain and Abel, is seen throughout history in the recurrent raids of the steppe- or desert-dweller on lands that are sown. Each gave rise to a social life, differing greatly from the other in its culture and in particular in its religious ideas and preoccupations.

In a pastoral life the decisive factor is climate. Since the herdsman's main concern is with changes of weather, the powers whose favours he wishes to win and whose anger he must do all that he can to avert are those of the sky. The gods of pastoral peoples were therefore personifications of various aspects of the heavens. The different branches of the Aryan race (if we may still keep this convenient, if much misused, name) in their migration into the lands in which they eventually settled in Europe and Western Asia and India, brought with them sky-gods of their earlier pastoral way of life—Jupiter, Zeus, Ahura Mazda, Varuna, and all their train of attendant deities—most of them male figures, as was natural in a patriarchal stage of social development. As the life of the herdsman involved much fighting—beating off raids of man and beast, raiding the herds of others, and plundering the rich lands of the peasant—the deities of such people were essentially warlike, endowed with the fiercer as well as with the finer characteristics of a hardy fighting race.

When, however, these Aryan invaders settled in fertile lands and adopted an agricultural life, the cults they had brought were modified by the beliefs and customs to which such a life gave rise. We see this no less clearly in the case of the Semitic people whose early history and legends are preserved in the Old Testament. Their habits of life and thought, as their early traditions show, were those of nomad Bedouin. *Jahveh,*[1] in whose name Moses gave them their law, was the storm-god of the mountains and the desert, a war-god, and one who required a disciplined life in his worshippers. From the time of their settlement in Palestine their religious history was one of continual backslidings to the worship of the local Baals. From these orgiastic fertility-cults of the agricultural peoples among whom they settled they were again and again recalled by a succession of prophets to the simpler cult and stricter morality of their old pastoral religion.

The herdsman when conditions become adverse is free to migrate and seek some spot where they are better, and his gods go with him, for the sky is over all. The peasant, on the other hand, being bound to one spot, feels himself entirely dependent on the gods of the particular locality, however cruel and capricious they may show themselves in threatening his crops with failure and himself with starvation. There is little room for wonder that the tiller of the soil has always been prone to superstition and to rites, orgiastic and often cruel, whose aim was to ensure fertility and to retain or recall the favour of these powers. To him it is the earth rather than the sky with which he is chiefly concerned. Sun and rain are needed to bring his crops to maturity; drought or storm, the inroads of beast or man may at anytime destroy the fruits of his labour; but all depends ultimately on the fertility of the soil that he tills and on the annual miracle of the rebirth of vegetation from its winter death.

Amongst primitive agricultural peoples the chief power that they worshipped and whose help they invoked by sacrifices and by rites of sympathetic magic tended to take the form of a Great Mother. Such a figure we see in many of the ancient religions that are known to us. Demeter,[2] Ceres, Cybele, Ashtaroth, Isis, and the unnamed goddess of the Minoan civilisation, are familiar examples; and the rude female figures that have come down from prehistoric times seem to be an

[1] For this, the more correct form of the name better known as *Jehovah*, see the note in Chapter IV (page 81).

[2] Demeter is, by derivation, Ge Meter, 'Mother Earth'; and this without doubt is the significance of the Great Mother goddess under whatever name.

earlier expression of the cult. Associated with the worship of the Great Mother there was often another deity, usually male—Attis, Adonis, Osiris—representing the vegetation-spirit that every year dies and goes down to the lower world, and must be recalled to life by the lamentations of the worshippers and by some form of imitative ritual.

In such ways as these, likenesses and differences in religious cults have been shaped by the similar needs and preoccupations of mankind and by the different conditions under which a living had to be secured. While food-production was necessarily the chief of these factors, it was not, of course, the only one. Two others in particular need mention. One is the fact of death and the need for disposal of the dead body. In a later chapter[1] we shall see how deeply religion was affected by the feelings and ideas that gather round this universal experience. The other is the mark left on religion by certain crafts which did so much to promote human advance. That of the potter, for instance (usually carried on, it would seem, by men rather than women), helped to shape the conception of a divine Creator who moulded the world and all that is in it, and made man from the dust to which his body must in the end return.

4. RELIGION AS REVELATION

The influence of environment and occupation can be clearly seen in those religions of which we have actual record. Some, as we have seen, were of the pastoral type; others embodied the cycle of ideas associated with agriculture. In most, however, owing to historical causes, there was some combination of the two. Races of nomad habits invaded settled lands where agriculture had long been practised. As new peoples were formed by the admixture of conquerors and conquered, there was a corresponding intermixture of religions. Such a process is to be traced in the Classical mythology, in which the Olympian gods dispossessed earlier deities. Sky-gods, that is, supplanted earth-powers that now took a subordinate place; but the worship of these latter still continued amongst the subject population and was eventually adopted as part of the official religion, or at least had to be allowed to supplement it. This primitive earth-religion, with its local cults and ceremonial of sympathetic magic, everywhere

[1] See Chapter IX.

tended to outlast the imposed religion of the conqueror and to break out again in some form of 'mystery' cult.

With the growth of a more settled civilisation, men came to attribute to their deities a rule of law and order instead of capricious and irresponsible will; and to see in them, instead of merely superhuman powers and passions, a moral nature in accord with their own developing ideals. Religion thus became something more than an attitude of submission to superior powers: it gave its authority to a standard of conduct recognised as imperative through its intrinsic rightness. Even if fear of divine anger at any falling away from this standard remained the strongest element in religious feeling, it was at least a fear that contained the nobler element of reverence. It was already on its way to a passionate aspiration towards what is felt to be highest, in which fear is swallowed up in love. With the widening of experience religion thus became more spiritual in feeling. It found expression not merely in a traditional ritual but in a conduct of life in accordance with moral ideals. Even though it has always contained much that is irrational and much that is repugnant to the more fully developed moral sense, we can see, in the main, an advance from cruder to more rational and more moral forms.

There is, however, another trend which is no less plainly to be seen in the history of all religions. This is the growth of traditionalism and the establishment of a rigid orthodoxy that will admit no change either in belief or practice, and thus is opposed to all further advance. Since so much was felt to depend on the exact performance of certain religious duties, the nature and proper performance of which were mysteries known only to the few, it was inevitable that religion should be under the control of a priesthood. It was equally inevitable that this priesthood should insist on an orthodoxy, both of doctrine and ceremonial, fixed by tradition, from which no deviation could be admitted. In all ages, therefore, the official guardians of religion have tended to oppose, as a falling off from divinely appointed procedure and revelation, any admission of new truth or any modification in accordance with a change of feeling. In the history of all religions the influence of the priesthood has thus led to spiritual ossification and the deadening of the religious sense which its function was to quicken.

But while in some periods of its history the religious sense of a whole community may be so dull as to be satisfied with the observance of merely traditional forms, there have also been times when it has been extraordinarily quickened, at least in individuals who have sought to raise their fellows out of such spiritual dullness and to lead them to truer beliefs and a better way of worship. Hence the opposition, so common in religious history, of the prophet and the priest.

The word 'prophet' (Greek, *pro-phetes*) has, in derivation, three meanings: (1) one who speaks *forth*, (2) one who speaks *for* another, and (3) one who *fore*-tells. It is this third meaning that is attached to the word in its common use; but originally—as applied, for instance, to the Hebrew prophets—it is the other two meanings that the name chiefly conveys: one who speaks out boldly as the mouthpiece of the divine will which is revealed to him. Because, in so doing, they constantly made assertions as to the results, good or bad, that must follow on particular courses of action or historic events, the third meaning has come to be specially associated with prophetic claims.

In the religious connotation of the word, however, a prophet is one who proclaims that traditional beliefs and practice can no longer satisfy a quickened religious sense, and sets forth his own vision of the divine nature and the divine will.

Of such reformers some have spent their force in initiating religious revivals by appeal to the crudest passions of mankind: revivals which, however widespread or intense in their appeal at the moment, have been shortlived in their effect or have left only a dwindling body of enthusiasts. But there have been others, however little they may have seemed to accomplish at the time, whose words and actions have borne continually increasing fruit, so that the religious feeling and practice of those who came after them have been permanently lifted to a higher level.

This is how all the great religions of the world have come into being. By their adherents they are held to have been divinely revealed, and in each case those who so believe hold that theirs alone is true and of supreme value, and all others at best faint approximations to the truth, lacking the full revelation on which the truth of religion depends. To those who see in all the religions of mankind, together with what is of permanent value, an admixture of much that is spiritually null, if not actively harmful, such a claim is no more—and no less—valid in one case than in others. Any doctrine of a revelation which set forth *once and for all* the one and only way of salvation, to be followed henceforth with unquestioning submission, is now, for most, impossible of acceptance. But a progressive revelation of spiritual values, a deeper insight coming to fruition here and there among various races and at various times—this is an undeniable fact of human history. Again and again the religious ideas and feelings of the time, shaped by tradition and by experience into a form embodying the conceptions and aspirations of the race to which he belonged, have been taken up in the mind of a religious genius; transmuted by his deeper feeling and more spiritual outlook, they have then emerged as something newly experienced, in which what had seemed familiar was touched to a new life and took on meanings then for the first time revealed. While each new form thus given to religion was itself the outcome of earlier forms and the flowering of a long-continued growth, the new outlook upon life and its mysteries was so far different from what had been before accepted as to seem not merely a new and intensely individual creation but a direct revelation proceeding from the divine nature of which it told.

In the course of evolution there have appeared from time to time combinations of conditions from which has emerged something new, in the sense that it could not have been foreseen from any knowledge of what was in existence up to that time. Thus at a particular degree of chemical complexity and under particular conditions life appeared; and so, too, new manifestations of mind and spirit have emerged at new evolutionary levels. If we accept emergence of this kind as an essential characteristic of evolution, there is no need to postulate a supernatural intervention in order to account for new departures in religion any more than in other lines of evolutionary advance.

Recognition of the fact of emergence does not, of course, give any explanation of the process. Like natural selection, emergent evolution is merely a descriptive term summing up in one generalisation a number of observed facts. Neither attempts to explain how it is that the conditions select what makes for a particular kind of advance, or why they should lead to the emergence of a new mode of being or a new apprehension of reality. To those who prefer the theological explanation it is open to attribute each advance to the direct intervention of a personal Deity. But if so, they must logically allow the same to hold good of *all* such advances, not of one revelation only.

Whatever the reason, it is a remarkable fact that the thousand years leading up to and including the opening of the Christian era brought a world-wide advance in the evolution of religious consciousness. During that millennium in widely separated countries ideas and ritual practices belonging to an earlier age were shaped into coherent systems of thought and conduct. Religion became at once more rational and more ethical. It took on a universal instead of a merely tribal and local significance. Of the great religions of the world today there is only one, Islam, of which the origin or reshaping does not fall within this period. In China, India, Persia, Palestine, Greece, appeared men of the greatest religious genius and highest spiritual reach that the world has known. When we recall how nearly contemporary were the greatest of the Hebrew prophets with Zoroaster, Confucius, Lao-tzu, Gautama, Pythagoras, and Socrates, we cannot but feel that here was an emergence of something new, a higher level of spiritual evolution, of which the culmination, for our Western world, was reached in the teaching of Jesus of Nazareth.

CHAPTER THREE

THE GREAT RELIGIONS (1)

1. TYPES AND TENDENCIES IN RELIGION

EACH of the great religions, whether confined within the limits of a particular region or race or accepted by great masses of mankind irrespective of geographical or racial conditions, has drawn its inspiration from the life and teaching of an individual founder, and bears the impress of what was most individual and characteristic in his spiritual outlook: whether, for instance, he was in the first place a thinker, a law-giver and social reformer, or one burning with passionate devotion to an ideal or overflowing with love for his fellows.

Thus in the first case—if the founder was above all a thinker—the religion that derives from his teaching is of the philosophical type, in which supreme importance is attached to the direction of life in accordance with an enlightened understanding of it meaning and purpose. Its aim is to clear away the mists of ignorance and error that blind men to the true meaning of life and to the course that they would follow if they were wise. If, however, the founder was more concerned with the practical conduct of life than with speculation, the religion shaped by him is of the type in which supreme importance is attached to matters of conduct, whether social obligations, or ritual observances due from the worshipper to the object of his worship or, at a higher spiritual level, observance of moral law regarded as expression of the divine will. In the third type the relationship of the worshipper to the Unseen rests upon an emotional rather than an intellectual apprehension of the supreme reality, and the evaluation of conduct is felt to be concerned most of all with the motive that prompts it.

But while a religion may be conveniently classified as belonging to one of these main types according to the importance that it attaches to thought or conduct or feeling—Buddhism, for example, to the need of enlightenment, Judaism to that of righteousness, Christianity to that of love—this must not be taken to imply that in any of them the other modes of experience are ignored. All religions afford some emotional expression of man's attitude towards the unseen world and the spiritual reality with which he feels himself to be in contact. All offer some system of belief, from the crudest to the more philosophical, as to the nature of this reality and the meaning and purpose of its activity. And all find expression for faith and worship in some kind of ceremonial and some regulation of conduct. Though there are marked differences between them according to the extent to which any of these modes of response predominates over the others, we must always bear in mind that whichever type a given religion may belong to, its main pattern is enriched and modified by the presence of the other elements, and it is only in a general sense that it can be said to be representative of a particular type.

Another feature to be noted as common to all religions is a certain similarity in their historical development. We may say, indeed, that there is a normal course followed by any religion, whatever its personal origin. The founder was spiritually in advance of his time; this is the mark of what we call genius in any kind of activity. The greatness of his new conception of religion could be recognised only by a few. To his teaching the majority of his contemporaries remained indifferent, even if they did not openly reject it and seek to uphold the existing orthodoxy by persecution of the new teacher and his followers. Only with time came a growing recognition of its value, and through the efforts of devoted followers the new religion won gradual acceptance by a continually increasing number of adherents. But with this enlarged acceptance there comes inevitably a change: something of the spirit of the founder is lost, and though the religion thus established may grow enormously in extent and influence, it carries within itself a tendency to progressive deterioration.

This tendency is due to causes inherent in human nature. A great spiritual advance beyond the accepted ideas and practice of the time makes demands to which only the finest natures can respond. Not only does the great prophet stand high above the mass of his hearers, but even the chosen disciples who are nearest to him cannot fully grasp the implications of his teaching or understand the message which they endeavour to pass on to others. Still more when the attempt is made to bring it within the apprehension of average minds, these are apt, by taking only that which appeals to them, to lose yet more of its value and significance. Besides inability to grasp it as a whole there are many influences at work which change its nature, as they understand it. However eagerly they may welcome the new teaching, they cannot wholly escape from the thraldom of traditions in which they grew up; and since these still exert a subconscious influence (which is all the stronger because it is not realised) the new ideas and the manner of their expression are shaped into something very different from the spirit and intention of the Teacher.

Moreover there is in human nature a ready credulity and love of the marvellous which renders all of us prone, under excitement, to accept for true anything that strikes the imagination, and to exaggerate it yet further in the telling. Every day we see new stories grow, as they pass from one to another, until they have lost touch with the facts; yet they are readily believed. So it has been in the history of all religions. The story of the doings and sayings of one in whom the flame of spiritual genius burns strongly is strange enough, compared with what ordinary people feel and how they act, to move all who hear it with wonder. Seeing how far removed he is from beings like themselves, they are prepared to accept anything, however marvellous, that is told about him; and in telling it again they tend to add, unconsciously, yet further marvels to the story. It is in this way that legends grow up about all great men, and most of all about those who are spiritually greatest. These were so far from being ordinary men that many found it impossible to believe that they were men at all. Hence the tendency in most religions to give to their founders, as manifestations of the divine nature, a place amongst the objects of their worship. In the process much is added to the narrative of their lives in order to bring this intrinsic divinity into clearer light. Similarly in records of their words additions have been made, either in some turn of speech given to authentic sayings or in explanatory phrases attached to them, in order to make explicit what the devout worshipper would assume to be their inner meaning.

FORM AND SPIRIT

As the number of followers of a religion grows there is need of a twofold systematisation which cannot but affect the meaning and spirit of the teaching as originally given. On the one hand there must be some formulation of the main points of this teaching as it is passed on from one to another. There must be some agreement as to what is of most importance and as to what is to be included in the tenets of the new faith. As presented by different disciples to different audiences it was inevitably exposed to variations of statement and interpretation; in time, therefore, it was necessary to recognise these differences and to reach some agreement as to the particular presentation that should be accepted as orthodox. Hence the need of creeds and doctrinal statements which tend to throw the emphasis on to forms of belief as of no less importance than the spirit which was the essence of the founder's teaching, and which is too often stifled by the forms in which it is swathed.

Secondly, there can be no large body of adherents of any faith without some kind of external organisation. It must provide opportunities of common action. It must ensure that what is done shall be in accord with the convictions and practice of those who were most closely in touch with the founder. Thus there grows up a hierarchy of leaders with a fixed constitution and rules for observance. This tendency is just as inevitable as the formulation of orthodox doctrines; and again the result is to throw emphasis on the formal and external organisation of a religion, while in the process the real meaning and purpose of the founder and the values that his life and teaching revealed are only too likely to be forgotten.

This seems to be the normal history of the religions whose growth we can trace in historical times, whether the founder is little more than a legendary name, like the Persian Zoroaster, or a historical figure, such as Confucius, Jesus of Nazareth, and Mohammed. In the story of their lives legend and historical record are mingled in varying degrees. It is not always possible to discover with certainty what was the core of their teaching beneath the accretions with which centuries of tradition and adaptation have overlaid it. In speaking of the religions that bear their names we have therefore to keep in mind that much in the later doctrines and practice of each is inevitably on a lower level, and may even be in marked contrast with the teaching of its founder.

THE GREAT RELIGIONS

2. ZOROASTRIANISM

It is noteworthy that the great philosophical systems, in which man has endeavoured to solve the riddle of existence by the exercise of his rational powers and to give himself a coherent and intelligible account of the universe and his place in it, have been for the most part products of races belonging to the Aryan division of mankind. Much folly has been written and enacted in recent times in the name of Aryan superiority; but where other claims cannot be substantiated, it would seem that we may ascribe to these peoples a tendency to intellectual curiosity and the rational organisation of experience. Whatever forms their religion may have taken, a marked feature of it in different branches of the Aryan stock is desire to understand the meaning of things, and to fashion some system of rational apprehension that shall satisfy this desire.

This philosophical element first appeared in the guise of mythologies—imaginative explanations, that is, of the facts of experience that aroused men's wonder. In its later form it ran riot in metaphysical speculation. Much of Greek philosophy was of a mystical character, which, when combined with Semitic religious conceptions, gave shape to the elaborate theological systems of early and medieval Christianity.

An example of a religion of this type is the old Persian cult still practised by a small body of fire-worshippers found in India. Though its adherents are now insignificant in numbers, the religion of the Parsees, which claims for its founder the ancient Persian sage Zoroaster,[1] was once the religion of the greatest empire that the world had then seen, and is of historical importance not only for this reason but because of its influence on the development of other religions. Of the life of the founder little or nothing is known for certain, or even of the time at which he lived, except that it must have been in the earlier part of the millennium before the Christian era. Nor is it possible to say how much in the religion that bore his name represents his actual teaching, or how much was added or altered by the Magians—

[1] This is the form of his name by which he is generally known. A more exact spelling would probably be Zarathustra, the form used by the German philosopher Nietzsche in the book in which he put his own ideas into the mouth of the Persian sage.

priests who, in adopting it, undoubtedly reintroduced some of the very elements from which he had wished to free it. Zoroaster resembled other great religious founders in starting from the general religious ideas of his time and race. The Persians, like other Aryan peoples, were worshippers of nature-powers, and especially those of the sky. In the old Persian religion there were many gods and hosts of demons, good and bad. Each man, it was thought, had one of these as his special attendant spirit: an idea which reappears in the Roman conception of an individual 'genius', and in the Christian idea of a guardian angel. To the Persians fire was always sacred, symbol of the sun and revered both as a life-giving element and as the means of sacrifice, the messenger which carried up men's prayers and aspirations to the gods. For this reason fire must not be defiled by consuming the bodies of the dead, any more than earth by burying them: they must be exposed on platforms to be devoured by birds of prey. Reverence for fire, as seen both in the sun and in the sacred flame, is still the most conspicuous feature in the worship of the Parsees.

Zoroaster, it is plain, looked at religion from the standpoint of a philosopher rather than of a priest. It was his object to purify it from the superstitions and idolatries that he found prevalent; but together with the simpler doctrine and practice that he taught, these old superstitions still remained and were always tending to creep back into the beliefs and ritual of those who called themselves his followers. To Darius, the great king who made the doctrines of Zoroaster the religion of his empire, these baser elements were 'the Lie' which was to be combated and overcome by the truth of Zoroaster's teaching. Most of the earlier gods were, in this teaching, relegated to the rank of demons. According to it, there had been originally neither time nor matter, but only an unchanging eternity of as yet undifferentiated existence, neither light nor darkness. In this metaphysical doctrine Zoroaster's philosophy has much in common, as will be seen presently, with that of the Hindu thinkers in which both Brahmanism and Buddhism had their origin. At last, with the birth of time, Zoroaster taught, two great powers came into existence. One was Ahura-mazda ('wise lord'), the power of light and good in all its forms; the other, Angro-maingu[1] ('hostile spirit'), the power of dark-

[1] In later literature these names were usually written Auramazda, or Ormuzd and Ahriman, and are better known under these forms.

ness and all that is evil. From the beginning of the present world-order there has been a continual struggle between them. In this struggle man is called upon to take his part, fighting on the side of truth and good against 'the Lie' that draws men's minds away from the truth, and against evil in all its forms. By his choice and by his actions each man is helping to bring nearer or to delay the final victory of good; for though the struggle must continue as long as time lasts, it is not everlasting. Eventually good will prevail, and evil will either be overpowered or in some way reconciled to good and swallowed up in it.

Since man's part in the struggle has thus a cosmic significance, it is of the utmost importance that he should understand its nature and meaning and should direct his conduct by this understanding. By the way he does this he will be judged. To Zoroaster is traceable the idea, afterwards adopted by Mohammed in his picture of the judgment that awaits men after death, of a 'bridge of separation' which is to give, to those who have taken the side of right in the struggle, access to the heaven to which their life has entitled them; while the evildoers who try to cross it will fall from it into an abyss below. In life, therefore, men must avoid all forms of evil and must take their place in the ranks of those who fight against it. This they must do not only by opposing what is evil in the actions of their fellow men, but by helping to destroy what is harmful in nature—animals and plants and everything else that is poisonous and dangerous to life. They must keep themselves free from all contamination such as that of corpses, which are given over to the spirits of evil. They must help to maintain all that is good and useful for life, and as symbol of this they must keep alight the sacred fire.

Such was the religion that Zoroaster taught. Its simplicity, however, could not be maintained. Under the influence of the Magians, who saw in it the lessening of their priestly power, much that he had rejected was reintroduced. Sacrifice was restored; purifications and penances which required the mediation of a priest were enjoined. Prayer became largely the repetition of magic formulas. Lengthy services, with hymns, prayers, sacrifices, and recitations of the sacred scriptures became customary during the hours of darkness from midnight till dawn (as is still the custom of the Parsees), this being the time when the power of the evil spirits whose home is darkness was held to be greatest. But at least the love of truth and honesty remained its central feature, and for these virtues its remaining votaries are still conspicuous.

A historical offshoot of Zoroastrianism was the widely spread cult of Mithras in the first centuries of the Christian era. Mithraism was a combination of the Persian religion with the ideas and practices of fertility-cults that were then so prominent. Its chief deity, Mithras, an embodiment of Ahuro-mazda in the person of the sun-god, was worshipped as the unconquered hero-god who saved his followers through his victory over the powers of darkness; not, as in other mystery-cults, through his death and resurrection. This victory was symbolised by the slaying of a bull, of whose flesh initiates partook in a sacramental rite through which salvation was to be attained. In this respect Mithraism bore a distant resemblance to Christianity. Through its prevalence among soldiers serving in the Roman armies, Mithraism was at one time the most serious rival for adoption as the official religion of the Roman Empire.[1] But Christianity prevailed, through its higher ethical ideal and the fact that its central object of worship was a historical personality instead of a merely mythological figure.

The influence of Zoroastrianism has also been a factor in the development of other religions. When the Persian conquest of Babylon brought the Jews of the captivity under Persian rule, under which the restored Jewish state remained for some two hundred years, their religion was affected by contact with Zoroastrian ideas, just as it had been by those of Babylonian origin. Whereas Satan first appears, in an Old Testament book showing that influence, among the servants of God as the 'adversary' appointed to test the goodness of men, in the later Jewish and in early Christian literature he has become the power of darkness and evil that for a time is lord of this world and matched, like Ahriman, on almost equal terms with God.

Amongst early Christian sects were the Manichaeans, who adopted the teaching of the Persian Mani. Like Zoroaster, he held that there are two great principles, good and evil, and that life, both of the

1 Its observances had considerable influence on those of Christianity: in the replacement, for example, of the Jewish Sabbath by the day dedicated to the Sun, and the choice of December 25th (the sun's 'birthday') to commemorate the birth of Jesus. See *Stoic Christian and Humanist*, by Professor Gilbert Murray.

individual and of the world as a whole, is a constant conflict between the two. Matter being intrinsically evil, the body and all its instincts are necessarily evil also; it is only possible to escape from the bondage of this evil by an extreme asceticism which shall subdue the flesh and bring it into subjection to the spirit. Other features of Mani's teaching had more resemblance to Buddhist or Christian tenets. During his lifetime it had been confined to Persia; but after the opposition of the Zoroastrian priests had brought about his death by crucifixion, his followers carried it westwards, and much of it found its way into Christianity. Manichaeism was finally declared by the Christian Church to be a heresy. But in spite of attempts to stamp it out—at times, as in the case of the Albigenses in the thirteenth century, with the utmost ferocity—it obtained a firm hold in many countries. It has influenced the development of Christianity to such an extent that the dualism of good and evil, God and the Devil, and the doctrine of original sin have remained an integral part of Christian theology as popularly understood.

3. HINDUISM

It is in India that the most conspicuous examples of philosophical religion have arisen. The main forms of religion practised in historical times in this vast and populous peninsula are the outcome of conceptions brought by Aryan invaders before history begins. They were shaped into their later forms alike by the geographical conditions of the peninsula and by the cults of the races native to it, whose ideas and practice, during the process of conquest and absorption, have deeply affected those of the conquerors. The deities worshipped by the invaders were sky-powers such as were universal objects of worship in the pastoral stage of development. In the course of time, as the pastoral manner of life was changed to one mainly agricultural, so also did these deities change their character, and they were supplemented or replaced by those of the native peoples with the beliefs and superstitions associated with cultivation of the soil.

Inevitably also the character of the invading race suffered a change. When subject to the enervating climate of the plains they lost something of the energy that under other conditions could be expended in a life of action and in achieving material and social progress. The

Hindu tendency has been in general to an attitude of passivity, showing itself on one side in a rigid social system of hereditary castes, and on another in contemplative thought in which life appears to be little more than a meaningless round of suffering and illusion and the only true wisdom consists in finding a means of escape.

The outcome of this historical development is a culture widely different from that of the kindred races of the West, and a religion that to our eyes is apt to seem an astonishing medley of profound philosophical ideas and the crudest superstitions. In this respect, indeed, Hinduism resembles other religions; but the unfamiliar character of the forms in which its ideas are embodied makes the fact more striking than in the case of religions which to us seem more reasonable because we have long been familiar with their imagery and modes of expression.

In the earliest form in which Hindu religion is known to us from the Vedas—hymns which come down from the middle of the second millennium before the Christian era—the kind of worship that they portray is simpler than that of later times, without animal sacrifices or images to which they were offered. The names of the chief deities are different from those now in use and show, by their resemblance to those of other branches of the Aryan stock, that when these hymns were written the separation was still comparatively recent. The Vedas are addressed to deities representing the sky, the sun, rain, and fire. Chief among these are Varuna and Indra, the latter being also a war-god, naturally a main object of devotion to a migratory people of the steppes invading the cultivated plains.

Besides these hymns there are also early writings in which is to be found a conception that underlies all Hindu philosophy: of a state of being, diffused through the whole universe, from which living things are, as it were, detached, and to which it will be their supreme happiness to be reunited. The ultimate reality is to be sought, that is, not in external nature, but in a spiritual world. In this conception Brahman, the whole of being, is impersonal—to be distinguished from the later Brahmā, the masculine form of the name, under which this universal being is personified and worshipped as a god.

In the Upanishads, the sacred writings which follow the Vedas in the next millennium, Brahman is also spoken of as the Atman, or spirit of the universe (*atman* being the breath or spirit that animates each individual). This is the first step towards a personification which took many forms, recognised by Hindu thinkers as embodying different aspects of the one divine Being. The main idea that runs through these writings is desire to be reunited with the universal spirit by pursuing the path of knowledge. This path involves the practice of many forms of asceticism and other means whereby man's spirit may be withdrawn from the confusion of life (which Hindu thought regards as merely *maya*, illusion) into concentration on the universal and unchanging reality in which the individual may hope ultimately to be merged.

There are various lines along which Hinduism has been developed, but each of these, whatever their differences, shows the same general principles that are characteristic of all Hindu thought. Amongst no other people has the conviction of the unreality of all that is impermanent and changing become so firmly established that, not only for the philosopher but for all alike, it forms the sub-conscious basis of their attitude towards life. The only reality is the unseen and unchanging; all that is material is transient and unreal, an external show that is only illusion. Even if science, therefore, is useful for the business of life, it is not a means of discovering truth; for it is concerned with the temporary and changing, whereas truth is only to be attained by contemplation of that in which there is no change. Nor is history any guide; for this also deals only with the transient, the cycle of events that has neither beginning nor end nor any purpose in its everlasting recurrence. Each separate life, so long as it is bound in the illusion of material existence, is part of a similarly recurrent cycle of births and deaths, in which the one connection that runs through them all is the law of 'Karma'. This is the law that the nature of each new life is decided by the last, and rises or falls in the scale of existence according to the manner in which the previous one has been lived. The only hope of escape from the recurrence of illusion is to reach a state in which all stimulus of feeling and all need of action are left behind.

In the great epic poems, the Mahabharata and the Ramayana, the ideas of Hinduism are presented in the form of myths. What to the philosopher could take the form of abstract conceptions must, for the great majority who are not capable of abstract thought, be humanised as the story of the doings of living persons. It is here, therefore, that we find not only the personification of Brahmā as a deity, but other deities as well representing various aspects of the complete divine personality. Chief of these are the great Gods of later Hindu worship, Vishnu and Siva, perhaps originally deities of the Dravidian races of Southern India. These, together with Brahmā, form a Hindu Trinity, which may be said to represent the three modes of mental activity. Thus, Brahma stands for divine knowledge, Vishnu for divine love, and Siva for the divine will. Hinduism is pantheism in its most thorough-going form, what to us seem good and evil being equally expressions of the divine nature. Siva is therefore at once creator and destroyer, representative of the duality that runs through life. Vishnu is held to have appeared on earth in various incarnations in order to help mankind. Krishna, the great hero of the Mahabharata, is one of these 'avatars', or appearances in human form, of Vishnu. Another is Rama, the hero who gives his name to the other epic. Possibly both are deified human figures whose exploits had become legendary.

Such embodiment of the divine spirit is not confined to the heroes of the myths. Hindu thought recognised that men also have in them some part of it, in greater or less degree. Those who belong to the Brahman caste have most, and are most to be venerated on that account. In this way the caste[1] system which prevails in India—an outcome, no doubt, of the original Aryan conquest, with the grades of rank, determined by occupation, into which the conquerors were already divided, and the relegation of the conquered into inferior grades—has received a religious sanction that makes any modification of it a matter of extreme difficulty.

From conceptions of this kind and their poetical expression in the great myths the various forms of later Hindu religion are derived, with their multiplication of deities, male and female, and the inclusion of rites that have survived from more primitive times. The fact that any deity, however monstrous in form or character, can be philosophically regarded as personifying some aspect of reality, and accepted as a means of bringing it within the apprehension of the ordinary worshipper, makes it easy to find a place for such survivals in the same way that pagan objects of worship have often been

[1] 'Caste' is not itself an Indian word. The original word for this classification was one meaning 'colour'; it is now denoted by a word meaning 'birth', implying that each belongs for life to the social grade into which he is born.

retained under the names and attributes of Christian saints. Hence the Hindu pantheon is peopled with beings more numerous and more diverse in form than are to be found elsewhere, at least since the heyday of Egyptian mythology. In consequence, to the Westerner who forms a superficial judgment from the representations of these deities as portrayed in art and from the customary rites that Hindu religion enjoins or allows, Hinduism may seem to be no more than a medley of primitive survivals and superstitions.

Take, for example, the worship of Siva, the personification, as said above, of energy that is both creative and destructive. He is often depicted in art as having many arms and as engaged in a dance, these being symbols of creative activity. As the god of fertility he is represented under the form of a bull; and in Hindu temples the organs of generation, in symbolic form, are prominent as objects of worship. His terrible wife, Kali, is the personification of all that is dreadful and destructive.[1] One of his sons, Ganesha, portrayed with the head of an elephant as the wisest of beasts, is the patron of all arts and crafts. Animal forms of deities, such as Hanuman the Ape-god, are relics of a primitive animal worship. A survival of this worship is also shown in the refusal to allow animals, and in particular the cow, to be killed even for food, a refusal which has been so constant a source of violence between Hindu and Mohammedan.

It is easy for Westerners, repelled by this pantheon of strange and often, to our thinking, obscene forms, to dismiss Hinduism as unworthy of serious consideration—'magic tempered by metaphysics', as it has been called. It is not so easy for us to realise that, to a thoughtful Hindu, much in Christianity might well appear in the same light. No religion can be judged only by its superficial aspect. In Hinduism, in its various forms, there have been saints and thinkers as truly and profoundly religious as any of other lands; and there are those who see in it today, in the universality of its philosophic outlook and in its all-embracing toleration, a medium in which other creeds can be reconciled and religious aspirations of every kind can find sustenance.[2]

[1] Probably Siva was originally the vegetation-spirit of the primitive agricultural religion, and Kali the earth-goddess, but regarded as a terrible rather than a kindly power.

[2] See, for example, *The Hindu View of Life*, by S. Radhakrishnan.

4. BUDDHISM

A world-religion that had its origin in India, though now found mainly in other Eastern countries than that of its birth, is Buddhism —the name, like that of Christianity, being taken from the title given to its founder. It is one of the chief developments of Hinduism; or at least Hinduism provided the soil in which it had its roots. For while the Buddha turned away from its multiplicity of deities and from the superstitious ideas and practices with which it had clothed itself, he inherited from it the philosophic framework of thought which he made the basis of his own teaching. Though rejecting the whole superstructure of the religion of his time, he retained the fundamental principle of an ultimate unchanging reality in which all is one. To him, as to other Hindu thinkers, the apparent separateness of the individual self was an illusion, and all that makes up the life of conscious personality was so much inperfection, from which we have laboriously to free ourselves in the course of countless lives. In these several lives what is passed on is not an identical 'self' (for the self is merely made up of the temporary elements of each separate life) but a stream of energy disturbing the eternal calm of pure being: a stream from which it is only possible to escape when the craving for existence is overcome. This philosophic conception underlies Hinduism and Buddhism alike.

Buddhism, indeed, in its original form, could hardly be regarded as a religion but for the fact that it was permeated throughout with feeling for the suffering of humanity, and that it enjoined upon its disciples a particular way of life. Attainment of escape from the suffering involved in life and its illusions the Buddha sought neither in metaphysical speculation nor in any kind of religious ceremonial, but in a 'middle way' based upon psychological analysis of the causes of suffering and the conditions under which ultimate release could be obtained. Buddhism was thus in origin a philosophic discipline rather than a religion; but in the course of its growth it has largely abandoned the austerity of thought of its founder. Like other religions it has elaborated a ritual of worship, and has given itself up to adoration of the Buddha himself and other divine figures—developments that are entirely alien from his teaching. It still remains, however, in essence a religion of thought, whose chief aim is to reach a right understanding, and thereby to attain a peace which can only come with the cessation of all desire. For this reason, as being above all an intellectual apprehension of reality and interpretation of human experience, Buddhism is the religion most fully representative of the philosophical type.

In the course of close on two and a half thousand years, and as the result of its transference to countries other than that of its origin, Buddhism has absorbed many alien ideas and practices, by which it has been profoundly modified, and has taken forms that have little to do with the teaching of its founder. And even before this took place both his teaching and the actual facts of his life were soon overlaid by tradition and legend. All that is now possible is to see certain main features which may be accepted as trustworthy.

'Buddha', it should be borne in mind, like 'Christ', is not a name but a title. It means 'the enlightened one'. The man to whom this title is given was born, about 550 B.C., of a royal line in North-east India. He is sometimes spoken of as Gautama, from the family name, sometimes as Siddartha, his personal name, or as Sakyamuni—'sage of the tribe of Sakya'—a title of honour resembling that of Buddha. There is no reason to doubt the tradition that he was trained as a prince and knew all the happiness that such a position, together with a happy marriage, could give; or that, at the age of twenty-eight, when he had chanced to learn how much suffering, from which none can wholly escape, is bound up with life, he left his home and went out as a wanderer, seeking wisdom by which suffering could be overcome. At first, like the founder (who may have been his contemporary) of the Jain religion still widely practised in India, he sought this in extreme asceticism. But neither in this nor in abstract philosophy could he find what he sought, and so he abandoned both these traditional approaches to wisdom for what he called 'the middle way'. It was after much wandering as a mendicant, while sitting deep in meditation under a bodhi (or bo) tree, that he found enlightenment and became the Buddha. There are others who have also been enlightened in the course of that unending recurrence of lives and universes which, as already said, is an accepted part of Hindu thought, but he became the supreme 'enlightened one' of the present world-order; henceforward to be reverenced as such by all who should accept his teaching, and always in art represented as sitting wrapped in eternal meditation.

By thus reaching enlightenment he was freed from the cycle of personal life and its suffering, and could at once have entered the eternal calm of Nirvana. This was the great temptation which he overcame through compassion for his fellow-men, renouncing the privilege of immediate absorption in the infinite, and living his life out in order to teach to others the truth he had himself found. To the disciples who gathered round him he expounded his doctrine, teaching them how enlightenment was to be found and escape from suffering won. This teaching was oral only. For this reason, to make it easier to remember, and no doubt also in accordance with the pattern of his own thought, it is set forth in numerical sequences: the four sublime truths, the eight-fold path, the five practical precepts, the three-fold training, and so on. The fundamental doctrines of Buddhism are laid down in the four sublime truths as to the nature and universality of suffering and the way of escaping from it. Sorrow, the transitoriness of all experience, the unreality of material evidence, and the illusions with which we are surrounded—these, which are the lot of all, are due to the dominance of self and its desires; they can be made to cease only by the annihilation of desire and the cessation of the personal self. Escape from the self, with its limitations and endless source of suffering, is to be found in following the eight-fold path: through attaining, that is, to right methods in belief, in purpose, in speech, behaviour, occupation, and effort, and in thought and the inward concentration upon reality which will bring detachment from the distractions of life.

In all this there is no merely abstract philosophy, but insistence on a way of life, as a means of escape from evil, no less complete than the insistence of Judaism on righteousness of conduct. But there is an immense difference both in the philosophic implications underlying the two demands and in the two lines that are to be followed. To the Jew the one certainty on which all depends is the existence of a righteous God, creator and ruler of the world; and the one thing that matters is to serve God according to the Law, both ritual and moral, that He has given to men. To the Buddha there was no such sanction for conduct. Accepting the Hindu conception of a universe, or a succession of universes, without beginning and without end, subject only to an eternal sequence of cause and effect, he saw no place for the intervention of divine power; if gods exist, they must be subject to the same laws as all else. He therefore stressed the futility of prayer and sacrifice and taught that man's salvation rests with himself, first in true thought about the nature of things, and then in the way of life that enlightenment shows to afford the best hope of escape from all that is evil.

While, therefore, he discouraged metaphysical speculation, he could only express his religious intuition in philosophical terms. The doctrines of 'Maya' and 'Karma' he took for granted, as well as that of the changelessness of absolute being. This being the only reality, all else is only a temporary becoming. There is thus no permanent individual soul. We are only temporary bundles of mental states, feeling, perception, judgment, and so on, always becoming something else even though, like a river, we seem to be the same. It is only when we realise how transitory is all sense and all perception that we can hope to escape from the recurrent wheel of life to which we are bound. Death is no release; for through death we only pass to a fresh life—a new flame, as it were, kindled from the old. It is not an individual soul which is reborn, but only the impress passed on of a self which is the composite result of past actions. Therefore, since in each new life we are what we have made this 'self' in the past, conduct is all-important as the outcome of right thought. Compassion and self-mastery are the virtues insisted upon above all in the five practical rules. The Buddhist must kill nothing, for all living things are struggling up the ascent of life. He must give gladly, and take nothing by force or fraud. He must not lie or bear false witness, and he must keep from intoxicating drink and from sensual indulgence, which, like mud in a river, defile and dull the mind. Those who do not keep these rules cannot even enter upon the path of enlightenment, but fall back to lower levels of life.

Conduct, therefore, is not, as to the Jew, the service of God in obedience to a divinely appointed law, but a means of escape from the wheel of life with its law of Karma, by which we suffer the destiny we have brought on ourselves. The goal to which the Buddhist looks forward is not added power or clearer purpose or fuller love, but peace from desires and impulses, a peace only to be won by the cessation of personality and individual consciousness. Just as before the world of life began, he holds, there was a state of pure being, formless and one, so also when life as a state of separate existence is ended we shall enter again into Nirvana when we are emancipated from the tyranny of self, and find peace in the absence of desire. Some have thought that Nirvana implies the annihilation not merely of personal feeling, but of all conscious being; but this is not a necessary interpretation of what is undoubtedly a difficult conception to grasp.[1] Buddhist teachers, anticipating the dialectical method of Hegel, have said that it is neither existence nor non-existence, but that there is a 'middle way' in which the two are reconciled. A favourite metaphor under which they present the relation between life here and Nirvana is that of a wave sinking back into the ocean from which it rose. Though in so doing the wave ceases to have an individual existence, it does not thereby cease to exist or cease to share the nature of the ocean. If, therefore, absolute existence is living spirit, Nirvana is the realisation of an identity with this spirit far fuller than any personal consciousness could be.

If Buddhism, like all the greater religions, lays down a way of life for its adherents, it is not that it regards either action or feeling as ends in themselves worth seeking. Activity of any kind, since it proceeds from desire which is the root and occasion of all suffering, is even at best a necessity that is to be deplored; its purpose is not accomplishment, but only escape from the need for activity. The morality enjoined by the five practical rules is the first step towards this end, without which there can be no starting on the path of deliverance. Beyond this comes, for those who are now fit for it, the real training, Yoga, of which the highest form is abstention from all external activity and an inward concentration upon reality. By such meditation comes knowledge of the cause of evil and the means of escape from it, leading ultimately to full enlightenment and release from the wheel of life. This is beyond the reach of the rank and file, who must be content with practising the simple virtues that are only

[1] Those who dismiss the Buddhist conception of Nirvana—the ultimate state of being—as a mere void, the most empty and meaningless of all objects of faith, forget that all systems of thought come eventually to a point at which thought can go no further, and what lies beyond can only be defined in negative terms—by the absence, that is, of qualities and limitations attaching to all objects with which we are familiar. Nirvana thus takes its place with the Absolute of philosophy, the Infinity of mathematics, the Unseen of faith, and the Ineffable of the mystic as conceptions in their nature inexpressible in terms that are derived from and applicable to our actual experience.

the preliminary stage, in the hope that by so doing they may, in future incarnations, attain to the higher stages.

There are some, however, who are capable of further training. It is right, the Buddha taught, that these should wish to leave the world of workaday activity and devote themselves entirely to this manner of life. Hence the prevalence of monasticism in those countries in which Buddhism has taken root. This is confined to the male sex; for to Buddhist thought, as so commonly in the East, woman is an inferior being who can only hope, by performing the duties of her inferior station, to be born again as one to whom the path to enlightenment will then be open.

The Buddha himself left no writings. After his death his sayings were collected by his disciples and handed down orally for many generations until, about a century before the Christian era, they were written down in the Pitakas ('Baskets of Tradition'). It was inevitable that they should be modified and expanded in the course of this transmission, and that much pious legend should have grown up around the facts of Buddha's life. By this time his teaching was widespread in India and missionaries had been sent out to carry it to Ceylon and Burma, where it still retains its more primitive form. Later it gradually lost its hold in India, through being either absorbed into the older Hindu cults or treated as a heresy to be expelled. By then, however, it had penetrated into China, where in spite of persecutions it was widely accepted. From China it spread into Korea and Japan on the one side and on the other into Tibet.[1] In the course of this dispersion and the many contacts thus brought with other forms of religion, Buddhism has departed widely from the teaching of the Founder. Thus there was a reintroduction of such rites as adoration of images, prayer, and repetition of formulas, which he taught his disciples to do without. The monks became priests, and temples were built in honour of Buddha in which elaborate ritual is performed.

There are now two main divisions of Buddhist thought and practice. Hinayana—the 'little vehicle', as it is somewhat contemptuously called to distinguish it from the 'great vehicle', Mahayana, of the

[1] Tibet remains one of the chief strongholds of Buddhism, but in its most depraved form, being penetrated through and through with the demon-worship which has always been prevalent there. Prayer-wheels and devil-dances make a strange combination with Buddhist doctrines.

majority—is the name given to the doctrines that are accepted by the southern Buddhists, which seem to be the older and more authentic. Hinayana Buddhism prescribes a monastic life of austere discipline and poverty, by which and by meditation on the illusoriness of mundane experience and the need of freedom from desires merit is to be acquired that will eventually win release from the wheel of life. It was this that was originally spread throughout China, and from China introduced into Japan in the seventh century. But such doctrines, arising from Hindu ways of thought and conditions of life, proved too austere when brought into contact with other cultures. The earlier Buddhist sects have died out, and later ones have adopted a greatly modified form of Buddhism, the Mahayana, in which allowance is made for the weaknesses and needs of those who find the 'way of the wise' too hard to follow. There are various sects, with differences of doctrine and practice; the general tendency is towards worship not only of the Buddha but of other beings also through whom eternal happiness may be won. These are the 'bodhisattvas' (somewhat resembling the part played by 'saints' in the development of Christianity)—those, that is, who like the Buddha have attained to enlightenment but, though they might then at once have entered Nirvana, renounced the privilege in order to be able to help others to follow in their steps. In some Buddhist sects the one most honoured is Amida, the Light of the World, who is held to have taken a vow that he would never himself accept the final release, but would establish a resting-place in a 'Pure Land' of happiness for such as could not themselves reach Nirvana. Into this paradise it is possible for all to enter through faith in the saving power of Amida, as shown by repetition of his name in a sacred formula.[1] It is a characteristic of this later Buddhism that, like Hindu religion, it can find a place for other deities (as aspects of the Buddha in different incarnations) and for other doctrines, to be explained as 'accommodation'—a way that is, of reducing higher truth to a form in which it can be grasped

[1] The honour paid to Amida probably represents the adoption into Buddhism of an older cult of sun-worship. To one of the largest divisions of Japanese Buddhism, the Shinshu sect, Amida is an all-loving personal deity, who took upon himself incarnation in the form of Sakyamuni in order to save men. There may be here an echo of Christian teaching. See *The Buddhist Sects of Japan*, by E. Steinilber-Oberlin.

at a lower level of intelligence. In some sects of Eastern Buddhism there is also a female figure, Kwannon, goddess of mercy, who holds a place similar to that occupied by the Madonna in Catholic Christianity.

To the more spiritually minded Buddhist, however, this is all to be accounted for as concession to those who know no better and cannot live on the heights of thought, while the teaching of the Buddha remains unaffected by it, as simple as it is profound. To such a one his religion is an increasingly selfless manner of life, as a help to the quiet of inward meditation through which he may hope in each succeeding life to rise to a higher level of existence, until at last he has sloughed off the last remnant of personal desire and can sink back into the eternal calm of absolute being. Viewed from without, this may seem only a religion of escape, a flight from actuality; experienced from within, it is the hope of release from the burden of life and the finding of peace.

CHAPTER FOUR

THE GREAT RELIGIONS (2)

1. CONFUCIANISM

OF religions of the second type, those that are primarily concerned with conduct, there are two pre-eminent examples: the established religion of China, and Judaism, originally the national cult of a small branch of the Semite race, which has become one of the most distinctive though still numerically the smallest of world-religions, and is more widely spread in extent, though not in numbers, than any other with the exception of Christianity.

Of these two the first may be said to be a religion of common sense, good feeling, and respectability. Of all widely followed religions the one that looks to the Chinese sage Confucius[1] as its founder shows fewest specifically religious characteristics and is, so to speak, the most secular of religions, in which the ordering of conduct is a more prominent feature than either philosophic thought or emotional intensity.

Like other religions, Confucianism is the outcome of the manner of life and temperament of the people among whom it arose. The Chinese civilisation is the oldest now existing. A settled way of life, with an unbroken, though much troubled, history that goes back for thousands of years, has established a reverence for the past and for the sages to whose wisdom what is best in it is held to be due. The mass of the people consists of peasantry, patient toilers, content with little, peaceful and docile. Living as they do in close dependence upon nature, of which they feel themselves a part, the objects of their

[1] This is the Latinised form, adopted in the West, of the Chinese Kung-fu-tsu, meaning 'Kung the Philosopher'.

worship have always been the powers of heaven and earth on which their livelihood depends. To these no temples were erected, but their worship was carried on, with simple rites, in the open air. Still closer as objects of reverence are the spirits of the dead, who are still counted as members of the family to which they belonged. Ancestor-worship has always been the core of the Chinese religion.

Into such an already old feudal society Confucius was born about 550 B.C. His life and teaching are known to us through his own writings and those of his followers. These writings and the later development of his ideas by Mencius (Meng-tsu) have always been regarded as the Chinese classics, the chief subject of study for all who sought political advancement. Confucius was by temperament a student; seeking wisdom in the writings of earlier sages, he gave much attention to sifting and arranging these, so that now they survive only in the form he gave to them. He was, however, not merely a student, but endeavoured as an administrator to put his ideals of government in practice. For this purpose he visited several courts; but though his fame was sufficient to ensure a welcome, he met with continual disappointments in the actual conditions under which he had to work, and finally retired to his native place. There he died (about 480 B.C.) and there his tomb is now held in high honour. The form of government that he inculcated was a paternal despotism, such as was practicable in the comparatively small states of his time. He attached the greatest importance to the example of the ruler, which should permeate the whole community through a rigid gradation of authority, to be maintained by observance of an elaborate ceremonial on the part of all, both towards superiors and inferiors. This insistence on the behaviour proper for the various relationships of life is the chief characteristic of his teaching.

Confucius laid no claim to possessing any religious revelation. While admitting the all-embracing presence of a divine power, 'Heaven', he seems not to have regarded this as in any way personal or as an object of more than a general reverence. On the question of a life after death he keeps silence; and though he did not deny the existence of spirits of the dead, his advice was to reverence them, but keep them far off. As regards ancestor-worship, he asked how, if we do not know how to serve men, we can serve their ghosts? He taught that happiness is dependent in part on external circumstances, but mostly on a right manner of life. We should not lay upon destiny what is in reality the outcome of our actions and can be altered by the exercise of our will. What matters above all else, therefore, is the pursuit of wisdom by following the example of the sages. Confucius did not claim to be himself a sage, like those he reverenced so greatly, or even to have attained to the ideal of a 'Superior Person'. By this he meant much what we mean by 'gentleman'.[1] This was the ideal to be aimed at, within the power of anyone to reach who will submit himself to the necessary training.

This training consists in the first place of study of the Chinese classics. It was characteristic of one who attached so little importance to metaphysical speculation or to mysticism that he should warn his followers against any kind of abstract thought or turning inwards to find subjects for meditation. Thought, he said; must have material supplied to it, and such material was best found in the ancient writings and in the records of the past. With this in view he compiled digests of what seemed to him most worthy of remembrance in the sayings of earlier thinkers and in the events of his own and earlier times. In this he was following his natural bent, for, as he said of himself, he was 'a transmitter rather than a maker'. And so successful was he that from his time onward the sum of all wisdom seemed to be found in his writings, which were henceforward to be the chief objects of study; while the earlier classics, except for his compilations, were neglected and lost.

Besides this training of the mind by study and by filling it with the wisdom of the past, no less important was the training of the will to the formation of right purpose and to expression in fitting behaviour. With the same practical predilection that he showed in everything, he insisted that the good will must be made visible in action which was the true expression of thought. When he was young, he said, he had judged men by their words, but now he judged their words by their conduct. So conduct is all-important; and the greater part of his teaching consists in laying down rules for the behaviour fitting for the various relationships of life.

All begins with the home. The greatest of virtues is filial piety, and the conduct due from son to parent is laid down in great detail. So too that which is due from wife to husband, her position being one of

[1] See note on p. 68.

complete subordination to him and to the needs of the family. Divorce is permitted for various specified reasons, and polygamy is allowed. Next in importance to the home relationships comes friendship. All need friends, and should choose those with whom they have most in common. For this relationship he laid down the 'golden rule' in its negative form: what we should not like done to ourselves, we should not do to others. This, expressed as it can be in Chinese by a single written character or 'ideogram', he made into a universal rule of life.

In accordance with the practical concern that he showed all his life for good government, he lays down many precepts for the conduct of the Superior Person as ruler. He must himself be beneficent and just, and by his example must secure these virtues in his subordinates. While his office is sacred, he himself is only to be so regarded as long as he shows himself worthy of his office; when this is not the case, the allegiance of his subjects is no longer binding on them and he may be deposed. Great stress is laid on the observance of ceremonial—the 'proper things', as Confucius calls them, in the behaviour of subordinates to higher authorities, of superior to inferior, and of equals to each other. He insists on the importance of such ceremonial behaviour not merely as an expression of the proper feeling that each ought to have towards others, but also as a means of calling out this feeling and establishing the right gradations of relationship which to him seemed essential in a rightly ordered scheme of things.

It was, no doubt, owing to this conservative tendency and the sanctity conferred upon authority that the teaching of Confucius was officially adopted, within three hundred years of his death, as the only true doctrine, and established as the State religion. For this purpose the old nature-worship and ancestor-worship were combined with it. The Emperor, as the Son of Heaven and therefore himself divine, acted as mediator between Heaven and earth and performed the rites on which the welfare of his subjects depended. Confucius was now also regarded as of divine rank, and worship paid to him and to other sages and leaders to whom various degrees of such rank could be given by the Emperor's command. The worship was simple, consisting of prayer and sacrifice, for the most part in the open air. There were no priests, all public rites being performed by the Emperor and the various State officials as a regular part of their duties, and those connected with ancestor-worship by the head of each family. The study of the Confucian literature henceforth formed part of the training of all officials, and examination in it was made a condition precedent to any government appointment.[1]

Confucianism is thus a religion that differs markedly from most others in that it has but little sense of the mystery of things, and makes little attempt at explanation of the origin and purpose of human existence and of the universe in which we find ourselves. It may thus be said to be the least religious of religions, being mainly a code of customary conduct[2]; but for this very reason it has, to a greater degree than others, retained the character given to it by its founder.

In this respect it may be contrasted with Taoism, the other religion native to China. Lao-tsu, the founder of Taoism, was an older contemporary of Confucius, whom the younger philosopher knew and revered, though he did not accept his teaching. The name of the cult is derived from Tao, 'the Way', by which Lao-tsu meant the way in which the universe works and so the ultimate reality in which all opposites are reconciled. To live in harmony with this principle is the whole wisdom of man. He must therefore refrain from all self-assertion and cultivate an attitude of quietism. Taoism, in spite of its metaphysical background, is not so much a religion of thought as one of mysticism and complete immersion in the divine unity of being. From the standpoint of philosophy it is a loftier religion than that of Confucius. But, as Shakespeare said, 'lilies that fester smell far worse than weeds'. The philosophic doctrine of Tao and all that it stands for, being far beyond the grasp of the majority of those who did it lip-service, soon degenerated into a mass of superstition and magic, with a continually increasing list of deities of every kind and the pursuit of an elixir of life as one of its ends. From this, at least, Confucianism has been saved owing to the lower range of its thought and the limitation of its scope to matters of everyday.

[1] It was only at the beginning of the present century that the Confucian Classics were dethroned from this position.

[2] Galsworthy, in *Flowering Wilderness*, has pointed out how closely this corresponds with the actual creed of the typical English gentleman. 'Most of our caste in this country,' he makes one of them say, 'if they only knew it, are Confucian rather than Christian. Belief in ancestors and tradition, respect for parents, honesty, moderation of conduct, kind treatment of animals and dependents, absence of self-intrusion, and stoicism in face of pain and death, these are the characteristics of the gentleman.'

2. JUDAISM—ITS HISTORICAL GROWTH

Preoccupation with behaviour, at the two widely different levels of ritual observance and righteousness of life, is no less characteristic of Judaism, with its two-fold allegiance to the Law and the Prophets. In giving them the Law, divinely dictated, as its followers believe, to Moses, the Creator and Ruler of the world thereby marked off one people from all others as being in a peculiar degree the object of His care and the exponents of His will. Judaism is based on the Mosaic Law; but this was supplemented by the teaching of a great line of Prophets, who showed that ceremonial observance, however complete, is not enough. Even more important, they taught, is observance of the law in the heart, which requires an inward righteousness with justice and mercy in all the dealings of life. It is this two-fold insistence—upon the formalism of the Law and upon righteousness as central both in the conception of God and in the religious duty of men—which stamps Judaism, notwithstanding the intensity of feeling with which prophets and psalmists and centuries of persecution have endowed it, as a religion of conduct.

It would be a mistake to speak of Judaism as though it had been the same religion from the time of Moses to our own day, just as it would be to disregard all differences between present-day Christianity and the religion taught by the Apostles in the first century of our era. There have been different stages of Judaism, if the name may be extended to include the religious development of Israel in the period before we can rightly speak of Jews[1]: first, the religion of the early Hebrews; second, that taught by the great prophets and shaped in the time of the Babylonian Captivity; and third, that inspired by the 'Apocalyptic' writers and taught by the Rabbis before and after the beginning of the Christian era. It must always be borne in mind in

[1] It is somewhat confusing that in speaking of the Jewish race we must give them different names at different periods of their history. In their early records they are Children of Abraham or, more often, Israelites—'sons of Israel' (whatever the origin of the name 'Israel' may be). To other nations, in Egypt or in Palestine, they were Hebrews, a name also of uncertain meaning; and this is the name given to their original language, in which most of their Scriptures are written. After the return from the Captivity, since it was only the land of Judah that was at first resettled, they became known as Judaeans, of which our name for them, ' Jew ', is an abbreviation.

speaking of any historical religion that it has passed through several such stages in its evolution.

Of the religions that exist in the world today, Judaism, although not one of the largest in the number of its adherents, is certainly one of the most important, both in itself and as the parent both of Christianity and Islam. Moreover, it is outstanding in the fact that it has a recorded history of some 3,500 years and that throughout this time it can show a continuous development in its main principles. For these we must look back to Moses, in the middle of the second millennium before Christ; for though it is possible to go back yet further, and to regard Abraham as its real founder, there is much in the earlier records that has evidently been rewritten in the light of ideas of later growth.

If the tradition may be trusted, Abraham left Ur, the home of his family on the Euphrates, and migrated into Palestine[1] in order to sever himself from the idolatrous religions of Mesopotamia and to be free to worship his own God. In this his descendants saw the beginning of their monotheistic religion. But it was of slow growth. We can see in the early records stories showing how they retained a worship of sacred stones and groves as well as of 'teraphim' (their household gods) right down to the time of the Kingdom. We see also a belief in magic and a readiness to practise the rites and worship the deities of the peoples with whom the 'sons of Israel' came into contact. The story of Abraham's readiness to sacrifice his son in obedience to a divine command is evidence of a cult from which a later age recoiled; though even then, as we learn from the denunciations of the prophets, there was a tendency to resort to it in times of danger.

Where all is legend, it is not possible to give any certain account of the origins of the Hebrew people or the Hebrew religion. We can only regard them as an amalgamation of Bedouin tribes, sharing the superstitious fears and observances of their race and time, until they were

[1] Like the people, their land has been known by different names at different times. In the Old Testament it is usually called the land of Canaan, and the name Palestine is rarely used. The name, though properly given only to the coastal strip (the land of the Philistines) was later extended to cover the whole country between Syria and the border of Egypt. This Jews always looked upon as the 'land of the Promise' made by God to Abraham for his descendants. In returning to it, therefore, to set up a State of their own, they are only, in their own eyes, claiming what is theirs of divine right.

welded into a people by Moses. The religion which he gave them was then gradually elaborated by their priests and purified by the prophets. The accuracy of the tradition that associates Moses with the escape from Egypt of a horde of 'sons of Israel' who had long been subject there, and the giving of the Law during a pause in their long wanderings, in the desert of Sinai, can neither be proved nor disproved. It is tempting to connect Moses and his monotheistic religion with the reformation brought about in Egypt during the reign of King Akhnaton, of the XVIII Dynasty. Under this enlightened monarch the worship of Ra and the whole Egyptian pantheon was, for a short time, replaced by that of the one god, Aton, on a far higher spiritual level. The time of the Hebrew invasion of Canaan seems to allow of such a connection, and it is accepted as at least probable by various writers.[1] There seems no reason to doubt that, in its main features, the tradition of the escape from Egypt under the guidance of Moses rests upon some basis of historical fact.

The God whom the Israelites henceforward worshipped as their own was associated in their traditions with Sinai and Horeb and Sin: with mountains, that is, of the southern desert through which they had to pass before entering the 'promised land'. This God, according to the tradition, was revealed under the name of Jahweh[2] to Moses when, in middle life as an exile from Egypt, he found refuge with an Arab tribe in the mountains of Sinai. When, later on, he led his people from Egypt and brought them there, the story tells how the presence of Jahweh was manifested in storm and how the Law was given to Moses on the mountain.

The Law, in its original form was without doubt very simple. As in the history of all religions, it became customary to attribute any subsequent developments to the first founder; and thus the whole of the elaborate ritual of ceremonial observance that was gradually built up by the priests in the course of a thousand years, and also the rules of

1 Of these the most recent is the late Professor Freud, whose last published work was an elaborate—though, to any but those ready *jurare in verba magistri*, hardly convincing—theory resting on this assumption.

2 It is not certain how the name should be written. In the old Hebrew script, which omitted vowels, the exact form of a word may be doubtful. It is, however, agreed that the vowels inserted in the form of the name, Jehovah, with which we are familiar, are not correct, and that it should be read as a dissyllabic name.

conduct that were found desirable during the like period of social development, were assigned to a direct revelation made to Moses.

From the time of Moses Jahweh was the tribal deity of the Hebrew people, and it was the constant endeavour of their religious leaders to make him the sole object of their worship. Jahweh was a deity of the mountains and the desert, terrible in power, who manifested himself in storm and in fire from heaven.[1] He was also a war-god, the 'Lord of hosts', who led them to the conquest of their national home and rescued them from its subsequent invaders and conquerors. At first they regarded him only as their special deity, who watched over them alone, and whose power was strictly local. Thus Ruth, coming from beyond the Dead Sea to live in Palestine, takes him then as her God. David, flying from Saul and seeking safety among the Philistines, feels that he is exiled from the presence of Jahweh. Naaman the Syrian, when healed of his leprosy, wishes to carry two mules' burden of the earth of Palestine to his own country, in order to build on it an altar on which he may sacrifice to the God he now recognises as supreme, who will thus have a footing even in a hostile land; and this is apparently approved by the Prophet Elisha. Jonah thinks that by taking ship to another country he can escape from the presence of the God whose commands he does not wish to carry out.[2] It was only at a later stage of Hebrew history, in the teaching of the prophets, that their God was recognised as not merely the god of the Hebrews but as Creator and Ruler of all the nations of the world.

In the earlier Hebrew literature Jahweh is represented as a Being with human attributes and passions. He walks in the garden of Eden in the cool of the day; he smells the sweet savour of Noah's sacrifice; he passes before the face of Moses, but while doing so he covers the eyes of Moses with his hand and only takes it away to allow his back to be seen.[3] He is harsh alike towards enemies and towards those of his chosen people who disobey his commands. The whole tribe of Amalek, because they opposed the passage of the Israelites through their pastures, must be entirely wiped out, 'both man and woman,

[1] The account of the circumstances surrounding the giving of the Law on Sinai (Exodus XIX) suggests experience, at some period in their nomadic existence, of a volcanic eruption.

[2] Ruth I. 16; Samuel XXVI. 19; Kings V. 17; Jonah I. 3.

[3] Genesis III. 8; VIII. 21; Exodus XXXIII. 22–3.

infant and suckling, cow and sheep, camel and ass'. The tribes of Canaan who resisted the Israelite invaders were to have no mercy shown them, but to be utterly destroyed. And when, in the case of Jericho, the order was not carried out to the letter, but a little of the spoil was concealed, it was held that Jahweh required not only the man who had done this and his sons and daughters to be stoned, but that all that he had should be burnt with fire.[1] A tribal god necessarily has the characteristics of those who worship him and displays their ideals and their faults alike on a superhuman scale. It is the distinctive mark and the supreme value of the Old Testament as religious literature that it shows the development of the Hebrew idea of God from this all too human figure of the earlier stories up to the lofty conception of the great prophets—a conception which has made Judaism one of the noblest religions of the world.

In these earlier books Jahweh is still pictured as one of many such tribal deities. In spite of the prohibition in the Second Commandment, there was always a tendency to set up some image of Jahweh as an object of worship.[2] Moreover, he is surrounded by hosts of spirits, some of them his attendants and messengers,[3] others demons, such as the desert spirit Azazel, to which the scape-goat, laden with the sins of the nation, was handed over on the 'day of atonement'.[4] Thus, it was easy for the Israelites, right down to the time of the Babylonian Captivity, to turn to worship of the local Baals—the fertility spirits of the land of Canaan, associated with stones and trees—and to adopt the deities of the surrounding peoples. Against this idolatry and the rites with which such deities were worshipped the prophets were always inveighing. Hebrew history, as they saw it, and as it came to be written in conformity with their teaching, was one long record of sin and punishment, repentance and restoration. It narrated successive backslidings from the true worship of Jahweh, punished by disasters that were signs of his anger against his people,

[1] Samuel XV. 3; Deuteronomy VII. 2; Joshua VII. 15, 24–5.

[2] E.g. in the form of a calf, in remembrance, no doubt, of Egyptian deities, Exodus XXXII. 4; 1 Kings XIII. 28.

[3] These 'angels' form part of the inheritance taken over from Judaism both by Christianity and Islam.

[4] Leviticus XVI. 7–22. The ceremony is not mentioned by any writer before the time of the Exile. It was perhaps derived from some similar Babylonian ritual of atonement.

allowing their subjection to alien conquerors, and successive restorations to his favour when the nation was brought back to the right way by reforming rulers and prophets. We see a priesthood established and a centralised worship set up, first at Shiloh and certain other places of special sanctity, and later at Jerusalem; for the building of the Temple, and eventually the destruction of the northern kingdom with its rival shrines, made Jerusalem the spiritual centre as well as the capital of the nation. The whole of the earlier tradition was then revised in order to bring it as far as possible into accord with this centralised worship and with the monotheism which priest and prophet alike upheld.

It is to this time that the Book of Deuteronomy belongs. This, though called the 'Second Law'—professing, that is, to be a summarised version of the Law as given in the preceding books—is in fact the first great codification in writing of the traditional Law of Moses, brought into harmony with the ethical teaching of the prophets. Justice and righteousness are set beside observance of a detailed religious ritual as God's requirements from his chosen people. When Jerusalem and the Temple were destroyed and a great part of the people carried into captivity in Mesopotamia, all that was best in them was concentrated upon keeping uncontaminated their monotheistic worship and the customs enjoined by the Mosaic Law. By so doing they felt themselves to be marked off from their captors and shown to be still the chosen people not merely of a tribal god but of one whom they now began, in their exile, to recognise as God of the whole world.

This concentration on observance of the Law was yet further emphasised after the Return from the Captivity and the reconstitution of the Jewish State. Those who took part in this reconstitution were the few in whom passion for the Temple worship and belief that Jerusalem was God's chosen dwelling-place on earth burned most strongly. As 'sons of the Captivity' they regarded themselves as the picked remnant of the Chosen People, and looked with scorn on Samaritans and all who had not shared their exile. The Temple was rebuilt and its ritual was re-established. After the reforms of Ezra, at some time before 400 B.C., this ritual was permanently fixed; and it is from this time that Judaism may properly be said to begin, with Ezra as its second founder. The Law was now completed by the compilation of the ceremonial portions, and the already existing Scriptures underwent a priestly recension which gave them their present form. The new Jewish State became a theocracy, under the guidance of the High Priest. After the Greek conquest of Alexander's time religious devotion was the core of an intensely nationalist feeling. This inspired the Maccabean revolt and established a brief era of Jewish independence, which finally had to give way to Roman overlordship and the appointment of a half-alien king backed by the Roman power. It was this same religious nationalism which prompted, in the first century of our era, revolt against the Romans and brought about the siege of Jerusalem, the destruction of the Temple, and the final dispersion of the Jewish race among other nations.

This second catastrophic ending of their national existence and of the Temple worship had an effect similar to that of the first. The fact that the Jews were once more exiles without a country or a religious centre intensified their devotion to the Law of Moses, both in its ceremonial aspect and in matters of custom and conduct. These were now their distinctive badge of nationality and the sign that they remained the Chosen People. For nearly 1,900 years they have lived as aliens amongst other nations, slighted and often subjected to savage persecution, yet with a racial vigour and ability that have enabled them to make their mark in every kind of activity to which access was allowed them, and retaining much of their religious fervour and devotion to their Law. This, as a modern Jewish writer has said,[1] 'constitutes their manhood. It trains their intellect. It is their recreation, their joy and their solace. It is their treasure and their guide.'

Judaism can be very differently estimated as practised by different exponents. At its lowest it is merely an adherence to formalities allowing of conduct in contradiction to all that constitutes its spiritual value. At its highest, purified by the persecution it has endured, and liberalised by contact with other creeds, it is one of the finest forms of expression that the religious sense of mankind has found.

3. THE PRINCIPLES OF JUDAISM

The Mosaic Law had from the first two aspects, ceremonial and ethical. It laid down the proper ritual for the worship of Jahweh, and

[1] C. G. Montefiore in *The Synoptic Gospels.*

it also laid down the kind of conduct that he required of his worshippers in their relations with each other. This two-fold aspect recurs all through Hebrew history, and is clearly marked in the growing opposition there shown between the priests and the prophets. Both stood for the pure worship of Jahweh; but whereas the priest saw this purity of worship chiefly as a matter of the proper traditional ritual to be followed, the prophet regarded it rather as righteousness of conduct extending far beyond matters of ceremonial worship. The contrast is of importance in marking the two tendencies of Judaism as a religion of conduct.

In the patriarchal times there had been no priests. The head of the family offered sacrifices and performed religious rites; and even after the settlement in Palestine this seems to have continued. But the Levites, as members of the tribe to which Moses belonged, had a special claim to such duties, and in particular those who could claim descent from Aaron, brother of Moses, who according to tradition was the first priest to be appointed during the journeyings in the desert. The High Priest could only be chosen from some branch of his descendants. The office seems to have been hereditary in one family, that of Eli, until Solomon substituted that of Zadok.[1] Throughout the duration of the Hebrew Kingdom there was a struggle to confine the performance of sacerdotal acts to the priests, to discourage the use of local 'high places', and to make the Temple at Jerusalem the one religious centre of the whole country. This was not fully accomplished until after the return from the Captivity. In the theocracy then established the priests were the recognised officials of the state as well as the guardians of religion. At all times, naturally enough, they magnified their office and insisted on the supreme importance of the ritual which was to be carried out by them or under their direction.

Unconnected with the priests were the prophets, religious enthusiasts who either banded themselves together in semi-monastic communities or acted on their own initiative. Of the former we learn that they were liable to fits of frenzy or to trances, in which their utterances were taken to be directly inspired; the truth of their words—for it

[1] It was probably from him that the Sadducees of the New Testament took their name, as adherents of the old religion in distinction from the new doctrines and meticulous practice of the Pharisees.

was recognised that there could be false prophets—being judged by the outcome. Some were well-known figures and exercised great influence. People came to consult them in their difficulties, as did Saul when seeking his father's lost asses, and Ahab before going to the battle in which he met his death.[1] Still greater influence was wielded by solitary figures such as Elijah; or the great prophets whose writings have been preserved, who spoke in the full consciousness of a divine mission. It is these of whom we think when we speak of the Hebrew prophets: men who felt it to be laid upon them to protest against acts of tyranny, and to recall backsliders, whether individual rulers or the whole nation, from idolatry and forgetfulness of Jahweh and his commands; and above all they were spiritual leaders who insisted that religion is a personal matter, and that there could be no true worship without righteousness of life.

Such a conception of the kind of worship that is most acceptable to God could not but bring the prophets more and more into collision with the priesthood. The sacerdotal view was never accepted by the greater prophets. To them what God needed was not so much the outward homage of sacrifice and ceremonial worship as service of the heart and uprightness of life. 'Will the Lord be pleased with thousands of rams,' asks Micah, 'or with ten thousand rivers of oil? Shall I give my firstborn for my transgression, the fruit of my body for the sin of my soul? He hath shewed thee, O man, what is good; and what doth the Lord require of thee but to do justly, to love mercy, and to walk humbly with thy God?'[1] In this way the prophets stand for the second and finer aspect of Judaism as a religion which recognises that conduct matters more than ritual observance. It is not surprising, then, that they should stand forth not only as religious reformers and as poets but also as statesmen, telling kings and rulers what course was in accord with the will of God, and denouncing the doom that must fall upon a wrong choice.

Like all of their race the prophets held that prosperity was the reward of right conduct and that misfortune must inevitably follow on wrongdoing. They looked, therefore, upon the troubled times in which they lived, and the doom that they saw closing first round the

[1] 1 Samuel IX. 6; 1 Kings XXII. 6.

[1] Micah VI. 7–8.

Northern Kingdom[1] and later round Jerusalem as punishment for neglect of Jahweh and his Law. But if defeat and captivity were punishment for apostasy on the part of the majority, the true service of a faithful remnant must meet with a no less visible reward. Their God had promised to his chosen people prosperity and happiness; these promises were yet to be fulfilled. More and more, therefore, we find the prophets looking forward to a restoration of the Hebrew Kingdom as a great power among the nations, because it was to be the great exemplar of the Kingdom of God, under a divinely appointed ruler.

Thus grew up belief in a 'Messiah'—the 'anointed one' who was to be entrusted with this task. At first he was pictured as a Son of David—a king of the royal line—who was to restore the material greatness of the Kingdom. Then, as this hope grew less, the Kingdom that was to be took shape in their minds as a kingdom of the righteous. They alone were to be preserved. They were to return to life on earth after a final judgment that would separate righteous from wicked, and would end the rule of the nations that did not accept the true worship of God. This new hope involved a belief in a return to life from the grave, a belief that finds no place in the Hebrew Scriptures earlier than the latest books admitted into the canon immediately before the Christian era. In a religion regarded as the organising principle of the daily life there had hitherto been little thought of any life but that here and now,[2] and emphasis was laid on material success as the reward of right-doing. But now that this assurance of material reward had been weakened by the course of events, the prophetic writings of the time took on an 'apocalyptic' character. They tended,

1 After the death of Solomon, most famous of the Hebrew kings, who displayed the costly magnificence of an Oriental sultan, the bulk of the people, unable to bear such a burden of taxation, revolted against his successor and formed a separate northern kingdom, with Samaria for its capital, while two tribes only, Judah and Benjamin, remained loyal to the 'House of David' still ruling in Jerusalem.

2 The earlier belief of the Hebrews was that after death the spirit descended into Sheol, a gloomy underworld where it had a miserable partial existence. It was long before the hope arose of a resurrection to life on earth, in the Kingdom to be restored after the judgment of the nations; a hope which gradually grew into that of life in some spiritual Messianic Kingdom. The earliest assurance of a resurrection is found in Isaiah XXVI. 19 and in Daniel XII. 2.

that is, to become revelations of the coming end of the present world-order and the restoration of the righteous after a day of judgment. These ideas, first appearing in the visions of Ezekiel, are seen more fully developed in those of Daniel, and in the book of Enoch, which was not admitted into the canon. The Messiah now became a super-human figure, though in human form, described as 'one like unto a son of man', who was to 'come with the clouds of heaven'[1] to judge the world and to have dominion over the remnant who should be saved.

The later Scriptures, whether those included in our Old Testament or relegated to the Apocrypha, show also a growing tendency towards religious meditation, as in the later psalms; and towards a philosophic handling of the problems of life, as shown in the 'Wisdom' literature. Creative effort now took the form of exposition and commentary. Under the rule of Persia, as later under that of Rome, there was no political independence, but no interference with religious independence so long as taxes were paid and order kept. Attention was therefore concentrated on the study of the Law and the interpretation of its teaching. This was the age of the 'Scribes', copyists and expounders of the Scriptures. Like Ezra, they were priests who, in addition to their occasional routine service in the Temple, would read from the Law on the Sabbath in the local synagogues and expound the passages they read in order to make plain what the Law enjoined and how it was to be carried out. A High Priest, Simeon the Just, living at the time of the Greek conquest, said that the three essentials of religion were 'the Law, the (Temple) Service, and the showing of kindnesses'. At no time was doctrinal belief, other than acceptance of the Unity of God, regarded as an essential. The whole emphasis was laid on doing the will of God as revealed to men in the ceremonial law and the code of ethical conduct.

Under Hellenic rule there was a period of religious anarchy when many were for accepting the Hellenic civilisation and abandoning the most characteristic Jewish customs. This only ended with the Maccabean revolt and the outburst of national and religious patriotism in the second century B.C. The Sanhedrin, or Great Council, was established for the direction of the restored Jewish State; and a succession of great teachers, the Rabbis, enlarged the work of the Scribes in

[1] Daniel VII. 13.

expounding the Law. The chief feature of their teaching was that they did not, like the Scribes, confine themselves to the text of the Scriptures, but gave decisions as to matters of conduct and custom of later development with which the written law did not deal. Thus grew up a body of oral tradition—the 'unwritten law'—supplementing and in some respects modifying the Mosaic Law in accordance with the needs and ideas of later times. As they could not appeal to the written text, the authority of the Rabbis was dependent on their personality and reputation. They taught as 'having authority and not as the Scribes', as was said of Jesus, and were in fact the successors of the prophets in the work of teaching the service of God by right-doing, the difference being that whereas the prophet claimed the direct authority of God from his message, the Rabbi based his judgment on conscience and reason, and gave a rational explanation of the course he laid down. These teachers—'the wise', as they were sometimes called—had no concern with prediction: and it was through their small regard for the apocalyptic writings of the time that these, with the exception of the visions of Daniel, were not included in the full canon of the Scriptures. It was, however, through their recognition of the 'unwritten law', and their inclusion in it of matters of custom and conduct which had no direct sanction in the Torah,[1] that Judaism was able to go on developing and thus could adapt itself to ideas and conditions other than those in which the Mosaic Law had been formulated.

The Torah thus found enlargement and variety of application in the oral teaching, the 'tradition of the elders', which was eventually reduced to writing in the Mishnah and the Talmud. Well-known Rabbis had their schools of followers. While much of their teaching was on a high plane of thought and practically helpful, some dealt merely with verbal niceties or with the ceremonial injunctions against which there are so many protests in the Gospels. In New Testament times we see a sharply marked division into sects. The Pharisees represent the party (the Hasidim, or 'pious'; in our translation of the Psalms often called 'Saints') that came into prominence in the Maccabean wars as zealous supporters of the Law and determined

[1] The Hebrew word 'Torah', applied to the first five books of the Old Testament, properly means 'Teaching'. But it has usually been translated as 'The Law', and this usage is followed here.

opponents of all attempts at hellenisation of the Jewish customs and religion. But though they opposed all foreign influences they accepted the new ideas as to a future life and the spirit world which had entered Judaism since the Captivity, largely, no doubt, through contact with the religion of Persia. Their chief characteristic was the most exact observance not only of the requirements of the written Law but of the oral tradition also. Opposed to them were the Sadducees, the conservative and orthodox party, who only recognised the Torah and the old religious practices, rejecting alike the idea of a resurrection and the need of so much burdensome ceremonial. In religious matters, therefore, they seemed lukewarm in comparison with the fervour of the Pharisees. Their interests were largely political, occupied with the maintenance of their predominance in the State. The Zealots, on the other hand, as their name implies, were fanatics in whom religious zeal was indistinguishable from hatred of the Roman rule. They perished, fighting to the last, in the final overthrow of the Jewish theocracy and the destruction of the Temple in 70 A.D. With the Temple disappeared also the need of a priesthood and the party of the Sadducees. In the reshaping of the decentralised Jewish religion—a religion not of the Temple but of the synagogue[1]—which was the result of the Dispersion, it was the Pharisaic attitude, as exemplified by the best of the Rabbis, that prevailed.

Of this later Judaism the main principle has always been observance of the Law of Moses in its two-fold aspect of a code of worship and a code of conduct. One of its most distinctive features is the proper observance of the Sabbath as a day of rest from every kind of work, to be devoted to religious exercises. Besides the Sabbath, there are also certain great days to be kept: the Passover, with its commemoration of the Exodus from Egypt, the greatest event in their history; Pentecost, originally a harvest festival, and then associated with the giving of the Law on Sinai; Tabernacles, a vintage thanksgiving; and the solemn fast of the Day of Atonement, last of the ten penitential days with which the seventh month of their year begins, in sign of contrition for any wrong-doing in the year past and of reunion with

[1] This (meaning 'meeting' and then 'place of meeting') was an outcome of the Captivity, when the Temple service was no longer possible, as a means of keeping up the study of the Law and such ceremonial observances as could still be carried out apart from the Temple.

God. In place of the old ritual of blood-sacrifices, the synagogue meetings now became the recognised form of worship, with an established liturgy. Stress also was laid upon certain 'works of the Law', fasting, almsgiving, and ceremonial cleanliness in such matters as ablutions and food regulations, not merely for their own sake but still more as 'the hedge around the Torah'; a means, that is, of emphasising the difference of the Jew from all those outside the Law, and an external expression of his devotion to the inner meaning of the Law itself. All such ceremonial is a step towards attainment of the true righteousness, 'keeping holy the divine name' (the divine nature, that is, in which man is privileged to share) in every act of daily life.

Of the principles that underlie the Law the first and greatest is that embodied in words which the Jew was to recite twice a day, the 'Shema', as it is called from the Hebrew word with which it begins: 'Hear, O Israel; the Lord our God is one Lord: and thou shalt love the Lord thy God with all thine heart, and with all thy soul, and with all thy might.'[1] Judaism is one of the great monotheistic religions which recognise in God the omnipotent Creator and Ruler of all things, who demands the entire obedience of mankind to His Law; an obedience to be willingly given as He is the Righteous One whose service consists in righteousness of life. Such an exalted Being it would be easy to reverence, but might be difficult to love, were it not that to Jews He stands in a special relation as 'the Shepherd of Israel'. They are the chosen people with whom He has made a covenant, and through whom His Law is to be taught to all mankind. Since man was created 'in the likeness of God' and so has some share in the divine nature, it is possible to enter into personal communion with Him. It is this partaking of the divine nature that makes it at once possible and obligatory to carry out the moral law, which is as universally binding upon man as physical law in the realm of nature. To its 'thou shalt' each is directly responsible, without reservation and without intercessor, for to the Jew it has been plainly revealed; it is his mission, by the example of his wholehearted service, to reveal it to others and bring them into the same relationship with God.

In the utterances of Messianic prophecy there is a description by an unknown writer (usually styled 'the second Isaiah' from the fact

[1] Deuteronomy vi. 4–5.

that his rhapsody on the return from the Captivity has been included in the collection of prophetic writings attributed to the historical Isaiah) of a 'Servant' of God who by his own sufferings was to bring healing to his people and to take their sins upon himself. Of the meaning and application of this description there have been various interpretations. To Christian readers it has always seemed exactly applicable to the founder of their religion, in whom his disciples thought all Messianic prophecy found its fulfilment. To others it has seemed to refer either to some contemporary prophet or, more probably, not to any particular individual but rather to the captive people whose life of humiliation might take the place of the daily sacrifice that could no longer be offered in the Temple; or at least to a righteous 'remnant' through whose sufferings in exile the whole Jewish race might be brought back to the true service of God and take up its mission as the Messiah of mankind.[1] Belief in such a mission for which they have been tried and tested in the furnace of affliction has supported many Jews in their long exile and the persecutions with which, throughout the centuries, they have been harried. In all ages the progress of humanity has been won at the cost of the suffering of its finest natures. Such suffering is the sign and proof of Messiahship; 'for whom the Lord loveth he correcteth; even as a father the son in whom he delighteth'.[2]

How far belief in such a mission can justify itself would seem to depend on the extent to which Judaism can adapt itself to meet modern needs and changing ideas. A religion which only looks back, seeking to perpetuate ideas and practices shaped in conditions that have long vanished, has little help for the present or hope for the future. But if much in the Torah has long ceased to have any application to changed conditions and has become only an encumbrance in the modern world, the principles to which it gave expression have not lost their force. The two great commandments of the Law, love of God and love of man, still remain as the summation of man's highest aim. It is, now as ever, a question how they can best find expression in a religion which shall include the whole of life.

[1] The same idea seems to be symbolised in the book of Jonah, who is delivered from a symbolical form of captivity in order to fulfil his mission, not of revenge, but to carry the message of religion to the Gentiles.

[2] Proverbs III. 12.

By the sixth century of our era the oral tradition, as systematically arranged by a leading Rabbi in the third century, together with the discussions held about it in the schools of various teachers, had been collected in the Talmud, and the Law was now complete. In the thirteenth century the great Jewish thinker Maimonides laid down thirteen principles which may be regarded as the statement of orthodox Judaism, although, except for the Shema, it has no creed and uniformity of doctrinal belief has never been regarded as essential. Briefly summarised, these principles include belief in God, the creator of all things, who is One, incorporeal, eternal, and alone to be worshipped; belief in the divine inspiration of the prophets, and above all of Moses, the giver of the Law, both written and oral, which being directly inspired by God is to be accepted in its entirety and without change; belief that God knows the thoughts and deeds of men, rewarding those who keep His Law and punishing those who transgress it; belief in the coming of a Messiah to regenerate the world; and in a future life.

While these are the beliefs of orthodox Judaism, not all of them are held by all Jews. There is a Liberal or Reform school of Jewish thought which does not accept the doctrine of plenary inspiration at any period of their history, but regards it as having always been partial and affected by the human agent through whom it was given. Each age, therefore, they hold, is free to re-interpret and re-express what has been handed down by tradition. Laws that were once needed at a particular stage of development are no longer binding when the old conditions have passed away. Their worth is to be judged by their effect; those only are still to be observed which still have a meaning and application to present conditions and prove helpful for life today. Revelation, Jews of this school hold, is progressive. They are ready, therefore, to accept new truth—such, for example, as the theory of evolution—even if it is rejected by orthodox Judaism as incompatible with statements made in the Scriptures.

Similarly, though they look forward to a coming Messianic age of righteousness, they no longer think that this is necessarily to be ushered in by a personal Messiah. The Messianic prophecies they regard as having been directed to events and hopes of the times in which they were uttered. The Messianic age, on the other hand, is one for which all can work to bring it nearer. Each by doing what is right can help to make the world better. In this way, now as much as ever, Judaism has a mission.

While Jews were treated by other nations as outcasts, existing only on sufferance in alien countries, it was a tenet of their faith that some day they would be restored to their own land, and prayers for return to Palestine were included in their traditional form of worship. Devotion may be no less genuinely religious even if, consciously or not, other feelings have a part in it. No one who saw Jews beating their foreheads against the Wailing Wall in Jerusalem in an agony of lamentation could doubt the sincerity of their grief and longing, whether it was the Destruction of Solomon's Temple that called these feelings forth or the loss of Solomon's kingdom and the hope of its restoration. Consciousness of belonging to a Chosen People, even if outcast and despised, was throughout the centuries nursed as a psychological compensation for the lack of a political existence and for the cruel oppression to which the race has been subjected. With emancipation and the grant of citizenship in other States, the desire for return to the Promised Land lost, in these countries, something of its force, and such prayers were omitted from the liturgy of the Reform school of thought. But the desire never died, and the harsh treatment to which, varied from time to time by savage persecution, Jews were subject in many lands kept alight not only an intensity of devotion to the religion which gave them a spiritual bond but a hope also, however remote, of a national renascence in the land of their Hebrew forefathers. Zionism, the movement that worked for a return to Palestine and the creation there of a Jewish State, seemed to many Jews a hopeless dream; and to some of the traditional schools of Judaism the strict observance of the Law, which was their pride, seemed likely to be weakened, if not forgotten, in absorption in political activity. But a powerful impulse was given to the movement by the establishment, after the First World War, of a 'national home' for Jews in Palestine under the mandate assigned to Britain. The political development, however, into a state under joint Arab and Jewish control on equal terms did not follow the lines intended. Arab alarm at the prospect of Jewish preponderance and Jewish resentment at restricted immigration led to hostilities between them and towards the mandatory Power, whose efforts to maintain order with impartial fairness only provoked violence and bloodshed and brought about the relinquishment of the mandate. In the open warfare that followed the Jews obtained mastery over the greater part of Palestine, and a Jewish State—a new 'Israel'—has now been set up and its independence recognised.

Though not a theocracy of the old pattern but a democratic republic, there is in the new State, with its parties of different aims and outlook, a certain resemblance to that at the beginning of the Christian era with its various sects, including Zealots who held terrorist methods to be justified in pursuance of their aims. There is now, however, no Roman army of occupation, and the new Israel is free to develop along its own lines. What these will be depends in part upon conditions imposed by its geographical position and political environment and by the troubled international situation. But still more depends upon the practical wisdom and upon the far-sightedness and faith of its leaders, who can now, by the creation of a State firmly based on a religion of conduct in accordance with moral law, take up the Messianic mission, set forth by the Prophets, of guidance and example to those among whom it is set 'for a light to the nations'.[1]

[1] Isaiah XLIX. 6.

CHAPTER FIVE

THE GREAT RELIGIONS (3)

1. ISLAM

IN the last two chapters we have been considering religions which stress the supreme importance of right thinking or of right conduct. Such a distinction, it must be repeated, is not intended to imply that in either type of religion the other aspect is ignored, or that in either of them emotion has little place. If the origin of religion is to be sought in those states of feeling with which in all ages men have faced whatsoever in their experience was beyond their comprehension or mastery, it follows that in all its forms religion must satisfy an emotional need and give some kind of emotional outlet. If this need and this outlet are associated mainly with matters of ritual and conduct or with questions about the meaning and purpose of life, the resulting religion can be assigned to one or other of the types of which examples have been taken. It may, however, be the emotional response itself, supplying the chief motive for activity in the various relations of life, and giving to religion its emotional colouring, that is felt to be of supreme importance. Such a religion may then be classified as belonging to the third type. Of this type—the one in which religion most often finds expression—in which feeling rather than thought holds the first places and conduct is to be valued by the motive that inspires it, Christianity and Islam are the finest examples.

Some kind of emotional expression is the commonest form taken by religion at all levels of mental development, whether among primitive or civilised peoples. Sound and movement have always been employed as a means of arousing and satisfying religious emotion and enabling worshippers to feel the actual presences of their deities.

The phenomena witnessed at dervish dances or at 'revival' meetings are little removed from ways in which primitive tribes find vent for their feelings. In such states of excitement we have religious feeling at its lowest level. If this were all it meant, religions of which such expression of feeling was characteristic could not, however widespread, hold any but a low place among the great religions of the world. But the emotion which can thus seek its satisfaction in some excitement of the senses can also, at a higher level of spiritual development, find expression in the rapture of the mystic, the heroism of the martyr, the devotion of the saint, and can give spiritual enrichment to the practice of social duties and to personal relationships. It can thus inspire the highest forms of religion, giving them a fervour and depth of feeling without which philosophies and ethical systems are lifeless things. Such religions, of course, will have their theological framework, their prescribed ritual, and their ethical code, for the fact that any religion has been long practised and widely accepted necessarily involves formulations of creed and conduct. But that which most deeply characterises them is the emotional attitude which they seek to intensify, and in which they find the main motive-power of life.

Of the two examples here taken we will begin with Islam; for though the later in date, it may be said, in its combination of legalism with a complete self-surrender and trust in the mercy of God, to stand midway between Judaism and Christianity. The fact that it is the most recent of the great world-religions, having its beginning at a time and under circumstances of which we have reliable record, makes it possible to trace its rise more clearly than in the case of those where the legendary element is so large. Not that this element is lacking even here; but it is at least easier to distinguish legend from fact, and so to see something of a process that has been common to all. And though Islam in the thirteen centuries of its growth and wide extension has undergone changes, its doctrines have suffered less change from the teaching of its founder than those of other religions.

Like Christianity, Islam has its roots in Judaism. Arab and Jew both trace their descent from the same ancestor, Abraham. While the Jew regards his branch through the line of Isaac, the 'son of the Promise', as the Chosen People, the Arab claims a higher rank as due to descendants of Ishmael, the elder son. In their common Semitic origin and traditions and in the fact that both peoples have the same desert background and have passed through similar phases of nomad and settled life, there is enough, apart from any question of direct derivation, to account for the resemblances between the two religions. Both are strongly monotheistic; both have their Law, the Koran in the younger religion taking the place of the Torah and undergoing a similar process of interpretation and expansion. Mohammed[1] claimed that he was restoring the religion of Abraham to its original purity, and that his message was the consummation of that of the great Hebrew prophets who had looked forward to his fuller revelation. Where Islam differs from Judaism, apart from differences of detail due to the historical conditions of his time, is in the special emotional force and direction given to it by the man in whose mind it took shape.

Mohammed was born at Mecca in 570 A.D. Mecca was already a holy city, associated with the story of Abraham and Ishmael, and a centre of trade and pilgrimage of such repute that for four months of every year a truce from all feuds and fighting within its walls had to be observed during the time of pilgrimage. The centre of its worship was the 'Kaaba', the square shrine containing the sacred Black Stone that from prehistoric times had been regarded as the symbol of Allah, the supreme deity amongst countless other objects of worship and superstitious dread. Mohammed was of good family, but orphaned in early childhood. Brought up in poverty by an uncle, he became caravan leader for a wealthy widow, Khadijah, and thus visited many parts of Arabia, Palestine, and Syria. Recognising his fine qualities, Khadijah married him; later she became his first convert, and remained his greatest help through the troubles of his life.

He was evidently a man of deeply religious nature, given to meditation and subject to trances, in which he heard voices and believed that divine revelations were made to him. But it was not till middle life that a chance happening made him regard himself as marked out for a divine mission. At a time when the Kaaba needed repair a dispute arose as to who should afterwards replace in it the Black Stone. It was at last agreed to leave the decision to divine appointment, in the person of the first man who might enter the sacred enclosure. This

[1] Of the various ways in which the name has been written, this is the one now usually adopted, though Muhammad would more nearly represent the Arabic spelling.

man chanced to be Mohammed, who took the honour thus laid upon him to be a proof of divine selection for a prophetic mission. He still, however, shrank from the task and fell into fits of depression; but the inner voices continued to urge him, and he was strengthened by his wife's belief in them. Next to her, his first disciples were a cousin and a slave whom he adopted; but the band of believers grew but slowly. When he publicly announced his message that 'there is no God but Allah' and declaimed against the idolatry rife in Mecca, he roused furious hostility against himself. Amongst the pilgrims, however, to whom he preached this message he won more adherents; and when, after the death of his wife and uncle, he received an invitation to establish his reformed faith in Medina, he fled there with his handful of followers from Mecca. This is the event—the Hegira, or Flight, from Mecca, in A.D. 622—from which the beginning of the Mohammedan era is reckoned.

From now on all was changed. The new prophet was acclaimed, and his followers grew rapidly in numbers and in fiery enthusiasm. Mohammed no longer doubted his divine mission or his own competence to perform it. He laid no claim to miraculous powers (these have, of course, been ascribed to him in the legends that soon grew up around him), and always spoke of himself as a man, though one specially favoured to be the recipient of divine revelations that set him above all who had gone before him and superseded their teaching. Hitherto he had counted Jews as fellow-religionists; but when they refused to accept his revelations he turned away from Judaism. He now taught his followers to pray, not, as hitherto, towards Jerusalem, but towards Mecca. Friday, not Saturday, was to be their Sabbath. Ramadan, a month of fasting, was to take the place of the Day of Atonement.

There was now also another and greater change of outlook. Up to the time of the flight to Medina, Mohammed had been a religious reformer with no thought of political power. Now, however, he accepted the opportunity offered him to reorganise the government in such a way as to form a kingdom of heaven on earth. Hence comes the special characteristic of Islam that it makes no distinction between religious and secular, ecclesiastic and civil matters. This is at once its strength, embracing as it does the whole of life, and its weakness, as tending in practice to subordinate spiritual needs to practical necessity, just as, in his last phase, Mohammed merged the prophet in the statesman and the conqueror. With the determination to overcome opposition and to win Mecca by force came new 'revelations' that transformed Islam into a fighting religion. Unbelievers must be converted at the point of the sword; fighting was a holy service, and death in battle brought with it the remission of all sins; all being predetermined, none could meet his fate until the appointed time. This is still the faith of Islam; and the proclamation of a *jehad*, or holy war, has power to raise it to a similar emotional pitch. By such means the zeal of his followers was fanned into an irresistible fury. Mecca was recovered, and all its idols except the Black Stone were destroyed. The allegiance of the whole of Arabia was given to the victorious prophet; preparations for still wider conquests were in train when, ten years after the flight to Medina, he died.

Mohammed left no writings of his own. During the last years of his life his utterances, which he believed to be messages brought direct from the mouth of Allah by one of his angels, had been noted down, as they fell from his lips, on any scrap of material—even palm-leaves or bones—that might be at hand. These were carefully preserved, with additions made from time to time by his own direction. After his death, as one by one those who had heard his teaching died, orders were given to collect all these fragments and piece them together to form a book. This was done by his chief secretary, and thus a standard text was formed, from which no departure was afterwards allowed. In the Koran, therefore, we can be more sure of having the actual words of the Prophet than in the case of other sacred books. The only question for the Mohammedan is not what the founder actually taught, but how to interpret and apply his teaching. Where it contains contradictions the principle laid down by Mohammed himself is to take the later utterance as correcting the earlier; but in a book put together as this was it is not easy to discover the true order, so that there is room for much difference of interpretation.

Looking, from a psychological standpoint, at particular utterances, it seems plain that they were prompted by the subconscious self in response to particular desires and needs. But this does not mean that Mohammed was aware of the personal nature of their origin, or was not sincere in believing them all to have been given to him by divine inspiration. To so intensely religious a mind, to which everything, small or great, was the work of God, all that came to him was equally inspired—concessions to human weakness, both in his followers and in himself, no less than the sublimest truths. Underlying all is a passionate belief in the Oneness and greatness of God, and a passionate desire to submit in everything to his will. Hence *Islam*, 'surrender' or 'submission', is the name given to the Mohammedan faith. The place held by Enlightenment in Buddhism and by Righteousness in Judaism is held in this faith by self-devotion to the will of Allah. The aim which the Prophet achieved was the purification of religion by the overthrow of idolatry and the establishment of monotheism. 'There is no God but Allah, and Mohammed is his prophet' is the whole of the Moslem[1] creed.

But with all his lofty idealism he could not free himself entirely from the beliefs and practices of his environment. There is much in Islam that is derived from the habits of the desert tribes as well as from Jewish and Christian sources. Angels and devils were no less real to him than human beings. He recognised the Jewish and Christian Scriptures as sacred books, though superseded by his own revelations. The great figures in Hebrew history, from Moses to Jesus, became Mohammedan saints, and Jerusalem remained a holy city, next in sanctity to Mecca. He taught that there is a future life of rewards and punishments, taking from Persian religion the image of the bridge across which the righteous will pass safely to Paradise while the wicked will fall into the abyss. He allowed, and himself practised, polygamy, but denounced the practice of infanticide. The Semitic rite of circumcision he retained. Religious ritual plays a comparatively small part in Islam; but five practical activities Mohammed enjoined as essential. Of these the most important is prayer—not petition for material gains but a confession of faith and complete surrender to the will of Allah—which must be made towards Mecca at fixed hours five times a day, or in no case less than three; and this must be preceded by ceremonial ablutions, either with water or, if none is available, with the desert sand. The other essentials are almsgiving, fasting from sunrise to sunset during the month of Ramadan, and pilgrimage, once at least in a lifetime, to Mecca. Wine and strong

[1] Moslem (or Muslim) is the participle of a verb of which Islam is the infinitive (as stated by Prof. Margoliouth in his *Mohammedanism* in the Home University Library). The root meaning is "submission" to the will of God.

drink the Prophet himself forbade; but it is only the most puritanical Mohammedans who observe the prohibition.

Islam is an emotional attitude towards the Unseen affecting the whole of life, but its requirements as to belief and practice are simple. Like Judaism, it is worship of an all-perfect Being, of whom no kind of representation is allowed; a pure monotheism, though subordinate powers are recognised as giving spiritual help or tempting to evil. The nature and will of this Being have been made known by successive stages of revelation, of which the teaching of Mohammed is the final form, though still progressive in that it needs to be interpreted and applied. It includes belief in a future judgment, as the final manifestation of God's glory. The life to come will be a continuation of the life here, in accordance with our good or evil deeds; but spiritual progress is unlimited, and spiritual blindness can be healed by suffering, for Allah is all-merciful. The few observances enjoined, possible at all times and for all peoples, are symbolic of abstention from evil and of surrender to the divine call. Since Islam is a universal brotherhood without distinction of class, it is the duty of the richer to give help to the poorer in proportion to their means. There need be no withdrawal from ordinary life, since all life is to be inspired and directed by religion. Salvation is the peace of soul that comes of being at one with God and man—the 'peace' which forms the ordinary Moslem greeting.

Of the characteristics of Islam the most striking, as already said, is the emotional intensity with which it was originally endued and is still held. The completeness of the devout Mohammedan's submission to the will of God, and of the devotion with which he carries out the duties that his faith enjoins, has always been remarkable; and most of all the fervour which impelled his followers to go out and force other nations to accept the teaching of the Prophet. There is nothing in history more wonderful than the speed and the extent of their achievement. Within fifty years from the Hegira they had overcome all western Asia and were beneath the walls of Constantinople. Within a century they had added North Africa and Spain to an empire, which now stretched from the Himalayas to the Pyrenees; and they were only prevented from overrunning the rest of Europe by the victory of Charles Martel at Tours. Their method was simple. Jews and Christians, as 'people of the Book', might keep their own religion if they submitted and paid tribute; all others must accept Islam or death. To many, even amongst the more favoured peoples, conversion was not merely a matter of necessity. Here was a creed that was simple, free from metaphysical and doctrinal subtleties, and not too burdensome in the duties that it enjoined. In its emotional appeal and in its promise of rewards to come in a Paradise of the senses, it was well adapted to ordinary human nature, the more as it associated religion with the fighting instincts. The astonishing success of Islam was due at once to what was good in it and to the fact that it was so near the level of the average man's spiritual development. To finer natures it appealed by its alliance with the higher level of civilisation in literature and science and art which it brought from Eastern centres of culture such as Damascus, Baghdad, and Cairo at a time when Europe was only emerging from the dark ages that followed the break-up of the Roman Empire.

But the fiery enthusiasm which was the inspiration of this amazing conquest of half the known world was the cause also of bitter feuds, personal and religious. Assassination was a common end of the early Khalifs—the 'successors' of Mohammed in the leadership, civil, military, and religious, of the adherents of Islam. Ali, the husband of the Prophet's daughter and one of his first disciples, was passed over several times; this fact, followed by his murder when Khalif and that of his sons, was the cause of the first great schism in Islam, when the Shiite sect, who upheld his claims as the true successor,[1] split from the Sunnites, the orthodox majority. The main strength of the Shiite faith has always been found in Iran (as Persia is now called) and has combined with national feeling to produce as deep a division between the Iranian and Arabic forms of Islam as that between Protestants and Catholics in the countries of Northern and Southern Europe.

In Islam, as in all religions, there have been many further divisions into separate sects, differing in points of doctrine and practice, though all are at one in the creed that 'there is no God but Allah, and

[1] The Shiites are now distinguished by allegiance to a divinely appointed and sinless leader—the Imam—instead of to an elected Khalif. The Imamate all Shiites hold to be hereditary in descendants of the house of Ali. The principal group, in Persia and Iraq, believe that the twelfth in the succession disappeared, but continues to inspire heads of the sect. He is the 'hidden' or 'expected' Imam who will some day reappear as the promised Mahdi, the Messiah, that is, of Islam.

Mohammed is His Prophet'. Contact with other religions and philosophies has led to the development of metaphysical speculation and of a strong element of mysticism in Islam. It has its saints—the Sufis—just as it has had its fanatics, such as the hashish-intoxicated followers of the 'Old Man of the Mountain' of Crusader times, from whom the word 'assassin' is derived, or the dervishes and followers of the Mahdis of later times. It has also its Puritans, like the Wahabis of central Arabia.

Islam, though intensely national in origin, is a world-religion in that it does not imply any kinship of race but the fellowship of all the faithful, of whatever country or nationality. Unlike other religions, it makes no distinction between the civil and religious aspects of life. To Mohammed every part of life was to be lived in submission to the will of God and was equally the concern of religion. All government, therefore, and every activity of public as well as of personal life, come into its scope and must be regulated in accordance with principles to be found in or deduced from the Prophet's own utterances in the Koran. When this is not enough, appeal is made to 'Sunna'—to tradition, that is, of the practice of Mohammed's contemporaries and successors. In the course of centuries great schools of Moslem law, like the Rabbinical schools of Judaism, have arisen in which interpretations and extensions of the Koran have been devised in application to every side of life. Thus after 1,300 years the flame of Mohammedan faith still burns strongly, and Islam satisfies at once the emotional and the practical needs of a large part of mankind.

2. THE LIFE AND TEACHING OF JESUS

Christianity, like Islam, was Semitic in origin and, like it, began in revulsion from the prevalent formalism and superstition of the time. Each breathed into religion a new spiritual life, raising it to a higher level of feeling. Whereas the central feature of Islam is a passionate affirmation of the all-pervading power of the one God, of man's complete dependence on the divine will, and of the complete devotion of the believer to the service of God as enjoined by the Prophet, Christianity, as we see it exemplified in its truest exponents, is the apprehension and expression of an all-embracing love. It is love, first towards God, in a relationship like that of children to their father, in which love and trust can be so complete as to leave no place for fear, and then towards our fellows, without distinction of kinship or expectation of return.

Not that Christianity, any more than other great religions, is the expression of one side only of our nature. Owing to its early association with Greek thought, it has a highly elaborated scheme of theology which attempts to give, in philosophical terms, an interpretation of human history and the purpose of life. It has also its traditional observances and forms of worship, derived from its parent Judaism or from the rites of mystery religions that were prevalent during its early growth. And it has inherited the Hebrew insistence on the ethical side of conduct as the necessary expression of religion. There have been times in its historical development when the chief importance has been attached to dogmas or to ritual; but the truest Christians have been those who gave to these things only a secondary importance and who found the core of religion in the spirit that underlies them. In this they have followed the example of their Master, who taught that it was not the beliefs that men professed or the forms that they observed which mattered most; even the external act, whether good or bad, being of less importance than the thoughts and feelings that led to it. Religion, he insisted, is a matter of the heart. It is in this sense that Christianity is to be regarded as a religion of feeling rather than of thought or outward conduct.

Like Judaism and Islam, Christianity is a historic religion: its doctrines, that is, are based upon recorded events and upon the recorded words of a prophet through whom, at a particular epoch, a new revelation was given to mankind. It is therefore of the first importance to know how much credence can be given to the records of the events and words in question. While in all cases there is the difficulty of disentangling fact from legend, there is less certainty, owing to the circumstances of their transmission, as to the words of Jesus given in the Gospels than to those of Mohammed recorded in the Koran. As regards Christianity, moreover, the difficulty is increased by the fact that, from the first, the life and teaching of the human Jesus were merged in the figure of a divine Christ.

To the adherents of a religion its founder is no merely human figure, but a revelation of the divine in human form. It is natural to feel that in one endowed with a supereminent spiritual sensitivity—a genius in religion comparable to but even more striking than that shown in art or in any intellectual or practical ability—there is a manifestation of something beyond the reach of ordinary men. It is easily to be understood, therefore, that this manifestation should be regarded as unique in the one who is revered as the giver of spiritual truth and the bringer of salvation to mankind, and that theologians should differ only as to the fulness of the manifestation and the manner in which the divine was united with the human nature. To adherents of the religion in question such matters are of vital interest and importance. Those, however, who wish to look at it, as at others, from a more detached standpoint are primarily concerned not with the attributes of divinity that the adoration of their followers has seen in such a figure, but with trying to penetrate, so far as is now possible, to the core of historical fact beneath the supernatural element in the legends by which each has been surrounded.

Of the life of Jesus—the 'Christ'[1] from whom Christianity gets its name—we know certain main facts, but beyond these little that can be considered as certain. In the accounts that have come down to us there are many discrepancies and much that cannot be accepted as historical. This is not surprising if we remember that they were written many years after the events recorded, and contain, besides personal recollections, traditions shaped by the interests and pre-occupations of those by whom they were repeated and to whom they were addressed. In order, for instance, to convince Jewish hearers that Jesus was the long-expected Messiah, who, according to prophetic tradition, must be of David's line and come from David's city (though Jesus himself seems to have disputed this belief[2]), stories were told with varying details, to show that he was born at Bethlehem. These stories, beautiful in themselves and accepted as literal truth by Christians, belong, like much else in the Gospel narratives, to the kind of legend that springs up round the lives of those who most deeply impress the imagination of mankind. All accounts, however,

[1] This, it should be remembered, is, like Buddha, not a name but a title. Christ is the Greek equivalent of the Hebrew term 'Messiah', *the anointed one*—one, that is, appointed to a divine mission. It was in the writings of the Apostle Paul that the name was first used with the implications it has since conveyed.

[2] See Mark XII. 35–7. For questions of fact Mark's gospel, traditionally said to be a record of the teaching of Peter, the first disciple chosen by Jesus, may be taken, as the earliest and simplest of the four, to be the most reliable.

are agreed that he grew up in the little Galilean town of Nazareth, in the home of his parents, the carpenter Joseph and Mary.[1] In his early manhood the fame of a new prophet, John the Baptist, led him to join the throng that flocked to the Jordan to be baptised. This experience, followed by a period of meditation in the desert, seems to have confirmed his sense of his own mission. Returning to Galilee he gathered round him a small band of devoted disciples and went about the villages and countryside, consorting mostly with the poor and despised, and proclaiming the coming of the 'kingdom of Heaven', of which the main principle was that God is our loving Father and all men are brothers.

His teaching was entirely oral, and it is not possible, for the reasons given above, to be certain of the accuracy of the words in which it has been handed down.[2] But of its general tenor there can be no doubt. He did not attempt to lay down a philosophical or ethical system, but taught by aphorisms, arising from incidents of the moment, and by parables. Of these many have been preserved in the Gospels, and from them we can learn what were the main principles on which he insisted. Some[3] press home the lesson that we must show to others the same mercy that we hope to receive for our own shortcomings, and that, while this mercy is freely given to all who will accept it, we must

[1] The tendency to heighten the story by the introduction of supernatural elements is clearly seen in the treatment of the parentage of Jesus. That a god should be born of a virgin mother was a familiar idea in Eastern cults, and this at an early date became part of the Christian belief. That Jesus was the Messiah, and therefore in a special degree the 'Son of God', was the central point of the Apostles' teaching. To their hearers this seemed to mean that he needed no earthly father, and that Joseph was his father only in name—in spite of the fact that the descent in David's line, assumed to be necessary for the Messiah, was reckoned through him. To Jewish Christians there was also a reason for insisting on his mother's virginity, since an Old Testament prophecy (Isaiah vii. 14) was interpreted to mean that the Messiah would be born of a virgin. In the Middle Ages, when the particular sanctity associated with virginity was at its highest, the 'immaculate conception' of the 'Mother of God' became an essential doctrine of the Church.

[2] Moreover, the Gospel narratives are written in Greek, and the recorded sayings are therefore translated from the Aramaic which Jesus spoke, and in some cases appear to have been expanded in order to bring out more fully what was taken to be their meaning.

[3] E.g. the two debtors (Mat. xviii. 23–35); the prodigal son (Luke xv. 11–32); the labourers in the vineyard (Mat. xx. 1–14).

not think that we are entitled, by anything we have done, to a larger share of it. Others[1] dwell on the need to make the fullest use of such gifts as we may have, and insist that the truest service of God lies in the acts of kindness we can show to our fellows. Others[2] again show the depth of his psychological insight. Realising that the majority of his hearers, however gladly they listened to his words, could not fully understand his meaning, he did not attempt to explain his parables to them, but gave fuller explanation to the inner circle of his disciples, who later saw a meaning in much they failed to understand at the time.

Jesus shared the ideas of his time about the attribution of disease to possession by demons and the existence of a personal power of evil, as well as the Jewish belief in the divine inspiration of the Hebrew Scriptures and the near approach of the end of the world which was to bring the establishment of the Messianic Kingdom. He seems to have taken no interest in history, politics, science, or art; but on all questions of religion and the will of God he spoke with the authority of one who was there at home. He showed the keenest insight into the thoughts and feelings of all with whom he came into contact. His boundless pity for all kinds of weakness would not let him refuse entreaties to use the unusual powers of healing that he possessed. These powers he did not regard as supernatural, but told his disciples that if only they had sufficient faith they also could acquire them by living the manner of life that he lived. The cures that he performed were always acts of spontaneous kindness, never for notoriety or to prove his claim to speak with authority of a prophet; and he was constantly trying to escape from this drain upon the spiritual energy which he wished to conserve for his true work of teaching.

He does not seem to have felt it to be his mission to preach to any but those of his own race.[3] It was to 'the lost sheep of the house of

1 E.g. the talents (Mat. xxv. 14–29); the sheep and goats (Mat. xxv. 31–46).

2 E.g. the sower (Mat. xiii. 1–9, 15–23) and the empty house to which the unclean spirit returns (Luke xi. 24–6).

3 On this point the Gospels are not consistent. There are passages (e.g. Luke xxiv. 47) in which he is represented as telling his disciples that before his 'second coming' the Gospel must be preached to all nations. But it may well be that since, at the time when the Gospels were written, this was being done, it was taken for granted that he had foreseen and commanded it; whereas such a story as that of the Syro-Phoenician woman (Mark vii. 27) and his injunction to his disciples (Mat. x. 3) show that he regarded his teaching as confined to Jews.

Israel' that he brought his message of the love of God and of mercy given to the repentant and the loving. Like the Hebrew prophets, he set little value on ritual, and taught that what matters most is not what we do but what we are. Quick to recognise good even in those whom others condemned, and no less quick to expose the complacency and hypocrisy of those who made a display of righteousness, he came into frequent collision with the official representatives of religion, and especially with the Pharisees, who attached more importance to the letter of the law and the rabbinical tradition than to the spirit which alone gave to law and tradition their value. It was the common people who heard him gladly and who were ready to hail him as the Messiah for whom the nation, chafing under Roman rule, was waiting.

By them, and even by his own disciples, the Messiah was thought of as a king who should drive out the Romans, restore the glories of the old Hebrew kingdom, and rule a world in which Jews would be the dominant nation, but such a conception was far from the thoughts of Jesus. That the Messiah was to come and to bring about a new kingdom he did not doubt; and it seems certain that he believed, as did some at least of his disciples, that he was himself to be the one sent for this purpose. But this he would not allow them to proclaim openly, whether through fear of political troubles that would arise from an outburst of popular enthusiasm or because their conception of the Messiahship was so different from his own. The Messiah that he felt himself to be was no earthly king, but rather the 'Servant' described by the 'second Isaiah', who was to be despised and rejected by his people and to undergo death at their hands, and thus to bear their punishment and be the instrument of their redemption; who would then, as in the vision of Daniel, return as the 'Son of Man' who was to judge the world and establish the Kingdom of Heaven.

It seems to have been in consciousness of such a two-fold mission that he went up to Jerusalem to challenge priests and Pharisees in their stronghold. There he was arrested, through betrayal by one of his own disciples, tried before the hostile Sanhedrin, and condemned to death on the ground that he had spoken blasphemy in something he had said about the overthrow of the Temple and its rebuilding by himself. That one who could treat the Law and the Temple ritual as he did should claim to be the Messiah seemed to them insufferable.

As they could not themselves carry out a death sentence, they handed him over to the Roman Governor on a charge of setting himself up as king. The Governor, Pilate, at first tried to save his life; but fearing a riot if he resisted the clamour of a mob now worked up to a pitch of fury by the priests, he finally gave way and allowed Jesus to be crucified.

To the disciples it seemed the end of all they had hoped and believed. But soon came a revulsion of feeling. He had spoken to them of overcoming death; and now they had proof, so they believed, that this was true in fact. The tomb, it was said, in which his body had been hurriedly placed was found two days later to be empty; and there were occasions on which he reappeared among them, to individuals or groups, as a living presence. Such experiences convinced them that he had indeed risen from the dead, and that they could look forward to his second coming as Judge to establish the rule of heaven upon earth. In this conviction they were transformed from the cowards who had forsaken and denied their Master when he was arrested, into zealous missionaries, spreading the good tidings of his resurrection as proof that a like victory over death was assured for all who believed him to be the Messiah, and of the glorious state that was soon to be theirs at his second coming.

We must not suppose that in doing this they had any intention of breaking entirely with Judaism. Jesus himself and all his immediate followers were Jews. However much he came into conflict with priests and Pharisees in regard to the kind of service that God required or the interpretation of the Torah, it was not the overthrow of the Jewish faith that was his object, but only its reformation. 'Think not that I am come to destroy the law or the prophets,' he said[1]; 'I am not come to destroy but to fulfil.' Like the Rabbis he regarded himself as entitled to interpret the Torah as his understanding and conscience directed; but with an authority greater than theirs, since he felt himself to be, through his divine mission and through constant prayers and meditation, in closer touch with the spirit of the heavenly Father. Like them he laid stress on the need of doing the will of God, but only in actions that were a true expression of the spirit, this alone being the thing of ultimate importance. Prayer, fasting, and almsgiving might

1 Mat. v. 17. Matthew's gospel, being written for Jewish Christians, naturally stresses this aspect of his teaching.

be worthless if done for show; what mattered more was to make use of every occasion for doing acts of loving-kindness. To refrain from murder or adultery was not enough; what mattered was to harbour no angry or lustful thoughts and feelings.

Other Jewish teachers before him had said that love of God and love of one's neighbours were the two great commandments of the law. He went beyond their teaching in wishing the one to be no mere adoration of supreme power and goodness, but rather an intimately personal relationship, the absolute trust and obedience of a child in which there was no place for fear or thought of reward; and in wishing the other to be extended not only to those who are bound to us by ties of affection and habit and common interest, but to all with whom we have to do, even strangers and those who do us harm. To Jesus religion was no mere ritual observance but essentially a matter of the heart. It is in his insistence on love as the central and all-important motive-power of religion that the essential character of Christianity is to be found. Throughout its history there has been much in it that tended on the one side to formalism and ceremonial observance and on the other to doctrinal elaboration. But in so far as it has followed the teaching of its Founder it has been the mission of Christianity to show that love is the essence of the divine nature and the supreme value in all human relations.

3. APOSTOLIC CHRISTIANITY

Though neither Jesus himself nor at first his disciples wished to sever themselves from the religious doctrines and observances of their nation, there were elements in his teaching which, together with the hostility of the official guardians of the Jewish religion and the natural trend of events, made the severance before long inevitable. Jesus had always made spiritual insight and the simple human affections the true criteria of right conduct, and had claimed authority to override the rabbinical tradition and even the Law itself when Moses had allowed some compromise 'because of the hardness of their hearts'. His followers therefore turned for guidance to his teaching rather than to the Torah. It was to him that they looked for salvation, and from him that they drew the new spirit of faith and hope and love in which their lives were henceforth to be lived. This substitution of a person for a system, an example to be followed rather than a code to be obeyed, was the chief distinction between early Christianity and Judaism. It widened into an irreconcilable breach when the Christ was presented as a divine figure, to be regarded as a manifestation of God himself, which to the Jew seemed rank idolatry. As long, however, as all the believers were drawn from the Jews, it was possible for them to continue the old observances and to think of themselves as a special sect, perhaps, but still within the Jewish fold. But when the Apostles[1] began to carry the gospel—the 'good news' about the Messiah who had risen from the dead, who could save from death those who believed in him and, at the approaching day of Judgment, would give them life in the world to come—to Gentiles[2] also, the question at once became urgent whether, as his followers, these must become subject to the Jewish Law, with all the burdensome requirements and taboos that it would lay upon them.

While the disciples at Jerusalem were inclined to insist on Jewish observances, Paul, 'the apostle of the Gentiles', as he calls himself,[3] championed the other view; and since the converts in other countries soon far outnumbered the Jewish Christians, this was the view that prevailed. Not only was it mainly through Paul's missionary efforts that the new religion was carried beyond Palestine and Syria to Asia Minor, Greece, and Rome, and so eventually spread through the whole Roman Empire, but it was in Paul's writings that its doctrines were first formulated, so that all subsequent developments ofChristian theology were based mainly upon his teaching.

By birth and training a strict Pharisee, Paul, who had no personal knowledge of Jesus, at first joined in the attempts to suppress the growing Christian community. It was on a journey to Damascus, in order to carry out a similar persecution there, that he underwent the psychic experience which changed his life; and from the bitterest enemy he became the most vehement supporter and exponent of the Christian faith. From his headquarters at Antioch[4]—he was, not

1 Those who had been 'disciples' during the lifetime of their Master became 'Apostles'—missionaries, that is—when they set out to make converts.

2 The Jews spoke of people of any race and religion other than their own as Gentiles—'the other nations'.

3 Romans XI. 13.

4 It was at Antioch that the name of 'Christian' was first applied to followers of 'the Way', as the new religion was then called (Acts XI. 26).

unnaturally, for long regarded with some distrust at Jerusalem—he went on long missionary journeys from city to city, preaching in each first to the Jews. When these rejected his message, he turned to those of other races, by whom it was widely welcomed. Women especially and slaves and those whom other religions treated as inferiors, but some also of those in high positions, received his teaching with fervour. Usually the Jews, regarding him as a renegade, stirred up furious opposition, so that he was constantly exposed to violence. But his burning zeal carried him through all hardships[1]; and it was mainly through his labours that, in spite of persecutions[2] by the Roman authorities, by the end of the first century of our era Christianity was firmly established in most of the cities of the Empire.

The earliest Christian documents, prior in time to any of the Gospels, are Paul's letters to the various 'churches'[3] he had established. In these there is little reference to the actual teaching or personality of Jesus. To Paul Jesus was not, as to the disciples, the loved Master whose words and example were their chief source of inspiration, but the divine Saviour, the 'Christ' through faith in the atoning virtue of whose death salvation was offered to all. The theology that Paul constructed was not a philosophic system, but a means of bringing to others the experience, such as he had himself received through his conversion, of liberation from the burden of the Jewish Law and from the sense of guilt. He had been brought up in the strictest sect of Jewish legalism, regarding the flesh as inevitably opposed to the spirit. For him the new religion was an escape; not, as to the Buddha, from a life of suffering, but from sin and death—the inevitable outcome of a law impossible to keep in full. A new life of faith and hope

[1] For his own account of the dangers and ill-treatment he had to face, see 2 Corinthians XI. 23–8.

[2] In the first of these, in the time of Nero, tradition says that both Paul himself and Peter, next to him the most vigorous of the Apostles, suffered martyrs' deaths at Rome.

[3] 'Church' is the term used in the New Testament to translate the Greek word (meaning 'assembly') applied to the first communities of Christians, who frequently gathered together for mutual help and encouragement as well as for common worship and in particular for the sacramental meal (the Eucharist—'thanksgiving'—as it soon came to be called) in commemoration of the last supper of Jesus and his disciples and of the communion of believers with their risen Saviour.

and love was made possible through the indwelling spirit of the divine Being who had taken upon himself the just condemnation for the broken law, and by his death on the cross had ransomed mankind from sin and its punishment. It was on the basis of Paul's teaching that Christianity, as a system of belief, was built. By the time the Gospels were written (or at least put together in the form in which we have them) Paul's letters were widely known and his doctrines accepted, and much in the synoptic[1] narratives is coloured by the Pauline conception of the Christ.[2]

The other main factor in shaping Christian theology is the Johannine presentation of Jesus as the Messiah. The figure depicted by John—whoever it may be, whether the disciple or another John, who wrote the fourth Gospel,[3] which is undoubtedly the latest of the four —differs greatly from that shown in the synoptic gospels, not only in the incidents of his life, which are so arranged as to make of it a divine drama culminating in the final Passover sacrifice, but still more in the discourses that the writer (like Plato putting his own speculations into the mouth of Socrates) attributes to Jesus. John's gospel is

1 The first three gospels are called synoptic ('taking a common view') because they narrate much the same incidents in the life of Jesus, and in much the same order. Matthew and Luke both incorporate most of the narrative of Mark, but add other material, some taken from an earlier collection of sayings of Jesus and some contributed by themselves. Matthew, writing for Jewish Christians, is specially interested in showing the life of Jesus as the exact fulfilment of Old Testament prophecy. Luke, writing for educated Gentiles, presents Christianity as a universal religion, and tells in a sequel—the Acts of the Apostles, which is chiefly occupied with the doings of Peter and Paul—how it was carried from Jerusalem to the capital of the Roman Empire.

2 Two of the writers whose names the Gospels bear, Mark and Luke, are mentioned in Paul's letters as being his companions. It is not surprising that, after coming under so strong an influence, they should show evidences of his way of thought.

3 The commonly accepted tradition is that it was written by, or from the dictation of, the disciple in his extreme old age, at the end of the first century. According to another tradition, however, he suffered martyrdom in middle life. The gospel would then be the work of one of his followers, perhaps the one traditionally known as John the Elder, of the Church at Ephesus. In either case (we may believe) it embodies the teaching and memories, however much dimmed by lapse of time or modified in transmission, of the 'disciple whom Jesus loved'. (This, in place of his name, is the way in which John is several times mentioned in the fourth Gospel.)

thus not so much historical as symbolic and interpretative, a presentation of the divine Messiah as seen through the eyes of a mystic. Jewish thought had long been familiar with a personification of 'the Word' of God—the divine fiat by which the world was called into existence—as 'Wisdom'. To John 'the Word' was incarnate in the person of Jesus during his life on earth. By his death, of which the sacrifice of the Paschal lamb had been a symbol, he had redeemed his people and was now present among them as a spirit poured out—this seems to have been John's view of the 'second coming'—upon the Christian brotherhood. He thus brought in to the Christian doctrine something of the Hellenic Judaism of Philo, a Jew of Alexandria in the first century, who was steeped in Greek idealist philosophy, and treated the Old Testament as at once a record of fact and an allegory, of which the spiritual interpretation was the more important.

The Christian Church has rightly called itself 'Apostolic'. For though it may be doubted if the Apostles would recognise much in the doctrines of the Church for their own (so greatly were they transformed in succeeding centuries by the way in which they were formulated and applied), nevertheless its doctrines rest upon their teaching; on that of Peter and John in particular, and above all on that of Paul, who, though not himself a disciple, by the intensity of his zeal won the chief place among the Apostles.

4. CHRISTIANITY IN ITS HISTORICAL DEVELOPMENT

The history of Christianity during the next 1,800 years falls into three main stages. First, in the early centuries, there was a gradual penetration into all the provinces of the Roman Empire and throughout all classes, in spite of bitter persecutions by the imperial authorities, who rightly saw in it a solvent of traditional beliefs and customs and a rival loyalty that might be opposed to that due to the State. This was also the time of its formulation into a doctrinal system of belief. Eventually it was adopted as the State religion, and in order to ensure compliance with their policy, the Emperors claimed to regulate not only the affairs of the Church, as being a part of the State, but also the theological disputes by which it was torn.

In the second stage, throughout the Middle Ages, the position is reversed. It was now the Church, constantly growing in wealth and power, that claimed to take the place of the Empire as head of a united Christendom. But already its unity was broken by irreconcilable differences between East and West; and power brought with it increasing worldliness and corruption within the Church itself.

The third stage is that, from the time of the Reformation onward, in which the modern world has taken shape. It is marked by the break-up of the medieval system and the growth of regional sectionalism, bringing at first fierce wars of religion inspired both by religious differences and by national consciousness. In reaction from this upheaval the tendency (until the set-back that we are now witnessing) has been towards greater toleration and the separation of religious from political activities; towards a growing recognition that religion is in the main a personal matter, and that questions of belief and worship are not to be decided by arbitrary authority, of whatever kind.

1. Christianity has never taken possession of the East to the same extent as did Buddhism and, later, Islam. Its rapid spread throughout the Roman Empire was partly due to the fact that old loyalties had been swept away by the Roman conquest of the Mediterranean world. Men were everywhere, throughout this world, ready to accept whatever offered an escape from an unsatisfying present and brought an emotional zest and meaning into life. Still more, however, was it due to the nature of the religion now offered to them: a religion that excluded no one, sinner, outcast, or slave, but welcomed all into a universal brotherhood. All believers were, in a sense, made equals. It gave to women a standing which was denied to them by other religions throughout the East, where women were regarded as inferior beings. And while it offered to the thinker an interpretation of life, it set before all a personal object of worship and love. With all this, it found place for old customs and beliefs, and, in its sacraments, for the reliance upon magic that ordinary human nature could not do without. Since converts were made chiefly from followers of pagan religions, it was inevitable that some tincture of pagan beliefs and practices should creep in. Existing festivals were so adapted as to become Christian anniversaries. The rites in which the old fertility cults dramatised the rebirth of nature in the spring were transformed into commemoration of the death and resurrection of the Christ, and the widespread worship of a mother-goddess influenced the growth of

worship of the Mother of Jesus. When the cult of pagan gods and heroes could not be wholly rooted out, these, together with wonder-working charms and localities, were eventually taken over with the substitution of Christian saints. In such ways Christianity paid the price for its wide extension.

With the growth in numbers came also the loss of its first simplicity and singleness of purpose. At first, when the scattered Christian communities were small, they were organised on a communistic basis, all contributing to the common need without distinction of wealth and rank. But as they grew larger, it was necessary to organise each 'church' with various officers under a superintendent—the later 'bishop'. With wealth and power, especially when Christianity was adopted as the official religion of the Roman Empire, came luxury and worldly interests. It is not surprising that so many of the most devout and simple-minded turned to the solitary life of the anchorite or the humble fellowship of the monastery, as much to escape from what they felt to be a travesty of religion in the Church as to avoid contamination by the world. This led, in pursuit of the holiness associated with extreme ascetism and denial of the body, to wild extravagances, like that of Simeon, living for years on the top of his lofty column, his body a mass of filth and sores, esteemed by all as the holiest of saints. In spite of such aberrations, and its own readiness to succumb to the tendencies against which it was a protest, the monastic movement helped to keep alive, through the troubled ages between the break-up of the Roman Empire and the emergence of modern Europe, something of real religion as well as something of the old learning.

From the earliest days of the preaching of Christianity it was inevitable that different teachers should present their faith in different ways, and their hearers should understand them differently. There were soon, therefore, various differences of doctrine: many of them on minor matters, but some on points where the leaders of the central Church thought it of vital importance to insist on uniformity. Thus arose the conception of an 'orthodox' faith, any large divergence from which was to be treated as a 'heresy'. Those who persisted in holding such a heresy were to be turned out of the main body of Christian believers or else, when the official Church was backed by the might of the Empire, coerced into submission. Whereas in the first three centuries Christianity had been subject to bitter persecutions,[1] in which great numbers had suffered martyrdom rather than comply with demands that seemed to them to imply taking part in idolatry and denial of the Christ, the Church now used the same weapon of persecution against heretics, and practised violence and cruelty in the name of One who had taught a religion of brotherly love.

The three creeds, still in use, in which the attempt was made to formulate doctrinal orthodoxy, are the outcome of theological controversies by which Christianity was torn in the early centuries. Each phrase in them represents insistence on some disputed dogma or condemnation of some heresy. The so-called 'Apostles' Creed' dates from long after the time of the Apostles. It gives, in bare outline, the minimum of what was held to be fundamental in Christian belief and of the traditional events on which the belief was based. But it left room for much difference of interpretation. In the fourth century a fierce controversy raged between the followers of an Eastern bishop, Arius, and his rival, Athanasius, on the question whether Christ, as the Son of God, was to be regarded as of the *same* 'substance' (essential nature, that is) as the Father, or, as the Arians held, only of *like* nature, but subordinate. In order to settle the dispute, the Emperor Constantine summoned, in the year A.D. 325, a Council of Bishops at Nicaea. At this he presided himself and, claiming the right to decide the question as a matter of political expediency, pronounced against the Arians. After much debate the Council drew up the 'Nicene Creed' as the first statement of the position henceforward to be considered orthodox.[2] The 'Athanasian Creed' is intended to define in more precise metaphysical terms the relations between the three Persons recognised in the doctrine of the Trinity.[3] Whether or not the wording of this creed is to be attributed to the disputant whose

[1] There were five great persecutions: in the first century, under Nero and again under Domitian; under Marcus Aurelius in the second, and under Decius in the third; and the last, under Diocletian, at the beginning of the fourth century, shortly before Constantine adopted Christianity as the State religion.

[2] It was not, however, for three centuries, and only after many wars, that the last of the nations that had been converted by Arian missionaries was brought over to the orthodox faith.

[3] This is in itself a conception far older than Christianity, appearing in different forms expressive of various attributes and functions of a complete personality. In defining the divine status first of the 'Son of God' and then of the

name it bears, it is highly characteristic of the bitterness of the controversies that raged round these metaphysical subtleties, and of the arrogant dogmatism of one who claimed that, even if he stood alone against the world, he alone was right.

It is not possible to do more than mention some of the heresies to which disputes on points of doctrine gave rise. They were mainly concerned with questions as to the divinity of Christ. If he was in the fullest sense God, how could this be reconciled with a rigid monotheism? And again, if in his life on earth Jesus was both God and man, how were the two natures united in a single person?

As to the first problem, various solutions were put forward: that he was Son of God only by adoption; that his was but a lesser emanation of the fully divine nature, or an aspect of it, and his human life a transient mode of its disclosure (the Sabellian heresy). These were all adjudged to be heretical, as denying the full divinity of Christ; and the orthodox doctrine, finally established by the victory of Athanasius over the Arians, declared that all three Persons of the Trinity were to be regarded as co-equal and co-existent in a single Godhead.

As to the other question, there was also much difference of view. Some held that the human nature was only apparent; the death on the cross, being impossible for One who was divine, merely seemed to have happened to a substitute figure. Others that there was but a single divine nature despite the limitations of its human activity and knowledge. Others again, that the two natures were distinct, but held together in a kind of partnership. (These were the Docetic, Monophysite, and Nestorian heresies.) The condemnation of these views led to the formation of separate Christian sects in the East, while the main—'Catholic' or 'universal'—Church, both in its Western and Eastern branches, held to the doctrine of two natures, fully human as well as fully divine, completely united in a single personality.

Other heresies turned on such questions as severity of church discipline, the amount of leniency to be shown to penitents, and the invalidation of the sacraments by the personal unworthiness of the officiating priest (Novatian, Montanist, and Donatist heresies). One of much

'Comforter' whom, in John's Gospel, Jesus had promised as an abiding presence and guide to his followers, there was much theological dispute as to how what to the plain man appeared to be three several persons were to be included within the unity of the single Godhead.

religious significance was that of Pelagius,[1] who rejected the doctrine of original sin and taught that we are condemned for our own wrong-doing, and that what is right to do we have in ourselves the power to do. In opposition to this, one of the greatest leaders of the early church, Augustine, bishop of Hippo in North Africa at the end of the fourth and early part of the fifth century, laid it down as an essential part of the Christian faith that man can only be saved by the grace of God given through Christ and (as symbolised in the rite of baptism) through his appointed representatives in the Church. This reaffirmation of Paul's doctrine of 'election by grace' was later carried to the extreme by the Protestant reformer, Calvin, in his teaching of Predestination, according to which the number of those to be saved is limited and preordained.

2. We cannot here trace in detail the growth of the Papacy, which may be said to begin with Gregory the Great in the sixth century. It is connected with the first permanent division of Christendom, caused by the separation of the Eastern and Western Churches. This, though occasioned by differences of practice and doctrine, was due to more fundamental causes, psychological and political. The Roman, with his practical bent to law and order, despised the intellectual subtlety and mystical fervour of the Greek and Oriental, by whom in turn he was regarded as a boor. The bishop of Rome claimed a primacy over the bishops of the Eastern Churches, both as having his seat in the capital of the Empire and as being the successor to the Apostle Peter, of whom, according to Matthew's gospel, Jesus had said 'Upon this rock I will build my church'. When the seat of empire was moved from Rome to Constantine's new capital in the East, the change only tended to enhance the Roman bishop's authority. While the Patriarch of Constantinople could now claim, as Metropolitan, to be Head of the Church, having behind him the Imperial power, the Pope became the virtual ruler of Rome, the city that still dominated men's imagination; and by his greater freedom from the Emperor's control the Roman bishop exercised what was felt to be a more spiritual authority. The rivalry between Pope and Patriarch came to a head in the Iconoclast ('image-breaking') controversy of the eighth century. Islam was then tearing province after province from the Empire and threatening to overwhelm Christendom. The Emperor Leo, regarding this as a

[1] For us he has the more interest in that he came from Britain.

divinely sent punishment for the sins of the Church and in particular for the worship of images which it allowed—a worship which, in comparison with that practised by Mohammed's followers, had the appearance of gross idolatry—ordered the removal of images and relics from all churches throughout the Empire. This order the Pope refused to obey, and in return laid a curse on the Emperor. The cleavage thus demonstrated between the Western and Eastern churches was only partially overcome when ikons (pictures, that is, but not sculpture) were reintroduced in the East. Other points of difference remained—they may be said roughly to resemble those between the Synoptic and Johannine presentations of the Christ—and the breach was continually widened by racial antipathies and by historical circumstances. Since the eleventh century the 'Orthodox', or Greek, Church has remained completely severed from the Catholic Church of Western Europe.

No small part of the energy of the Popes was spent in struggles with successive heads of the new Western Empire—the so-called 'Holy Roman Empire'—established by Charlemagne, for the dominant position in Christendom. These struggles and the ever-growing wealth and temporal power of the Church, with the luxury and corruption that accompanied it, have little to do with religion except in so far as they tended to weaken the authority of the Church in the minds of those to whom religion meant something very different from this, and so led eventually to the break-up of its unity in the West. The development of Christianity in the Middle Ages, for all the splendour of its cathedrals and the great part played in affairs by its prelates, cannot but seem in great measure the story of a progressive deterioration and abandonment of most of what was finest in its Founder's teaching. But if there is no little truth in this view, it is not the whole truth. We must not forget all that the Church was doing in the service of humanity, or the reality and fineness of the religion that was being lived by great numbers of its adherents.

In regard to slavery, for instance, the value that Christianity attached to the individual soul, without distinction of external conditions, did much to create a state of feeling in which the institution could not flourish. So too the attitude of Jesus towards poverty and sickness and his ideal of brotherly love were never wholly lost, but led to such practical forms of charity as the establishment of hospitals and the relief of distress. With all their intolerance and violence, the ages which produced so many saintly figures were not ages in which religion was bent only to worldly ends. The very worldliness of those in high places led to reactions towards something more in accord with the Apostolic teaching and example. Francis of Assisi—to take one example—himself lived, and taught those who gathered round him to live, a life of poverty and service and love to all. From this grew up the Orders of the Friars, the 'brothers' who went about preaching and helping the very poorest in the true spirit of Jesus, until in time these orders also grew rich and worldly and lost the spiritual impulse that had inspired the movement. It was Christians such as Francis or as Catherine of Sienna, working among the plague-stricken and spending herself in efforts to heal the feuds and troubles of the Church, or as the childlike Thomas a Kempis, living the quiet life of a secluded monk and writing the *Imitation of Christ*, which breathes the very spirit of religion, who showed that Christianity was still a living thing, not as a religion merely of metaphysical subtleties and elaborate ceremonial, but as a religion of the heart, a love of God that shows itself in love of man.

Contact during the Crusades with the superior Islamic culture led to a renewed study in the Western Universities of Greek philosophy, and to the attempt, culminating in the work of Thomas Aquinas in the thirteenth century, to place Christianity on an unshakable philosophic basis by combining the teaching of Aristotle and Greek science with Christian revelations. This 'scholastic' philosophy is still, in the main, the accepted foundation of Catholic theology, although much in its presumptions about the universe was eventually made obsolete by the advance of scientific knowledge. It included, for example, the Ptolemaic astronomy, which seemed to explain all that was then known about the movements of the heavenly bodies. When this was questioned by Copernicus, the theory that he put forward was condemned by the Church as inconsistent with Christian doctrine. But denial of the truth could not be maintained. This and similar blows to the Catholic claim to infallibility were amongst the causes leading to disruption of the Western Church.

3. The Reformation, as the breaking away of the northern Churches from Rome is called by those who see in it a movement towards a simpler and more genuine Christianity, was brought about

by several converging tendencies which marked the close of the Middle Ages and the birth of the modern world. One of these was the intellectual awakening associated with the rediscovery of Greek learning, which made men look with new eyes both at the surrounding world and at the stored wisdom of the past. Scholars turned to the critical study of the Scriptures in their original languages, and by translating these into his own spoken tongue made it possible for a layman to study them for himself, instead of accepting the dogmatic interpretation of the Church.

Another thing which weakened the central authority of the Church was the growing nationalism which made those who were conscious of a geographical and racial unity, with a native culture and vigorous life of its own, impatient of any kind of foreign control; a nationalism reinforced by the greed of those who wished to enrich themselves with the spoils of a Church which could be attacked as both alien and corrupt, and by the indignation of all who were genuinely horrified by the corruption they saw in high places, and who refused to submit to the pretensions of those who openly flouted their Master's teaching.

Denunciations of alien claims and of the evil lives of dignitaries of the Church led to questioning of the source of the powers that they claimed. Thus Wycliff, in our own country, from protests against taxation by the Pope went on to deny the 'miracle of the mass' by which, according to Catholic doctrine, the priest brings about the transubstantiation of the bread and wine in the Eucharist into the body and blood of Christ. The followers of Wycliff were suppressed; but others in various countries took up the demand for moral and doctrinal reforms. The German monk, Luther, became leader of the movement when he denounced the sale of indulgences.[1] Luther's passionate individualism demanded personal assurance of salvation, to be sought in reliance upon the Scriptures and faith in the Redeemer rather than in dependence upon the Church. His object was to reform its abuses rather than to create a separate religious community; but his doctrines of justification by faith and of the priest-

[1] These were a method of raising money resorted to by the more worldly Popes. In theory an indulgence was merely the remission of penance to such as had sincerely repented of a sin; in practice, however, it came to be treated as a complete pardon, which could be obtained for a money payment, not only for a sin that had been already committed but even for one that the purchaser intended to commit.

hood of all believers could easily be pushed further. It was a French lawyer, Calvin, who carried the revolt to its logical conclusion. When invited to Geneva to reorganise, like Mohammed at Medina, the Protestant community there, he gave it a constitution in which there was no distinction between secular and religious authority. Whereas Luther had appealed most to the New Testament, and dwelt on the need for love as well as faith, Calvin was entirely Hebraic in outlook; his theocracy was based on Old Testament ideas and examples. In his insistence on the divine transcendence he rejected all religious symbolism and ornament as coming between God and the naked soul, and enjoined a stark simplicity of worship and a rigid morality. Since time is but a passing episode in God's existence and past, present, and future are all one to Him, He must, Calvin argued, have complete foreknowledge and must have foreordained all. Hence the logical necessity of predestination—the teaching of Paul and Augustine on the need of 'election by grace' carried to the logical extreme. Such a fatalist doctrine might seem to take away all motive to effort; but it has more often proved, as in the case of Islam, to fill those who believe that they are among the saved with an unconquerable energy and self-reliance.

Under the influence of these and other reformers the whole of the Western world was split into opposing camps: on the one side Protestants, who rejected the authority of the Pope and the sacrificial virtue of the Mass, and on the other Catholics who upheld the old doctrines. The struggle, supported by secular rulers from political as much as from religious motives, became one of States and nationalities as well as of creeds. Long and fierce wars waged in the name of religion showed that neither of the opposing faiths could coerce the other into submission, and the cleavage has remained permanent. Southern Europe and the lands it colonised or conquered have remained at least nominally Catholic; while in Northern Europe and its colonies Protestantism, in one or other of its various forms, prevailed.

The Reformation, in its religious aspect, was essentially a demand for freedom of thought and conscience. It upheld the right to a rational interpretation of the Scriptures, and salvation by personal faith and its effect upon the individual life rather than through the mediation of the Church. This demand could not be satisfied by substitution of a new creed or a new form of worship in place of the old if these were to be equally binding upon all. As long as officials of the

Church were regarded as holding their authority directly from the Apostles and as being the only interpreters of their teaching, there could be no escape from uniformity of belief and practice except on pain of excommunication as outcasts from the one and only Church of Christ. But once appeal was allowed from official decisions to the individual reason and conscience, each was free to decide questions of doctrine and conduct for himself, and to join with those of like mind in forming a church of higher authority as being, in their eyes, more truly in accord with the Word of God. It was inevitable, therefore, that the reformers should split up into separate religious sects.

In one respect, however, contradictory though it was to their own principles, they were only too apt to be alike—in their intolerance of other doctrines than their own. If Catholics tried to stamp out Protestant heresies by burning the heretics at the stake, Protestants retaliated, when they had the power, by the like treatment of Catholics, and even of other Protestants who differed from themselves. It took some two centuries of bitter struggle to teach the lesson, both in matters of religion and in the relations between religious and secular authority, that beliefs cannot be permanently imposed or convictions permanently crushed by force. The lesson, indeed, has not yet been fully learned. While in some countries toleration is practised (more, perhaps, as a matter of expediency or indifference than as the necessary outcome of the Reformers' claim to freedom of thought) there are those in which the State asserts its right to dragoon the churches and to compel its subjects to subordinate religious convictions to their political allegiance.

In our own country a characteristic compromise has been reached. While there is an established national church, it is sufficiently tolerant to allow within it a considerable divergence of views; and outside it there are many nonconformist bodies, still more widely separated on points of doctrine and religious observance. The position of Christianity today is thus presented in epitome, with its differences of belief and practice, ranging from those of the Catholic Church and of the Anglican ritualists who differ but little from it, to the Society of Friends, in which there is no priesthood, but each individual is to be guided by such 'inner light' as is given to him, and will best show himself to be a follower of Jesus by the life he leads and by personal devotion in bringing help to those who are in need.

CHAPTER SIX

FORMS OF WORSHIP

1. RITUAL

RELIGION is the contact of the human spirit with an unseen world, a contact which gives rise to some kind of worship. In all religions certain observances have been practised as means of bringing the individual worshipper and the community as a whole into a closer relationship with the Unseen, and intensifying the communion thus established between them. This is the meaning and purpose of the various liturgical forms of ceremonial worship. In the cruder religions they are hardly distinguishable from magic. At a higher stage, besides being a means of obtaining divine help in the conduct of life, ceremonial worship provides expression for feelings such as awe, dependence, gratitude, adoration on the part of the worshipper. Some such means of expression seems to be a need of human nature. If there are those who can dispense with any kind of ritual observance, this is not possible for all. Even when a great teacher such as the Buddha has insisted on the uselessness of religious ritual, his followers have in time overlooked this part of his teaching and have either adapted to their use existing forms of worship or established others in his honour.

In all religions certain observances have been enjoined, both for regular practice and for particular occasions, as traditional means of approach to the divine Powers. These observances have in general a communal character. In any primitive society and at all times of crisis —when we revert to primitive states of feeling—dependence of the individual on the group is felt to be so complete that the common welfare is the supreme consideration. It is for the community that the help of higher Powers must be sought, and this can be more effectively done by community of action. At such times the individual feels most at one with his fellows; in sharing the mass-emotion produced by a common purpose and a common ritual his own religious emotion is intensified to the highest pitch. To strengthen, by giving it expression, this community of feeling with out fellows has remained a reason for retaining public worship even when religion has come to be recognised as mainly a personal concern.

In all communal worship there must be a recognised procedure, whether under the guidance of a recognised leader or performed by him on behalf of the rest. From early times, when priests were little differentiated from medicine men and sorcerers, they were thought alone to know, through the possession of esoteric doctrines handed down to them, under what conditions the unseen powers could be safely approached and by what means divine help could be invoked or divine anger averted. It was essential, therefore, to follow their instructions and to entrust to them the conduct of acts of worship in order to avoid errors of ignorance or negligence. The tradition thus established has always been maintained, not only by the priesthood itself, with its tendency, as in all professions, to exalt the sanctity of professional routine, but also to a large extent by the laity, with its submissive respect for esoteric knowledge and the authority of the expert. One result, however, of the Protestant revolt against the claims of the priesthood to mediate between God and the individual soul has been to diminish the importance attached to communal worship and its traditional ritual; so that, as we see at the present time, such worship, if not wholly neglected, is confined to a few special occasions, and the spiritual need of which it was the outcome has to find other modes of expression.

Religious ritual has a double purpose: first, to serve for protection to the worshippers, by avoidance of anything that might offend the deity approached and by ensuring a proper state of body and mind in which to come; secondly, by the influence of special surroundings, ceremonial, and mass-suggestion, to stimulate the worshipper's religious emotion and strengthen his spiritual life. For the former purpose it provides some kind of 'sanctification'. Special garments to be put on by the worshipper (still seen in the traditional wearing of 'Sunday clothes') and ablutions, actual or symbolic, enjoined by various religions before taking part in acts of worship were originally intended to avoid offence to the deity by care for outward cleanliness. In later interpretation they symbolise an inward cleanliness and sincerity, in which the preoccupations of ordinary life are put off and evil in act or thought is washed away before coming into contact with divine holiness. For a like reason in many religions periods of fasting are required, and a life of ascetism and celibacy is regarded as essential for those—for priests above all—for whom such contact is to be closest and most continuous.

The other purpose of ritual is, by giving them outward expression, at once to stimulate and satisfy the religious emotions of the worshipper. Its appeal is aesthetic rather than intellectual. For this there are two reasons. In the first place there is an intimate connection between the religious sense and the sense of beauty. While recognition of the value of truth is closely bound up with practical experience of the utility of accurate observation and sound judgment, and that of moral good with the advantages derived from fair-dealing in all social relations, in the apprehension of beauty there is an immediacy of response independent of any process of reasoning or thought of use, a sense of contact with reality felt to be divine which brings it into close relationship with religion.

The second reason for the aesthetic element in religious ritual is that this derives from primitive (and therefore universal) tendencies in which the subconscious has a larger part than the rational mind. In all ritual much is achieved by repetition and by suggestion, and much by appeal to the senses. It is only in highly intellectual forms of religion that the surroundings and manner of worship become matters of small importance. From early times worship has been held to be most efficacious when performed on special sacred sites and in buildings made architecturally impressive by massiveness or intricacy of construction.[1] By the use of symbolic representation and devices akin to magic everything is due to produce a 'numinous' effect and arouse responsive feelings. Incense, music, incantations—all contribute, whether as a narcotic or a stimulant, to suspension of conscious thought and to concentration of feeling in the act of worship.

[1] Megalithic structures found in various countries seem to have been used for the worship of sky-powers and, as at Stonehenge, arranged to show astronomical facts such as the rising, on a particular date, of the sun or some conspicuous star.

The most universal expression of religious emotion is through some kind of activity combining sound and movement. Dancing is now to us little more than a means of social recreation, but among primitive peoples, as with children, it is the natural mode of expressing any kind of emotion; and as sympathy and imitation are most readily induced in this way, sound and movement are specially appropriate for any common expression of religious feeling, since it is thus rendered more intense and so at once more satisfying in itself and more likely, in the belief of the participant, to achieve its purpose of affecting the power to which it is addressed. Noise and movement are characteristic features of the 'devil-dances', 'corroborees', and other manifestations of religious excitement amongst the most primitive peoples that still survive. Tom-toms and bull-roarers and other musical instruments are employed to raise the excitement to the highest emotional pitch, as well as to create and sustain the magic influences that are to be excited. The excitement thus aroused finds its chief outlet in dramatic dances enacting in symbolic forms the events that are desired.

What was at first mainly noise, though with a rhythmic quality that gave it a strong emotional appeal, was gradually elaborated into the various kinds of music, instrumental and vocal, that usually form a large part of any religious ceremony. The singing of hymns, processional or stationary, is a later version of the primitive song-dance; and instrumental music, from its more corybantic forms up to church-music written by the greatest composers, has always been a powerful agent in producing and sustaining religious feeling. Speech also serves the same purpose when treated musically and arranged in familiar cadences. In all traditional forms of worship the repetition of formulas plays a large part, representing, though in a form more in accord with later ideas, the incantations with which the primitive worshipper sought to keep off malign influences and to constrain the unseen Powers to grant his desires.

However modified in accordance with changing habits, the expression of religious emotion through movement has continued to have a part in the ritual of worship. From the extreme form of whirlings and prostrations practised by dervishes and Oriental devotees to the genuflexions and ritual movements of those who participate in the Mass, or the change of posture in the course of any traditional form of church service, the difference is one only of degree. As in a drama-dance, the posture adopted symbolises the mental attitude of the worshipper. The Jew stands to pray, as a sign of reverence from a subject in presence of the king. The Moslem, in his utter submission to the will of Allah, prostrates himself as a suppliant before a sultan. The Christian prays kneeling in sign of humility and awe, as a lover may kneel in presence of the object of his adoration.

But while the purpose of ritual is thus to heighten religious emotion by giving it appropriate expression, and to call it up at will both by positive suggestion and by shutting out all distracting influences, there is an ever-present danger that it may defeat its ultimate object—the renewal and enrichment of religious experience—by attaching to externals an importance that may easily lead to substitution of the symbol for the actual experience. From some degree of this reversal of its purpose it is difficult—in most cases, indeed, it is hardly possible—for those who take constant part in traditional forms of worship, and in particular for an official priesthood, wholly to escape.

2. MODES OF WORSHIP

Ritual is concerned with helpful conditions and external aids to organised worship; the setting, as it were, for the various modes in which throughout human history such worship has found its commonest expression. Of those forms that mark momentous occasions in the lives of individuals or that for historical reasons are of special importance in particular religions, something will be said in the final section of this chapter. At present our concern is with certain means—sacrifice, prayer, praise, and the use of sacred writings—through which men everywhere throughout the ages have sought to maintain a fitting and helpful relationship with the unseen world and to give expression to their religious feelings.

1. Chief among those employed in ancient times was sacrifice. Although in the great world-religions it has now, in its original form, but little place, yet in the wider sense of any kind of offering made to the Deity it still forms part of religious practise. It furnishes, indeed, a good example of the way in which a traditional observance that has come to offend a more highly developed spiritual sense can be so transformed as to retain only a symbolic meaning.

Sacrifice as originally practised, had two purposes. The first was to sustain and strengthen the life of nature in its seasonal changes by means of the vital force of some living thing made one with it by the sacrificial act of killing. Since to primitive man it seemed clear that life was dependent upon blood, he poured blood upon the ground in order that the earth fertility might be renewed and increased. There are many traces of the sacrifice of human victims, representing the fertility spirit of nature, so that their blood might revivify vegetation in the coming spring and renew the fertility of flocks and herds. Connected with this belief was the widespread custom of putting to death the king ('tribal chieftain' would better express the position, as with Homer's kings and most of those in the Old Testament) or a victim substituted for him, either at a fixed period or when his natural vigour showed signs of waning, since in him as in a living symbol the vigour of the community was thought to be gathered, and must not be allowed to grow feeble before it was transferred to a younger man. In like manner, in order to promote the vigour of the family and of the flock, the sacrifice of the firstborn[1] was a custom frequently practised in primitive communities; as also the burial of children in the foundations of buildings.

Nor was it only the fertility of the earth and the vigour of animate things that must be continually renewed by this means. The spirits of the dead, in order to retain vigour and ability to help the living, needed offerings of blood as well as food. By like reasoning, supernatural Powers also needed freshly taken life for their sustenance. Moreover, food so shared with them, as at a communal meal, strengthened the bond of union between them and the human community, and was thus a means of securing their favour.

Here, then, was a second purpose of sacrifice. Just as subjects brought offerings to their rulers from motives mingled of fear of his ill-will, hope of his favour, and gratitude for his protection, so did the worshipper bring gifts to his deity from similar motives. Even if the first-named object—that of averting possible envy or malevolence—may have been predominant in primitive times, others later came to hold a larger place in man's attitude towards his deities. The practice

[1] Like so many primitive customs it still survives, but in a greatly modified form, in the dedication of the first fruits of the harvest, though this is now regarded as an act of thanksgiving.

of sacrifice was now rationalised as a recognition of man's complete dependence on the unseen power. It thus became a symbolic act, the nature and meaning of which were adapted to the spiritual level of the religion in which the practice was retained. The deities that men have worshipped have always been shaped in thought and imagination to some resemblance of the worshippers themselves, and thus have been projections of their own feelings and ways of life. To a savage it is natural to imagine a god who delights in bloodshed and demands human sacrifice. To the more civilised man such a demand, so far from being natural, seemed no longer credible, and the offering of some other kind of life was held to be sufficient as proof of readiness to give whatever might be required.[1] And from this, with a further advance of civilisation, it became possible to reach a conception of sacrifice as something in which the taking of life has no part.

The symbolic meaning of sacrifice is to be seen in the ritual, as recorded in the Old Testament, of those forms in which it was practised by the 'children of Israel' from the time when they were a nomad tribe up to their final dispersal and the destruction of the Temple. Of these forms there were three: the 'guilt-offering', an act of atonement for the inadvertent commission of any breach of the divine law; the 'thank-offering', an expression of gratitude for some special mercy conferred upon the worshipper; and the 'burnt-offering', an acknowledgment of continual dependence upon God. The ritual demanded that the living thing to be offered should be brought to the altar to be dedicated, and then killed by the person making the offering; the part of the priest was to catch the blood and sprinkle it upon the altar and worshipper in sign that a victim had been offered and (in the case of the guilt-offering) accepted in place of the worshipper's own life; thus atonement had been brought about and a blood-relationship, as it were, established with the obligations that it imposed upon both sides. The burning of the victim, in whole or in part, with the smoke going up to heaven and carrying with it the prayers of the worshipper, belongs to the ritual of a pastoral people making offerings to sky-powers. Of guilt- and thank-offerings only part was burnt, the rest being taken by the priest for his own use or

[1] The change of feeling is shown in the story (Genesis XXII) of the command to Abraham to sacrifice his son, and of the substitution, also by divine command, of a ram in place of the human victim.

given back to the offerer as occasion for a joyful feast with his friends; but the burnt-offering was so-called as being burnt entire, as symbol of readiness to give back to the Deity a portion of what he gave for the sustenance of man. It therefore included meal, oil, wine, and salt, as well as the flesh of the victim offered. Amongst those people in whose diet flesh plays no large part, other necessaries of life and other gifts of nature, such as flowers, have been the most frequent offerings made as an act of gratitude in setting aside for the giver something of what he gives. This practice has persisted into our own times, though in less recognisable forms such as tithes paid to the Church on the value of farmland, or gifts at harvest thanksgivings to be used, after serving as church decorations, for the benefit of the poor.

In most of the great religions almsgiving has always been regarded as an act of worship, the making of an offering acceptable to God. To the Christian, for example, the words of the Master bring assurance that what is given to the poor is given to the Christ himself. Nor is almsgiving the only way in which the practice of sacrifice has been sublimated in the course of religious evolution into forms that are remote from the blood-offerings of earlier stages. One such has been the dedication of wealth to building or endowing churches, colleges, almshouses, and hospitals. Fasting and asceticism have been other forms it has taken, in the belief that God's service requires a voluntary renunciation of pleasures which, even if themselves harmless, may lead to forgetfulness of higher duties. However narrow a conception of service this may be, it yet marks a spiritual advance, when it is realised that the finest form of sacrifice is to be found not in the surrender of external objects, however precious, but in the subordination of self and its desires to some higher purpose.

2. Prayer has always from early times been an essential part of religious worship and one whose use, like that of sacrifice, has changed with the development of the religious sense. While often no more than a magic incantation, it has also been the means by which those of the highest religious genius as well as countless others of normal endowment have found spiritual nourishment and sustained their powers. A great religious teacher such as the Buddha found no place in his own practice for prayer—as commonly understood, that is: for the meditation that he practised and enjoined can be in itself one form of prayer—but although he taught his disciples not to put trust in its

efficacy, ordinary human nature could not do without it, and prayer has kept its place in Buddhist worship no less than in other religions.

Belief in the existence of supernatural Powers on whose activity the life and welfare of man were dependent naturally led, in any time of need or danger threatening the community, to appeal to these Powers for help and protection. In the presence of any forces that could not be mastered by the exercise of normal strength and skill, whether natural calamities such as famine, pestilence, drought, flood, fire, or the threat of overpowering danger from enemies, the only hope was in the intervention of higher Powers that could be induced by some kind of pressure to stay the impending disaster. Such pressure was sought through some kind of dramatic presentation, in song and action, of the end desired, as a means of suggestion to the powers that could bring it about; or through incantations and charms employing special forms of words and accompanied by the proper ritual known to those skilled in this lore, by which the attention of powerful spirits could be compelled and their aid secured. In the common use of petitions addressed to the deity as a means of securing attention to particular needs enough remains of such semi-magical procedure to make the petition seem more likely to be effective if presented in a form hallowed by tradition. This has usually included some set formula, at least at the beginning or conclusion of the prayer, together with a particular posture for the suppliant; often also some kind of special preparation such as the ceremonial ablutions of the Moslem or the use of holy water on entering a church, or on occasions of great moment fasting[1] as an adjunct to prayer. The need of repetition has also been stressed as a sign of persistence; this in practice may easily become a process hardly less mechanical than the prayer-wheels of Tibet, in which it has been carried to its logical conclusion.

In order to avoid the danger of a merely mechanical repetition of set formulas, the tendency of the 'free' Christian churches has been to abandon a fixed liturgy and use extempore prayers in public no less than in private worship. In so doing it is only too easy, while avoiding one danger, to fall into another, and for beauty of form and the

[1] Besides being a means of preparatory 'sanctification' of body and spirit before coming into the divine presence, fasting has also been used as a means of inducing deities to attend to the worshipper's prayers, just as prisoners may try to bring pressure to bear upon the authorities by a hunger-strike.

hallowing of long association to substitute what may be trivial in thought and crude in expression. While personal feeling finds its sincerest expression in words of its own rather than in any formula, in public worship, which is the expression of common feelings and common needs, familiar forms of prayer shaped by long usage would seem in general to be more appropriate.

The use of prayer has been universal in the history of mankind, both in the form of private petitions for the satisfaction of some present need or for help in some personal trouble, and in public petitions for the safety and welfare of the community as a whole or of those individuals on whom its safety and welfare have seemed to depend. But while it remains a traditional part of public and private worship, belief in the efficacy of prayer, in the sense of petition for divine intervention in the course of nature and of human affairs, is everywhere on the wane in proportion to the spread of scientific knowledge and the growth of a scientific outlook.

To anyone who accepts the determinist conception of the physical universe presumed and supported by science, there is no place for any kind of prayer which supposes that laws of nature, whether on a large scale or a small, may be reversed or modified to suit human desires. In the Western world even churchgoers doubt the efficacy, for instance, of prayers for rain; nor do they think that plagues and flood and other such evils are to be met by prayer rather than by efforts to combat and control them. There is a growing recognition that in prayers for the sick or for help in adversity it is not any miraculous intervention that can be sought, but rather a strengthening of those who offer the prayer in order to meet with resignation and courage whatever may come.

For though modern thought rejects the possibility of any interruption of physical process in answer to prayer, this need not imply that the prayer is wholly meaningless and unwarranted, but rather that the answer to it is to be found in the resulting attitude of spirit and the increased clarity and strength of purpose that it can bring. To those who hold that our spiritual values give assurance that material processes are not the whole of reality, and that an increasing freedom of will and power of spiritual apprehension are characteristic of life and of human evolution in particular, there is nothing opposed to scientific truth in the use of prayer as a means of finding spiritual strength and courage, and of directing whatever power we possess to affect the course of physical and social events. Prayer in this sense is not the asking of favours, but a means to a closer relation with spiritual reality and to obtaining the spiritual sustenance that this closer relation can give.

By revealing the power of suggestion and auto-suggestion in bringing about a desired end, psychology gives warrant for the repetition, in private or together with others, of familiar forms of prayer, so long as such repetition is inspired by sincerity of desire and belief in its achievement. To put thoughts and desires into words is a means of clarifying our ideas and purposes. Prayer thus offers a way in which we can become more fully conscious of our higher impulses and of the finer possibilities of life, and can learn to see more clearly, and to feel more strongly how we may bring our daily life into some accord with the vision that comes to us at our best moments. It also offers a means of self-examination and admission of shortcomings and weaknesses; such confession, besides being a check on personal pride and on pride of race, place, or class, can bring relief from a sense of guilt and give a new starting-point by renewal of hope and resolve. In such ways prayer can still prove of help—even to those who do not think of it as petition addressed to a personal listener—in strengthening us to press forward to the fuller spiritual life that is the goal of religion.

3. In addition to prayer, praise of the deity addressed has always had a large part in organised worship. Just as the pomp of court ceremonial and splendour in the surroundings of royalty are intended to reflect and heighten the glory of the sovereign, so also the beauty and impressiveness of buildings dedicated to worship, the gorgeous vestments of priests[1] and ceremonial processions, music and singing, are intended to show the greatness of the deity worshipped and the honour due to him, and to heighten the feeling of adoration on the part of the worshippers. So too, just as an Eastern ruler carved on public buildings or on rocks a record of his exploits, temples and churches have been adorned with sculpture and painting commemorating sacred figures and events from religious myth and legend from a similar motive as well as being a means of instruction for the illiterate. And as sovereigns are greeted by their subjects with loyal

[1] These show a transformation of the primitive use of ceremonial painting, masks, and other disguises, whose purpose was to keep off evil spirits.

shouts and acclaimed in national anthems, so also in public worship outlet has been given to the feelings of the worshippers in ejaculations, formulas, and songs of praise. The singing of hymns—in which the tune is still of greater moment than the words in giving expression to the singer's feeling—has therefore always been a prominent part of communal worship.

4. In addition to its purpose of stimulating and giving expression to religious feeling such worship has also an intellectual aspect. Religion appeals to all sides of human nature. With the growing importance of knowledge and the development of reason as guide of conduct, it has addressed itself more and more to the understanding as well as to the feelings. Hence the need of some means of making known the traditional basis of a particular religion and teaching its specific doctrines. Of such means the chief have been the reading and exposition of sacred writings; dramatic representation of sacred scenes or of religious experience and moral principles under allegoric form; and commemoration, at recurrent festivals such as the Jewish Passover and the Christian Good Friday, of momentous historical events. Frequent repetition of formulas and summaries of belief is also employed, in order to impress on the minds of the worshippers truths the acceptance and understanding of which are held to be of greatest importance.

There survive sufficient portions of the sacred texts of now dead religions, such as those of ancient Egypt and Mesopotamia, to show how early in the growth of civilisation records were kept of religious forms of this kind, on which the due worship of the gods and the welfare of the community were held to depend. All the great religions of historical times have their sacred books: the Hindu Rigvedas and Upanishads, traditional accounts of the life and teachings of the Buddha, Chinese classics embodying the teaching of Laotse and Confucius, the Jewish Scriptures, the Mohammedan Koran, and the Christian Bible. Reading portions of these sacred books is frequently associated with the forms of worship practised in these religions; and exposition of the doctrines and ethical implications found in them is a recognised part of the duties of an official priesthood.

In Jewish and Christian worship this use of sacred literature has come to have a specially important place. In a religion largely occupied with ceremonial observances such as were laid down by the Mosaic

Law few could be sure of knowing fully what were its requirements or how it was to be interpreted in all its applications. Hence the need to consult those who, like the priests, were occupied with the ceremonial or, like the scribes, being familiar with the Law through making copies of it, could be expected to expound its meaning and application to any particular case. After the first destruction of the Temple and the removal of a great part of the nation into captivity, now that the traditional sacrifices could no longer be offered it was doubly important for the exiles to maintain this national and religious individuality by rigid observance of all that was laid down in the Law and enjoined by the prophets. Hence arose the practice of a weekly meeting—the synagogue, as it came later to be called—for the purpose of a common worship of prayer and praise at which portions of the sacred writings were read and expounded. Those who returned from the Babylonian captivity brought back this custom with them, so that it became a regular part of the worship of the new Jewish State; and after the overthrow of this State by the Romans and the final destruction of the Temple it has remained the characteristic feature of Jewish worship.

The custom of a weekly meeting, at which the Jewish practice was in the main adhered to, was retained by the first Christians. Besides the use of prayers and religious formulas and the singing of psalms and hymns there were readings from the Jewish Scriptures, from letters from the Apostles on points of doctrine and conduct, and later from the Gospels as well, when these had been put together in order to perpetuate memories and traditions of the life and sayings of Jesus. When in the course of time divergencies of doctrine within the various Christian communities became marked, creeds were drawn up to be repeated at these services as a statement of the essential doctrines of the Church. A sermon also came to be a regular feature, in which points of doctrine could be argued and expounded and matters of belief and conduct impressed on the hearer.

3. SACRED BOOKS

In each of the great religions certain collections of writings are regarded with special reverence, either as having been divinely inspired and therefore, in a literal sense, the word of God; or as containing records of the early growth of the particular religion and of the acts and sayings of its founder and the chief among his followers; or as collections of devotional utterances and other writings, imaginative or historical, in which its chief doctrines are to be found expressed, or which provide the material out of which they have been constructed. In connection with the use of such writings for devotional purposes something should be said as to the character of sacred literature in general and the way in which it has been regarded.

In most cases—the Koran is a notable exception—sacred books are the outcome of a prolonged process of accretion extending over many centuries, until a time came at which a definite selection was made from the whole mass of material and the 'canon' finally established. Additions made during this period of accretion were commonly attributed to ancient writers, thus giving them an authority like that of the earlier writings. It has been the task of modern scholarship to show how a sacred literature grew and took shape, assigning its various strata to the times and conditions in which they were produced instead of accepting all alike as of equal authority and value.

There are certain dangers to religion inherent in the very nature of religious literature. They are of two kinds, one arising from the nature of myth and the use of metaphorical language, the other from belief in verbal inspiration and from uncritical acceptance of the sacred text.

1. The literature of a religion whose roots go back into a distant past begins, as a rule, with hymns and myths picturing the relations of divine powers with each other and with mankind. Myths were the work of poetic imagination, the earliest form of literary expression of men's feelings and beliefs at a time when, as with children, imagination ran riot before the development of the critical faculties. We must not look, therefore, in these early myths for a coherent and logical system of belief. They are rather to be regarded as attempts to give some explanation of the strange facts of experience and the conception of unseen powers to which such experience had given rise. Myths belong to the dream-world of the child and the artist; they are the outcome of a sense of wonder, and give imaginative satisfaction to those 'questionings of sense and outward things, blank misgivings of a creature moving about in worlds not realised' that have always troubled the thoughts of men in the childhood of a race—whenever, that is, they began to have leisure to think and to put their wonder into words.

In the development of a religious literature two things have helped to shape the conceptions it embodies. In the first place, as actors in the stories told of them, the unseen powers had to take, in the imagination of the teller and his hearers, some tangible shape. This, even if monstrous—the most obvious way of representing what was superhuman—must not be beyond recognition. Animal or human shapes, or some combination of the two, were therefore taken; but even if the form was that of an animal, the actions portrayed and the feelings by which they were motivated were necessarily human. Anthropomorphism is a condition imposed by art on religion; for even if an unseen power can be *conceived* as without form or organs of sense and action, it can only be *represented* by imagery of some kind that suggests to hearer or beholder motives of action and means of contact such as he is familiar with in himself and in those like him. The likeness in which a divine being is thus presented is certain to include those traits, noble or otherwise, which at that stage of his development man has most admired and envied or feared. Once established in the imagination and hallowed by the glamour of art and the weight of tradition, such a figure is apt to remain in the currency of thought and to continue to shape the conception of deity after men have outgrown their cruder ideas, and even if in human affairs they no longer honour traits or allow the unchecked expression of passions attributed to the gods of their traditional worship.

Another inevitable feature of early religious literature was the use of 'picture-language'. Metaphor is characteristic of poetry in every age as a means of making more vivid to hearer or reader what is to be conveyed, and arousing his imagination to match, or at least to apprehend in some measure, that of the poet. What he now does of intention, the poet then did of necessity. In the effort to find expression for ideas and experiences for which he had as yet no words, he was forced to resort to metaphor without being conscious that he was doing so. He did not know how to describe a process of reflection except as a man speaking to himself, or a thought coming into his mind except as the voice of someone—of God or an angel, or it might be of Balaam's ass. Much of the language of religion is of this kind. Much of the miraculous element both in myth and in what purports to be history is due to the fact that the first narrator only had at his command language which seemed to imply more than was actually intended.[1] Thus metaphor, the language of religion as well as of poetry, has helped to make of it a mystery removed from normal experience. Once enshrined in poetry and legend beliefs, however little credible, have come to be accepted without question and have coloured subsequent thinking with a like unreality, until anything that is hallowed by tradition can be held to be true.

2. The fact that certain writings have come to be looked upon as sacred has seemed to put them, both as regards origin and use, in a different class from all others. In many cases those whose words are recorded in them believed that these words came not from themselves but from a divine Power that was using speaker or writer as mouthpiece. This verbal inspiration that the prophets claimed for their message was held to apply also to other utterances which time and tradition had made an object of veneration. All alike were thus looked upon as depositaries of divine truth from which nothing must be withdrawn, nor could any additions be made except to enhance their sanctity. Interpretations differing from that officially accepted or attempts to show, on historical or moral grounds, that all had not a like religious value, have commonly been denounced as dangerous heresy.

This attitude towards sacred books has had disastrous effects. An uncritical veneration of writings regarded as verbally inspired led to the treatment of each statement, detached from its context and without regard to its original intention, as an absolute truth. When any portion of a sacred text can thus be detached and used as a basis for belief or argument, there is no limit to the abuse of reason and conscience to which it can be put. As Donne said: 'Sentences in scripture, like hairs in horses' tails, concur in one root of beauty and strength, but being plucked out one by one serve only for springes and snares.' In this way any conception of the divine nature can be supported and any belief or act upheld as a manifestation of the divine will. Moreover, the method of treating in isolation widely varying statements by

[1] For example, one who wanted to express a hope either that the day would be long enough for the work in hand, or, as others interpret the story, that the storm by which the enemy were discomfited would continue, must be said to bid the sun 'stand still' (Joshua x. 12); and one who was helplessly wave-tossed in the darkness must be described as being in 'the belly of hell' (Jonah II. 2); then later tellers or hearers of the story took the phrases as literally intended, and saw in them a miraculous lengthening of the day, and a 'great fish' in whose belly the prophet uttered his prayer.

the founder of a religion, or by those who have carried on his teaching, has strengthened the tendency to split up into sects holding different points of view for which sanction has thus been found.

The habit of regarding certain writings as being different in kind from all others, so that everything contained in them must be accepted as unquestionably true, has exercised in all ages a narrowing influence upon intellectual growth. It has compelled belief, as a matter of obedience to divine command, in statements of fact and in the validity of systems of ideas and conduct to which full assent could not be given by those who were free to follow the dictates of reason and conscience. Or else, when this began to be realised, it has led, in the treatment of those parts of the sacred writings that could no longer be accepted in their original meaning, to an exercise of casuistry which has been detrimental to intellectual sincerity. If appeal has constantly to be made to writings belonging to an earlier age, embodying another stage of civilisation and another order of thought, in order to decide what should be believed and what line of conduct should be followed under conditions that have completely changed, such an attitude is only possible at the cost either of a petrifaction of mind that prevents all attempts at adaptation to changed conditions, or of the complete dissociation of religious belief from the affairs of daily life and the principles on which these are carried on.

4. SACRAMENTS

Besides the foregoing modes of worship in common use in ancient and modern times, there are also certain specific liturgical observances employed upon particular occasions. Apart from those needed for dealing with any pollution that might have been incurred, these are chiefly rites of initiation into some new state of relationship of the individual with his fellows or with God.

In addition to ritual sanctification (by means of ablutions, special garments, fasting, and so forth) required before entering the divine presence for public or private worship, religion has also been concerned with a more general sanctification of the daily life. This has had the three-fold object of removing any grounds of offence to the unseen powers, of freeing the individual from guilt that, even if involuntary, would be a danger not only to himself but to others, and of enabling him to give the fullest service of which he is capable both to the community and to its divine ruler.

In the Mosaic Law, for example, much is laid down in detail as to what is clean and what is unclean both in food and in other matters of daily life, and specific ceremonial is enjoined by way of protection and of purification. It is easy to understand how in most ages the idea of pollution has attached to corpses and to everything connected with the disposal of the dead. Sex also is a matter which has been hedged around with taboos. There is a deep-rooted tendency to treat its manifestations as unclean, needing religious sanction and purification, as seen, for example, in the 'churching' of women after childbirth, which lingered down to our times.

When man had reached the tribal stage of development, he was accustomed to find sanction for all that he did in the will of the tribal deity, and to account for any tribal custom by a myth in which it was instituted by the deity himself. Ritual which originally had a more practical purpose now took on a religious significance. Marriage, for instance, was a matter of such moment for the continuance of the community that it must become a divine ordinance; thus what had been a magic ritual for keeping off evil spirits and ensuring fertility grew into a means of invoking the blessing of the guardian deity. So too with death. At first the chief concern of the survivors seems to have been to allow the spirit of the dead to depart freely, and to prevent it from returning to haunt the living. Later, however, this concern underwent transformation; it became the chief object of the rites to ensure the welfare of the spirit and to bring consolation to the mourners. With the growth of belief in a fuller and more glorious life in another world the change was complete; a ritual that began as a means of allaying fears became now an expression of religious faith.

Besides birth, marriage, and death, the attainment of puberty is not only a landmark in the life of the individual but also a matter of concern to the community to which he belongs. From both points of view, therefore, this has been made an occasion for some ceremonial by which a new member was to be formally admitted to the adult social group and its responsibilities. And since membership involved fresh religious obligations and a special relationship with the divine guardian of the community, the tendency of an official priesthood has been to stress the religious nature of the ceremony. This led to another consideration. If the religious status of the individual, as an object of divine care and a participant in a divinely ordered relationship, depended upon a religious ceremony, was it not wiser to perform the rite of admission at the outset of life, instead of waiting till the maturer age was reached? If so, since the infant cannot be conscious of what is involved, others have to act on his behalf until, on reaching the age of discretion, he can take upon himself the responsibilities undertaken in his name. Where infant baptism is practised it is therefore followed at the beginning of adolescence by some ceremony of confirmation of the vows then made for him.

From the initiation ceremonies so widely practised among primitive peoples to mark the admission of boy and girl into the full fellowship of the tribe,[1] it was natural enough that the idea should be similarly extended to other occasions in the life of the individual and the community. Such an occasion is the dedication of an individual to some service of great social import: the accession of a monarch, for instance, or the acceptance of office by an important functionary; and even more, of course, entry to the priesthood or the taking of vows when entering some religious community or undertaking some action, such as a Crusade, with whose object religion is closely concerned. In the historic religions occasions of this kind are marked by specific forms of religious ceremonial. Certain of them, as being of supreme importance to the individual and to the community, are in Christian worship distinguished from other liturgical forms as 'sacraments'.

In its ordinary usage the Latin word *sacramentum* meant an oath: in particular, the soldier's oath, taken on enlistment, of allegiance to his commander. It could therefore be aptly used as a religious term to denote, at any ceremony of initiation, the solemn promises made to God to carry out the new responsibilities then being undertaken. The ceremonies involving a solemn promise of the kind to which the term 'sacrament' is applicable have varied in number at different times and in different branches of the Christian religion. In the Catholic Church, for instance, baptism and its later confirmation, matrimony, ordination to the priesthood, and the supreme unction given to speed the soul on its journey to the other world are all regarded as sacraments

[1] These still survive in the rites of initiation into secret societies of various kinds, from bodies of international standing, such as Freemasonry, to college fraternities.

—as divinely appointed means, that is, of entry into new spiritual experience in which the initiate undertakes, whether of himself or through others, to maintain the fullest allegiance to the divine Power through whose grace the possibility of salvation is given to him.

Whatever the sacraments recognised by the various Christian Churches, one that is admitted by all of them in the special form of liturgy—called in Catholic worship the Mass and in Protestant Churches either Holy Communion or (in the Greek term originally used for it) Eucharist—which has been, from the time of the Apostles onward, the central feature of Christian worship. As applied to this particular observance the term 'sacrament' has a fuller meaning which links this with other rites of a not dissimilar kind in various 'mystery' religions.

In his letters to newly formed bodies of Christian converts the Apostle Paul made frequent use of the Greek term 'mystery'—esoteric knowledge revealed only to the initiate—to denote a truth that had been, as he says, 'kept secret since the world began',[1] but had now been revealed in the person of the Christ, together with the new sense of joy and freedom from guilt brought to the believer by faith in his saving power. When Paul's writings were translated into Latin the word chosen to translate 'mystery' was *sacramentum*, so that 'sacrament' has now been invested with something of the ideas associated with the 'mysteries' then widely practised.

As the term is used by the classical Greek writers, 'mysteries' were secret rites and 'mystics' those who had been initiated into them. The Orphic and Eleusinian mysteries were a kind of religious freemasonry in which, besides ceremonies of initiation, there were further rites in which only the initiate could take part. Those celebrated each year at Eleusis seem to have included (though, as they might not be divulged, we have no full record of them) a dramatisation of the myth of Demeter and Persephone. As there shown, the story became not merely a personification of the burial and rebirth of the seed, but a symbolic representation of human experience, with its wanderings in darkness and the possibility of rebirth into higher life. Some such symbolism can also be seen in the 'mysteries' practised in other religions, such as those in the Persian worship of Mithras, in the Syrian cult of Adonis, or in the Egyptian worship of Isis and Osiris.

[1] Romans xvi. 2; see also 1 Corinthians ii. 7 and Ephesians iii. 9.

Through imaginative participation in the sufferings and joys of the divine figures portrayed in these myths, the 'mystic' came to feel that his emotions were purged and his spiritual experience enlarged, and that he was in some special degree a sharer in the divine experience and a recipient of divine grace and spiritual strength.

In some of these 'mystery' cults there was a further symbolism embodied in a sacramental meal. The victim offered for sacrifice was looked upon as in some sense the deity himself whose death and rebirth were being commemorated; the flesh and bread and wine of which the worshipper partook represented—or rather, to the mystic, became in actual fact—the flesh and blood of the dead and re-risen deity, by partaking of which he strengthened the bond of communion and drew into himself something of the divine nature.

This 'mystical' belief, deeply rooted in the Eastern Mediterranean world throughout which Christianity was spread by the Apostles, entered into the Christian practice of the Eucharist. Originally a common meal at which believers came together to 'break bread' in commemoration of the Last Supper shared by Jesus with his disciples, it soon took on the character of a 'mystery' in the two-fold sense of an initiation into a new life and a means of salvation.

In this sacramental sense, the Eucharist is the central act of Christian worship, combining in itself a commemoration of the historic events on which the religion is based, a renewal of the sacrifice made for mankind by the divine Saviour, and of the believer's participation in that sacrifice and in the salvation that it offers; and finally a means of closer communion, for all who take part in it, both with the source of spiritual life and with their fellow men.

CHAPTER SEVEN

GOD

1. MONOTHEISM

UNDERLYING the historical religions that have taken strongest and most extended hold upon mankind are certain fundamental conceptions, for the most part held in common though taking different forms: crystallisations, so to speak, of the apprehension of spiritual reality which is the essential element of religion. Such conceptions are: God, immortality, salvation, righteousness, worship. Not all of these, as we have seen, are equally matters of concern in all religions; but in some form and in some degree they enter into all. In the account that has been given of the chief characteristics of the greater religions these conceptions have so far been taken for granted. We have now to look at each of them more closely in order to see something of their development.

In all religions the most fundamental conception is that of an Unseen Power, of which the whole of experience, material and spiritual, is in some way manifestation and outcome. This Power Confucius was content to leave undefined, using only a vague term such as 'Heaven'. The Buddha went further in denying that any knowledge of it is possible. He advised his followers, therefore not to concern themselves with speculation about it, but only with what could be accomplished by human effort. For the great majority of Buddhists, however, this counsel has proved too hard. They have found objects of worship in manifestations of the divine in personal form. Buddhism has thus come into line with other religions in which the Unseen Power is worshipped as God.

To endow this Power with personal attributes is the outcome of a tendency so deeply rooted in the nature and working of the human mind that it may be looked upon as universal. When man emerged from the animal level and began to reflect upon his experience and wonder why things sometimes behaved in other than normal ways, it must have seemed obvious that what he saw happening had an origin like that of his own actions: it must be due to some impulse of will or desire either on the part of the object thus acting or of some sentient being using it as he himself used a stick or stone. Not that in such an assumption there was any conscious process of reasoning. Confronted as he was on every side with forces, some conducive to life, others seemingly hostile, can we doubt that even before reflective thought was possible the feeling evoked not only found outlet in some response containing the germ of ritual behaviour, but clothed itself in some kind of imagery? Later—in the course, that is, of unnumbered generations—as the power of reflection developed and language came to the aid of imagery, it became possible to give expression to nascent ideas in the picture-language of myth. It was the interaction of ceremonial and myth, instinctive response and imaginative presentation, which has given form and content to the various stages in the evolution of religion. Of this evolution an index of advance is to be found in the conceptions of Deity that men have held.

Advance has been along two lines: the one from belief in multifarious supernatural agencies to belief in a single supreme Power; the other from a crude to a more spiritual conception of the divine nature itself and of the attributes held to belong to it. The one aspect of deity is the subject of this section, the latter that of the one that follows.

Of the one line of advance some of the earlier stages were traced in a previous chapter.[1] It was there pointed out that the forms and activities attributed to the gods worshipped by any people were closely connected with its main preoccupations, and especially with the main source of its food supply. Natural conditions were personified in myths that sought to account for their influence and for the rites by which their favourable action was to be assured. Another source of ideas by which myths were shaped was belief that the dead continued to interest themselves in the affairs of those they had left. The corpse buried beneath the hearth or in some corner of the

[1] Chapter III, sections 1 and 2.

peasant's field was regarded as still sharing the ownership of house and land; and the dead ruler in his more elaborate tomb remained guardian of his country so long as the due rites were paid. Thus their memory was kept alive, their doings heightened in retrospect, and outstanding personalities tended to become legendary figures endowed with superhuman powers. Stories repeated from generation to generation may well have played a part in giving form and character to local deities and to tribal gods who, as embodiment of group-authority and upholders of group-tradition, inevitably took on amongst their attributes the characteristics and ideals of their worshippers.

We can see also how conceptions of deity were profoundly influenced by historical and political developments. When a nation extended its sway by conquest over other countries, it was natural to suppose that this was rendered possible by the greater power of its god over those that were unable to defend their own communities against him. Thus the conception could become familiar of a hierarchy among divine powers, with a supreme ruler among them in the same relation to others as that of a 'king of kings' towards subordinate kingdoms. When the ideal of a universal empire was brought within the bounds of possibility by the conquests of a Darius or an Alexander and largely realised by the power of Rome, what had been only a philosophic concept or a prophet's vision of a single divine ruler of the universe could now find wider acceptance.

The process was helped by two further factors. In the first place, those brought into close contact with peoples of other countries, and thus made familiar with their strange deities, tended to identify any that seemed to have similar characteristics with their own. It was thus possible to see in them, although worshipped under different titles and with different rites, so many embodiments of the same deity. And secondly, with the growth of moral sensitivity, the greater was the influence of spiritually minded thinkers and reformers who denounced the multiplicity of supernatural Powers that were objects of the common worship, and the unworthiness of the attributes with which they were endowed.

Several tendencies have thus combined to establish belief in one supreme deity, a belief that is common to various world-religions.[1]

[1] It must, however, be borne in mind that to the majority even of those who accept it as an article of their creed, monotheism does not rule out belief in the

Judaism was the first to reach the conception of a single God, Creator of the universe and Ruler of all the nations in the world. But even in Judaism this was of slow growth. Before the time of the prophets the Hebrew people had been commanded (in accordance with the revelation given, so their tradition said, to their ancestor Abraham) to worship one God only as their national deity. But they accepted the fact that other peoples also had their tribal and national deities, whose power was exercised within their respective borders; and even in their own land of Canaan there remained the local gods of the earlier inhabitants to whose worship there was a constant temptation to resort.

Worship of a single national deity has been called *henotheism* to distinguish it from true monotheism—the recognition that there is one God only of all lands and all peoples. This further development was the work of the great prophets; and it was this, together with their insistence on the spiritual character of the divine nature and of a truly acceptable worship, that has given to Judaism its place among the greatest of world-religions. A like place, as exemplifying monotheism, is held by Islam. While both religions admit the existence of other spiritual agencies, whether angels or demons, they look upon these as subordinate creations of the one supreme Deity; and both alike refuse to regard Christianity as monotheistic in its worship of a Godhead in which different Persons are distinguished.

At the other extreme among the great religions is Hinduism, which, with its immense patheon of deities in a multiplicity of shapes, animal as well as human, is the most complete survival of the polytheistic stage of religious evolution. To the thoughtful among its adherents the fact of this survival is of little moment. To them the multiplicity of deities is only apparent. The ultimate spiritual reality, the soul of the universe, is in its all-embracing immensity wholly indescribable; only to be imaged under an immense variety of forms, personifications of forces of nature and of moral qualities. An apparent polytheism may thus be defended, or at least explained, as only an inverted monotheism—a recognition that every attempt to present the unimaginable to human comprehension is equally valid and equally

existence of other supernatural beings. Whatever the creed they profess, it is only the more thoughtful and more spiritual natures whose religion can be called monotheistic in the fullest sense.

insufficient. It is not for Christian thinkers to deride such an attitude while themselves maintaining that the existence of three Persons in the Trinity is compatible with the assertion of divine Unity. To the Christian apologist, the Trinity is not merely a three-fold personification of different aspects of the divine nature. In his insistence on the historic manifestation of a separate personality manifested in the earthly life of Jesus and still continued in the risen Christ, there appears to be, if this held to be compatible with an absolute monotheism, a contradiction which special pleading may conceal but cannot, to the plain man, overcome.

2. DIVINE ATTRIBUTES

Man, said Voltaire, has created God in his own image. This is true if by 'created' we understand the process of shaping and reshaping, in accordance with the needs and ideals of every age, his conception of an Unseen Power, and his attitude towards it. Roughly summarised, the process has been one of change from a capricious exercise of arbitrary power to a rule of justice and a fatherly care for the spiritual welfare of mankind; and from a slavish attitude of fear to a willing service of devotion and love. Of the human response in worship something will be said in a later chapter; here we are concerned with what has been felt to be most fully characteristic of the divine nature.

Man's conception of God is the outcome of two kinds of experience: his contacts with the external world and the life of human relationships. His gods have always been embodiments both of external power and of human qualities. In lands subject to disasters on a great scale brought by storms, floods, and earthquakes, it was natural to think of the Unseen Powers as pitiless and rejoicing in destruction; and while a settled climate, with regularity of recurrent seasons bringing now good now harm, tended to give a fatalistic colour to religion, unreliability of weather conditions seemed to be the outcome of divine caprice, requiring constant propitiation by entreaty and offerings. With the growing realisation, however, of uniformity of causation in nature and the increasing need of law and order brought by settled life, the gods that man worshipped could now be conceived as requiring an obedience due not merely to arbitrary power but to established law. With the further realisation that the distinction between human beings and other animals, and between one man and another, lay not merely in physical differences but still more in the possession of mental and spiritual qualities, these qualities became increasingly necessary attributes of deity. Whereas superior strength could be symbolised by the forms of animals or embodied in monstrous shapes, these higher qualities, even at a superhuman level, required for their embodiment a human form.

In times when nomad peoples were invading settled communities and when city states were extending their dominion by conquest, their deities were inevitably thought of as endowed with the characteristics of conquerors. It was as a terrible figure, therefore, that the tribal or national deity was most commonly imagined, endowed with a fury which, towards enemies, took the guise of righteous triumph rather than cruelty; while from subjects he exacted complete submission and claimed their all as his due. It was no less natural to think of such a Being as harsh than to think of nature as hostile and of social obligations as maintained by force. But as leader of the community, on whom depended the welfare of all its members, he was the embodiment not only of power but of right, the law-giver demanding a certain standard of conduct, and the judge dispensing justice and punishing disobedience. With more settled conditions and the greater spiritual sensitivity thus made possible, this second aspect of deity could take greater prominence: the attributes of a conqueror could give place to justice in the ruler and mercy in the judge, with a corresponding change of attitude from servile submission to a willing loyalty on the part of the worshipper.

To us of the West there is no better text-book of religious evolution than the Bible. In this we can trace, in the history of a single people, the growth from a conception of God as a jealous and cruel tribal deity to that of a compassionate and loving Father. In spite of the priestly recension of the earlier Hebrew Scriptures in order to moralise the old stories and to give a more spiritual picture of the Deity than was there presented, enough is left to show that Jahveh was originally a figure endowed with terrible attributes, merciless alike to enemies and to those members of his chosen people who did not give complete obedience. In the Psalms and the prophetic writings we see the growth of a larger and finer conception. Here he is increasingly presented not only as a God whose power extends over the whole earth and who cares for all the peoples of mankind, but as one among whose chief attributes are justice and mercy, and one who desires the like qualities in his worshippers. It is still, however, the imagery of kingship that is most often employed; the relationship of mankind to God is regarded as that of subjects to an autocratic ruler. In the New Testament we see the further development of a sense of kinship between human and divine nature, making possible a more humanistic religion. To the teaching of Jesus most of all is owing the conception of that relationship as one of children to their father; and it was the disciple who entered most fully into the spirit of his teaching who summed this conception of the divine nature in the saying 'God is love'.

Here, then, in traditions and records that cover some two thousand years of religious evolution, we have, in this change of conception, a measure of man's spiritual growth. Not, of course, that this growth has been continuous. Evolution does not work in that way. It does not follow an unbroken line of advance, nor do all the lines that are followed prove to be advances. Some have no survival value. Some lead to degeneracy. There are reversions to an earlier type—as we see today in the deification of a nationalism which sets up its new tribal gods, as jealous and as cruel as any of the old. But just as we can trace a general trend of biological, and in particular of human, evolution, so also can we see in this an increasing apprehension of spiritual values. The new revelations of spiritual insight brought by the great religious teachers are, so to speak, mutations by which a further advance is made possible. There may be long periods in which one such advance is extending over a wider field and adjusting itself to fresh environments, or else, it may be, coming to an end or sinking back into degeneracy and failure. But in one respect spiritual evolution differs from biological. A gain once made cannot, while the remembrance of it is enshrined in tradition or in some form of art and literature, be wholly lost. Long after the forms in which it was first embodied have been laid aside like outworn garments or even treated with contempt and obloquy, the spirit which inspired it lives on and may be rekindled in other ways of life.

As with every kind of perception, in the apprehension of the divine there is an interplay of objective and subjective elements—the reality which is given and the degree in which this is apprehensible by the senses, physical and spiritual, of the percipient, and in which it is modified by association with the prior content of his mind. It is thus that the conception of God has grown with the growth of knowledge and with the development of thought and feeling. From physical manifestations of an unseen Power—nature in its most overwhelming and awe-inspiring forms—the general trend of religious evolution has been marked by a growing apprehension of divine holiness in which our highest values have their source and consummation. With each extension of our knowledge of the universe we gain a further glimpse of reality as physical energy passing far beyond our comprehension of its nature or its purpose. Science can only stand awed in the presence of the immensity it reveals. Religion with the inner eye of faith sees in this immensity a spiritual power at work in evolution, transforming the material and utilising it as a condition from which higher values may emerge.

The forms under which men have tried to present God to the imagination are necessarily anthropomorphic. They can only be projections of ourselves and the values that we feel, since it is only from what is known in actual experience that we can form any conception of the unseen reality which religion holds to underlie all being. But in all anthropomorphism there is a childish element that must in time be outgrown. Much that in every creed offends the thinker is due to this element; for in speaking of spiritual experience, the only language possible being that of metaphor, hypostatisation of metaphors and abstractions is a tendency that few can escape. An eventual reaction against these tendencies, whether consciously recognised or only felt subconsciously, is a factor in the decay that overtakes all the creeds in which religion has found expression. But if every such expression is in time outgrown, there remains a sense of something beyond—call it what we will—that continually seeks to reshape expression for itself. Under the jibe of Ingersoll that 'an honest God is the noblest work of man' there is a profound truth, if by God we mean the highest that we can conceive and feel.

While the trend of religious evolution has thus advanced from a crude anthropomorphism to a spiritual conception of deity, there has at the same time been another that may at first sight seem contradictory, in an increasing shift of interest from the supernatural to the human. The word 'supernatural' may be used in two different senses, according to the meaning assigned to the term 'nature'. This may be restricted to include only the order of reality investigated by science —whatever is capable of observation and experiment, and more particularly of exact measurement and mathematical treatment. This order, as the scientific investigator realises, is far from constituting the whole of being. There is much that lies beyond it—the qualities of things, the meaning of life, the purpose of the immense and intricate interplay of the forces he investigates. If it is this further sphere of experience that is designated 'supernatural', then the term may properly be applied to the concepts of religion, and experience of this kind has a definite and vastly important place in the sum of reality.

More often, however, the word is used to imply something that completely transcends not only external nature but also human experience and the values that it apprehends. It is in this sense of 'supernatural', implying something entirely apart not only from 'nature' but from human nature as well, that there can be said to be an advance in the transference of interest from the supernatural to the human.

To an omnipotent Being, terrible alike in power and in righteousness, existing apart from a world created and maintained by his divine will, the only fitting attitude was one of distant adoration and humble submission. From this it was a spiritual advance, bringing closer contact of the Unseen with humanity, when it could be believed that this Being had taken human form, whether in a single figure or in a succession of such incarnations, in order to help mankind in their weakness and to bring to them a means of attaining spiritual life. For in this belief something more was implicit. In such figures we see the highest to which humanity has yet attained. They are the crests, so to speak, of waves in the tide of spiritual evolution. In them we have some vision of an ideal humanity that we call divine, embodying the spiritual urge that inspires the struggles and aspirations of mankind.

In this turning from projection of human fears and desires upon a supernatural background to apprehension of a spiritual reality made manifest, if only in part and uncertainly, in man's nature and potentialities, religion has come down from a supernatural world to this world of ours. There is here no contradiction; for if it is true that religion is response to a sense of something more than the visible world, it is no less true that for us, while we are here, it is in this world and in the relations, actual and possible, of our human life that God is revealed.

3. IS PROOF POSSIBLE?

While in earlier ages there has been frequent controversy as to the nature and attributes of the supreme divine Being, the existence of such a Being has usually been taken for granted. With the development of the physical sciences, however, with their picture of a mechanical universe, the grounds for this belief came to be more widely questioned. In such a picture there seemed to be no place and no need for any such assumption; by many, indeed, its falsity was upheld as a necessity of scientific thought. In the first flush of the triumph of scientific knowledge and method over tradition and religious obscurantism it seemed that truth lay wholly on the one side and error on the other. Every fresh advance of knowledge, it was assumed, would show still more clearly that all could be explained in accordance with physical principles, leaving no room for any supernatural influence or for the existence of a divine Being. Of this, however, we hear comparatively little now. The further that science penetrates into the secrets of the universe the humbler does it become in presence of so much that is beyond comprehension, and the less certain that any merely material explanation can suffice. It realises that to attribute the evolution of the physical universe, and of life and its values, either to the workings of blind chance or to a self-imposed necessity is merely to confess our own ignorance. Theories of evolution may give what is at best a partial description of the facts; none of them gives, or can attempt to give, any explanation of the origin or ultimate meaning of the process. Beyond all that we can know lies the immensity of the unknown. A sense of something beyond knowledge is a necessary condition of human experience.

But mankind, always clamorous for certainty, is ready, when knowledge fails, to frame hypotheses and to find reasons for assurance of belief in their validity. In matters of religious beliefs, which the majority are ready to accept on trust and hold without question, acuter minds have long been occupied with attempts to find this assurance. Doubts as to the existence of God have arisen from time to time, whether through discrepancy between received beliefs and facts of common experience or from philosophical speculation. They have been met in three ways: by appeal to tradition, to reason, or to the believer's own inner certainty based on intuition and experience. A few words, then, as to the nature and validity of each of these kinds of attempted proof.

1. Official exponents of religion have usually been content to base assurance on tradition, whether in the form of ancestral wisdom hallowed by custom and accepted as beyond controversy, or of sacred writings recording the words of men divinely inspired and therefore to be regarded as the very word of God. To this authority they appeal as sufficient ground for belief not only in the existence of a Supreme Being, but also in the truth of particular statements as to manifestations, in nature and in history, of his power and will. Here lies the weakness of authority of this kind. If particular statements can be disproved, the validity of the whole system, and of the assumptions on which its authority rests, is open to question. And this is so today, more than ever before, in regard to authority of this kind. To those who accept the methods and findings of science—and these now include the vast majority of civilised mankind, whether themselves capable of forming a rational judgment on the matter or not—tradition alone, however sacred, can no longer be accepted as proof of the truth of any religious belief. On the other hand this does not mean, as some are ready to assume, that the existence of God is *dis*proved by the weakening of traditional authority, or by the fact that much in the sacred writings of all religions must be rejected as untrue. All that it means is that, while we may feel no less certain of the existence of God, the God of our belief is not to be defined by traditional assertions we are no longer able to accept; for our certainty we must have other grounds.

2. Thinkers have sought this certainty in logical arguments for the existence of God and in the fundamental assumptions on which they are based. By some God is identified with the universe as an impersonal activity, self-ordered, without beginning and without end. To Oriental philosophy resting on this assumption the question does not arise: in so far as we have a sense of reality we cannot but be aware of the existence of God, since God, as so defined, is the entire

and only reality. By others God is regarded as the spiritual whole of which the universe known to us is a part. Of the existence of the material universe we are directly aware through our physical senses; of that of the greater whole we are similarly aware through our spiritual senses. Religious thinkers would also add, through divine revelation, involving the further assumption that the ultimate reality is personal.

That there is an ultimate spiritual and personal reality, God, is the basic assumption of Judaism, Islam, and Christianity; and, further, that the material universe is a creation of the divine will and as such is rather to be contrasted than identified with its Creator. If rational proof of the existence of such a Being, antecedent to the sensible universe and wholly transcending it, is required, it has been offered by reasoning on one or more of three lines. One of these is the 'ontological' argument: that the very fact of our being able to form the conception is in itself a guarantee of the existence of God. As Anselm, the originator of this 'proof', put it: Nothing greater can be conceived than God; but to exist is greater than not to exist; therefore God must exist, or a greater could be conceived. Another is the 'cosmological' argument: that as every natural event is the outcome of a preceding cause we are bound, in tracing things back to their antecedent causes, to come eventually to a First Cause, itself uncaused and therefore outside and above the order of nature—that is, to a Supernatural Being.

To such arguments the Scholastic philosophers, seeking metaphysical support for scriptural truths, attached much weight. Today they have little, seeming rather to be examples of the philosopher's candid description of metaphysics as 'the finding of bad reasons for what we believe on instinct'. The third, or 'teleological' argument, makes more appeal to common sense. This sees in the evidence of design to be found everywhere in the natural world proof of a conscious purpose, partly seen to be good and assumed to be wholly so, and therefore of a mind that formed that purpose and directs its realisation. This argument has been contemptuously set aside as refuted by scientific demonstration that mechanical complexity might be the result of the blind interplay of natural forces, and that natural selection rather than conscious design could be held to account for the whole process of organic evolution. It has been suggested, for instance, that, according to the theory of probabilities, given a sufficient length of time in which to play about with a typewriter, a monkey, out of the random combinations of letters that are possible, could, without knowing what he was doing, produce the particular sequences that make up a sonnet of Shakespeare.[1]

Even if this might be so, and if all the complexities of organic evolution might be such a chance product, could this, it may be argued in reply, in any conceivable way account for the general trend of increasing organisation, with the further spiritual evolution which is its outcome? A merely mechanical explanation of the universe is now less commonly put forward than in the last generation; men of science are more inclined to postulate an activity of mind in inorganic nature as well as in living things. But even if not demonstrably false, neither is the teleological argument able to give proof of a conscious purpose on the part of an all-wise and all-good Creator, as it was once held to do. For one thing, we are now familiar with the fact of unconscious mental activity and unconscious purpose. And for another, even if the ordered complexity of the universe may seem to be proof of design on the part of a Being immeasurable in power, there is much in it which challenges belief rather than offers evidence that this Being is also good.

Such proofs, indeed, can give no intellectual certainty, for they rest on the very intuitions the truth of which they are advanced to prove. Reason can only say: if *this* is true, then *that* is necessarily true; but its 'ifs' are themselves assumptions. An attempt to show that there is something outside the universe as we know it in nature and ourselves must fail, for we cannot know what is by definition beyond knowledge; at most we can only feel that there is something more than we can know. Attempts on the other hand to show that we are right in attributing to the whole of reality qualities of which we are aware in ourselves can only succeed by taking this feeling as sufficient assurance of its own certainty and of the reality of that to which it is directed. And this is just what we cannot help doing. Apart from it no proof is possible. The only argument that carries conviction is one that appeals to the validity of the intuitions of mankind and to the great mass of human experience—so long as in making this appeal we

[1] Mentioned as a conceivable possibility, though not as a serious argument, by Sir James Jeans in *The Mysterious Universe*.

remember that, while the data of a finite experience may point to something beyond itself, of this they cannot give *logical* proof.

3. If, therefore, we ask for proof of the existence of a spiritual Being (whether apart from or including the material universe) who is endowed with all kinds of perfection, such proof is not to be had by means of any intellectual process; it is only to be found, if at all, in the emotional experience of the mystic. All experience is finite; but it can grow, and, as far as mind and spirit are concerned, no *a priori* limits can be set to its potentialities of growth. If the name 'God' stands to us for that reality of which we have direct experience—the sense of existence, with all that we know or feel of the power and beauty involved in it, and with all the potentialities of what to us is good—then there is no need for logical proof of that of which we have direct apprehension. The wider the range of our experience and the greater the universe, material and spiritual, of which we are aware, the more assurance can we feel of a reality at once including and transcending experience; a reality to which mankind at every stage of its growth has tried to give symbolic expression in its conception of God.

4. GOD, TO SCIENCE AND FAITH

If there is nothing in our experience that evokes our reverence and claims our worship in thought and act, argument about the existence of God is meaningless; to one who has such experience, it is unnecessary. It is more pertinent to ask: why continue to employ a name fraught with associations with anthropomorphic figures of the past? But is it possible to dispense with a name that has meant so much to mankind in every age? Just because it has, from age to age, been enriched with new meanings, its continued use keeps to the line of religious evolution which has always sought to reinterpret its symbols in accordance with the knowledge and feeling of the time. So too with the emotional enrichment that has gathered round it. Philosophy and science make their appeal to the intellect, not to the heart, and cannot, for most of us, touch the springs of motive and call forth devotion and love. Religion needs, as it has always needed, an object of aspiration and of worship; and this it has always thought of as God.

It is easy to see how crude and childish are the forms in which other civilisations than our own have portrayed the objects of their worship;

only custom makes it less easy to see this in the religious imagery with which we are familiar in our own art and literature. In giving clearer perception science is doing a service to religion. The conception of God such as found expression in the words of a Hebrew prophet or in a figure limned by a Renaissance painter seems now wholly insufficient to symbolise the cosmic immensities of energy in comparison with which a human figure, however magnified, sinks into insignificance. So, too, any attempt to express the Godhead, whether as a single figure or as some mystic union of personalities, in terms not of unimaginable power but rather of spiritual values, soon carries us beyond the possibilities of imagination and of any kind of language. Yet the recognition of these limitations and the dissatisfaction that we must feel with any of the symbols that can be employed are signs of a spiritual advance. The religious sense grows by drawing into itself every extension of intellectual and spiritual activity, and thereby makes each previous synthesis insufficient for its needs.

The modern mind is moulded by the scientific outlook and cannot be content with myth and sentiment. Physics, biology, and psychology all have something to contribute to any idea of God which we can feel to be tenable. It must include the stupendous energy at work in the physical universe, in the full scale of its relations from the unimaginably great to the unimaginably small, both alike beyond man's comprehension and expressible only in the mathematician's symbols. It must also include the fact of evolution and give to it a sense of something more than an aimless round of happenings that have no meaning beyond themselves. Above all it must include the emergence of mind and the spiritual values which are the highest reach of thought and feeling; in which, even more than in power and complexity of being, the Godhead has seemed to be revealed.[1]

Such a line of approach is in marked contrast with the older in one respect. Philosophers and theologians have defined their conception

[1] Such a combination of ideas, it may be said, is already presented in the Trinity of the Christian creed, which may be interpreted as symbolising the supreme spiritual reality under its three aspects: as transcending experience, as immanent in the universe, and as manifested by incarnation in human life; or (in briefer summary) as power, purpose, and love. So interpreted, it might serve as a symbol to include the main constituents of what the conception of Godhead has come to mean to the spiritually minded of many creeds; but only if freed from the particular doctrinal implications which so many are now unable to accept.

of God as the one perfect Being, eternal and self-sufficient, 'with whom is no variableness neither shadow of turning'. They have exhausted all the resources of language in the attempt to express perfection in its every aspect and every attribute. But this postulate of absolute perfection carries with it certain implications. What is already perfect, and by its very nature must always so remain, is incapable of change of any kind, as otherwise its perfection would not yet be complete. But a static conception of an eternal and unchanging divine perfection is only possible of a Deity apart from and wholly external to the changing universe of physical events and human experience. This universe may be the creation of such a Deity, set going and kept in movement as one object of his concern, as of an engineer with a piece of machinery or a child with a toy; but it cannot be a part of his being, nor in any degree share a nature which by definition is incapable of change.

Such a conception might satisfy the thinker seeking to find a First Cause, itself uncaused, outside the universal flux of causation and change; or of one content to dismiss the sensible universe as mere appearance and illusion. It might also satisfy the worshipper looking up to the divine perfection as an unfailing strength on which to rely, an unchanging truth and right beyond the welter of effort and failure. But as a philosophic conception such a static condition of perfection, external to the universe of which alone we have any experience, has become remote from a scientific outlook which is above all dynamic and sees in *process* the underlying principle of existence. Energy, physical and spiritual, is the fundamental mystery which we cannot penetrate; a power, incomprehensible in its origin and nature, that we see and feel at work in the universe around us and in our own experience. This, as well as the unknown beyond, must be included in our conception of God.

Does this mean that any such conception may be replaced by the idea of a vast machine, self-started and self-directing, bound to continue running through its different phases of activity until its energy is exhausted and—as the principle of entropy seems to foretell—until all is finally reduced to an inert equilibrium in which there can be no further change and no life of any kind? To those to whom mind and spirit, being the product of material structures, must cease to have any kind of being when these structures have perished, such a view of the universe and its fate may seem inevitable. But not to those who see in them emergents that show the direction in which evolution moves: emergents that point to something beyond the world of present experience, something for which the physical universe is only a starting-point and means of growth. To the question *why* the course of existence should be one of evolution, and still more one of spiritual evolution, neither science nor philosophy can give an answer; any answer that is given can only be one of faith. Whether we approach the question from the side of philosophy or from that of religious experience, there is need of a conception of God as that towards which the process is directed.

Is there here an answer to the much disputed question whether God is to be regarded as immanent in the universe or transcending it—a question that has momentous practical implications? In the one view—pantheism in all its forms—all that exists, both in external nature and in the spirit of man, is expression of the divine nature and the divine will.[1] In the other the universe as known to us is but an incident in the creative thought of God—no more, as oriental imagery has expressed it, than the footstool beneath His throne; the spiritual world in which He has His being is one differing in kind and infinitely greater than anything we know or can conceive. If we accept a pantheism confined to the physical and spiritual universe that is known to us, or that can be known, in nature and in man, the outcome is a religion of humanism whose view is bounded by the world about us and its aim directed to the making of a heaven on earth. The other view, pressed to its logical conclusion, is that of the mystic and the ascetic to whom the concerns of the present life are worthless or harmful as distracting the soul from its true concern with another kind of existence, and whose highest aim and greatest happiness are found in withdrawal from the present and the external into a timeless state of contemplation and emotional fulfilment in the presence of spiritual reality.

Those are the opposite poles of religion. Do we have to choose

[1] While philosophy has tended to regard the universe as the visible expression of an immanent unseen Power, most religions have dwelt rather on the transcendence of the object of their worship. They have been unwilling to accept a doctrine of immanence which seems to make God not only responsible for the existence of evil but himself possessing a nature in which evil has a part. This problem is one of the questions discussed in the following chapter.

between them? Are not the two views only differences of emphasis, aspects of the same supreme reality? There is place—and, if life is to be lived at its fullest, there is need—for both. A spiritual reality, however transcendent, could have little meaning or value for us if it is not present in all we are and do, and concerned with this present life of ours on which depends all the future both for ourselves and for the world whose destinies are in our hands. At the same time, though we must walk with our feet firmly planted on the earth and heedful of all that it offers for our enjoyment and use, we need not therefore keep our eyes fixed solely on the ground with no sight or thought of the heavens above us. Those have done most for their fellows who have found strength and guidance in communion with a higher world of being. The religion that we need is a humanism inspired and enriched by the sense of a transcendent spiritual reality.

What, then, of the further question, which to religion has more than a philosophical interest: is this supreme reality too vast and too remote for any personal relationship, or may it be approached by the worshipper, in the words of William James, as 'not an It but a Thou'? To religion, from the earliest animistic interpretation of experience up to the conceptions of Deity embodied in the great world-religions, there has been little doubt. It is only the Confucian, with his concentration upon human relationships, and the Buddhist (if he follows his Master's injunctions), by whom the question can be dismissed as unnecessary or meaningless. The stronger the feeling of the worshipper, the greater the need of a personal object of worship with whom he can feel some degree of communion to be possible. To philosophy, on the other hand, there is no such emotional need. It has long recognised that in shaping his metaphysical system each thinker does but give to it the impress of his own mental make-up; and this recognition has been reinforced by science, which makes plain how inevitably religious feelings and conceptions have been embodied in forms that can only have to reality a relation like that of a child's first drawings to that which they profess to portray.

On the crudity of all anthropomorphic religion there is no need to insist; it stands clearly revealed to all in the light of modern science. What could be uncritically accepted when the earth was held to be the centre of a limited universe created for the sake of man and to serve his needs, becomes, in face of the immensities of which today we have some little cognisance, a riddle before which understanding and imagination are alike helpless. We may well ask can such life as is possible for some brief moments, on a single planet of one of the smaller suns in one of innumerable starry systems, have any possible relation to the purpose of such a whole? And can there be in that whole a consciousness like our own that has any kind of human feeling for each individual of one of these transitory forms of life? To believe this would seem to justify the old *credo quia impossibile.* Yet we cannot believe that spiritual evolution is no meaningless 'epiphenomenon' of a meaningless process taking place in one tiny corner of the universe. We must suppose that in the nature of reality, incomprehensible as it may be, there is something that is in accord with the evolution of human consciousness, something of which our spiritual values can give us partial apprehension.

To many the new orientation of thought given by a scientific outlook seems to take from the conception of God all that is of most value in what the name has hitherto implied—those attributes that men have sought to express in such human terms as King and Judge, Father and Friend—and to leave only some impersonal order of events which may arouse our awe and wonder, but cannot call forth any warmer human feeling or give any sense of personal contact. It is true we can no longer be content to think of God in such terms as in an unscientific age satisfied men's feelings and raised no more question than they do with children. But this does not necessarily mean that such a conception must be replaced by that of a mechanism, to be expressed only in terms of mathematics, moving through some self-ordered cycle of increasing and diminishing complexity, blind, purposeless, indifferent to values thrown off like sparks from some tiny part of its vast movement. It need not mean that we can have no sense of communion with a living Whole with which, in our own nature and purposes, we feel ourselves to be in some degree of kinship. If God is to us the realisation of our highest values, any conception of the divine must comprise the highest of which we are aware in our own experience. And this highest to us is inseparable from the social relationships implicit in personality Thus we reach the paradox that while God cannot be confined within the limitations of a person, yet that which to us is dependent upon personality seems to be an essential element of the ultimate reality.

Religion is the quest for this ultimate reality which we call God. It begins in the assurance of something beyond the material environment and beyond the life of the moment. 'Beyond', that is, in the twofold sense of that which lies beyond the furthest reach of our present knowledge and spiritual apprehension, and also of a potentiality which has not yet been realised. No matter in what form the conception of the divine is embodied, if it implies something beyond ourselves, beyond our present powers and our present conditions, to which to lift our eyes and hearts and to which to direct our strivings, to this, so we may hope and believe, we can approach more nearly. Meanwhile in our highest values we have some glimpse of that 'far-off divine event' to which evolution points. These spiritual values it has commonly seemed natural to think of as consciously given by a pre-existing mind. Today a humbler attitude is more consistent with our knowledge and our ignorance. They seem rather to mark the emergence of a purpose that is growing to consciousness, pointing to an ultimate reality that is not yet revealed. Religion is our sense of a purpose dimly apprehended, in realising which our participation may be a small yet essential factor.

Yet the need of something more remains. Do we find, either in the vistas of immeasurable energy opened up by science or in a philosophy of emergent evolution, all that the life of the spirit needs for its sustenance? We need something that is neither incomprehensible nor incapable of sympathy to which to turn for guidance and comforting assurance. This we can find only in some personal Being possessing the warmth of human feeling, one not too remote to give directions to the perplexed and to set an example that can be followed. Hence the tendency of religion to embody the Unseen Power that it worships in some imaginable form endowed with human attributes. To a maturer religious sense any crude anthropomorphism cannot but seem unworthy of the divine reality it seeks to portray. Even if it were possible to find some form under which it could be presented to the imagination, such a superhuman Being would be too awful to approach. Religion has therefore turned, for the most part, to some less remote and less awful figure as exemplar of the divine nature in whom human feeling could find an object of adoration and a source of spiritual strength and guidance. From such figures in every age men have drawn help and inspiration, and have found satisfaction for an instinctive need of human nature in a personal embodiment of the divine. From this neither the spiritually nor the philosophically minded need dissent; but only from the claim that here is the full revelation of divine reality and the sole means of approach through which salvation can be found.

CHAPTER EIGHT

SALVATION

1. THE NEED OF SALVATION

PAIN, suffering, evil in its many forms are amongst the most familiar facts of experience. They are the inevitable counterpart of pleasure, well-being, and of all that we find good. As with heat and cold, light and dark, and all other contrasts in sensation, the apprehension of any kind of good necessarily implies a corresponding apprehension of its opposite. We may think of this opposite as due to withdrawal of what is good until a zero is reached; more often we think of it as positive experience of what is bad, with degrees of goodness and badness measured on a like scale on either side of a central point of indifference. Such a scale of values has no meaning, we must remember, except in application to the experience of sentient beings. In the physical universe a thing is not in itself better or worse by being in one state rather than in another—solid or gaseous, coherent or unstable, in slow or rapid motion—but only when considered from our point of view, whether it serves or hinders our aims. Things are good or bad only to one who benefits or suffers from them, either actually or in imagination, and who perceives their relation to his desires and purposes.

Apprehension of evil, then, is the price paid for the possession of sensitivity. Evil, like good, is an accompaniment of consciousness, and varies in kind as well as in degree according to the level of life attained. If by good we mean all that makes for the fullest life at its different levels, then evil is whatever brings harm or loss to life, whether of body or mind or spirit. At the level of the bodily life sensation brings apprehension of pain, which is no less effective than pleasure as a spur to effort, and even more necessary, in the world as we know it, as warning of harm and danger to be avoided. Evil at this level is injury caused by violence or disease, discomfort due to some ill adaptation, the burden of long-continued or excessive effort needed to overcome obstacles, or lack of satisfaction of bodily needs and loss of vitality by weakness and decay.

In looking at the animal stage of evolution we are apt perhaps to over-rate the extent to which the life of wild nature is clouded by pain and decay and death, and to read our own feelings—judgments of cruelty and the like—into a process that is wonderfully adapted to produce the utmost variety, vigour, and beauty and, in spite of pain, abounding joy of life. In wild nature, where any weakness leads to speedy elimination, health and vigorous performance of function are the rule: death is usually swift, and pain is not intensified by any long expectation or remembrance. As the price of our partial escape from the necessities of animal life, we have exposed ourselves to lingering disease; and so also, in return for mental powers which give us so much greater control of nature and fulness of life, we have to pay the price in all the added possibilities of mental pain. 'We look before and after, and pine for what is not.' We know doubt, anxiety, fear not only of death and dangers that actually threaten but of possible ills (a fear which does so much to make life mean and miserable), the ache of unsatisfied desire, the bitterness of disappointment and failure, and grief at the loss of what one has held dear. Like bodily pain, mental suffering can be a spur to effort and can bring enrichment of life and strengthening of character; but it can also, if unremitting, sap vitality and bring the apathy of hopelessness.

But it is at the level of spiritual evolution that the consciousness of evil is keenest, in suffering and doing wrong, in the pain of moral conflict and the worsting of higher impulses by lower; in unbridled lust and cruelty, in weakness of will, cowardice and betrayal, or in deceit and hypocrisy and cold-hearted cynicism. At this spiritual level harm done to the moral life by misuse or loss is evil in the fullest sense; whether we think of it as crime—wrong done to the community by breaking its laws; as vice—harm done without full knowledge or deliberate intention to injure; or as sin—the wrong which is done in spite of better knowledge and against the dictates of conscience. We may see in resistance to evil a condition of spiritual growth, just as we see in pain a necessary spur to the effort on which bodily life depends. Neither evil nor pain, however, are any the less unwelcome on this account. Our moral nature, in so far as it is aware of what is evil, shrinks from it no less than our animal nature shrinks from pain. Our first instinctive reaction to anything that we apprehend as bad is to escape it by avoidance; if we cannot do this we seek to resist and overcome it. Life is thus, at all its levels, a struggle constantly renewed either to escape or to overcome all that threatens to lessen vitality and to take away that in which, at any level, it finds its fullest satisfaction.

In the earliest stage of human evolution, as with the higher animals, the outcome of the struggle is seen in the instinctive reactions of flight or pugnacity, submission or self-assertion, with their associated emotions of fear and rage, which are the normal ways of response to threats of harm. Such instinctive responses to what he first feels and later comes to recognise as being harmful to life are at all stages man's first reaction to unpleasant experience; but with the growth of intelligence he has learnt that something more is needed. Instinct, unaided, acts blindly, both in being narrowly directed to a single end and in failing to make use of means by which, if intelligently controlled, its purpose can be more efficiently attained. And further, with the growth in complexity of social relations a merely instinctive reaction to experience is not only insufficient; it is often at variance with social needs that have a stronger claim than the personal impulses of self-preservation and self-assertion. Thus the sense of evil has come to have a greatly widened scope, including moral as well as physical harm and loss, and needing to be met by other than merely instinctive reactions.

One way in which primitive man met it was by turning to the help of magic in any situation too complex to be satisfactorily dealt with by an immediate instinctive response or by the traditional activity derived from experience. It was pointed out in an earlier chapter that in the forms used by religion in all ages something of the ideas and procedure of magic, both as a prophylactic against evil and as a means of exorcising it, has been retained. This is, so to speak, the underside of all religions. Alien though it is from the spiritual insight of the great teachers, no religion can escape debasement from the grosser alloy of magic brought into it by the bulk of its adherents.

There can be little doubt that with primitive man, as with the child, the sense of wrong-doing arose in connection with restrictions and taboos imposed in the interests of the community. With the growth of belief in the existence of higher Powers that required from their worshipper certain standards of conduct from which it was only too easy to fall, the sense of wrong-doing became a sense of sin in doing what was displeasing to these Powers. The only escape from sin lay in gaining from the Deity he had offended forgiveness for past faults and failures and aid against falling into them in future. It was essential, therefore, that he should know what was the divine will: what he must do and refrain from doing; and, further, how he should approach the Deity and by what means he could best hope to win favour and forgiveness. Here lay the strength of the priests, the official guardians of religion and intermediaries between Deity and worshipper. They alone knew the divine will or could interpret it as expressed in traditional writings or in oracles and portents; and they alone could perform the necessary ritual, and instruct the worshipper what ritual he must himself follow, by which the Deity could be approached and propitiated.

Among the strongest driving-forces in religion has been the need that man has felt for help in the struggle against evils without and within. He has turned to religion in the hope that through it he could win this help and find salvation from sin and from whatever doom may be the penalty of sin. One of the charges brought against religion has been that it is only a way of trying to shuffle off the consequences of our actions and escape into a dream-world from the hard realities of life. There is much in all religions to which the charge is applicable. To many of those who have done it lip-service religion has been no more than such a means of evasion of unpleasant realities. To yet more it has been an escape from doubt and uncertainty, from the need to decide what they should do and from responsibility for their choice: an escape welcomed by the inertia in ordinary human nature which loves to feel itself at one with others and to rest on the authority of a church or a leader. But there is more in religion, even as a means of escape, than this. The philosopher in his study or the artist in his ivory tower, no less than the thoughtless inheritor of comfort and security, may pass lightly over the problem of evil and may ignore the greater part of the misery and waste of life involved in the doing and suffering of wrong. But to those who have known, in actual experience or through sympathy, some part of its crushing weight, nothing that brings the comfort and hope which religion has brought to untold numbers can be dismissed as mere illusion. Salvation from evil has always been the promise of religion; and however much its meaning may change at different stages of spiritual growth, such salvation remains one of the deepest needs of man.

2. MEANS OF SALVATION

Whether so called or not, the idea of salvation has held a large place in all religions under two main aspects. In one, the more negative, salvation is release from the various evils of life: from pain and sorrow and the pressure of material wants; from the malice of evil powers; from the fear of death and of what may follow death, from the dominance of sin and the alienation from the divine purpose and divine love which sin entails. In its more positive aspect it is a way of life in accordance with the divine will and enriched with the joy and peace that the sense of release from evil brings. Since this is dependent upon and may be expected to follow naturally from the other, it is with the means of escape from evil that religions have usually been most concerned.

The ills from which they have offered release may be summed under three heads. First, there is *pain* in all its forms, bodily and mental, the harms to which all living things are exposed, and the griefs that are the shadows of our emotional life, the darker in proportion to its intensity of feeling. These ills men have always sought to avert or, when this was not possible, to mitigate and heal by the aid of religion. On its lower levels they have resorted to charms and repetition of prescribed formulas; at a somewhat higher to sacrifice and prayer; while at a higher level still they have learnt to make them bearable by resignation to a divine will and even to welcome them as part of an ultimately beneficent purpose, or at least to regard them as transient and light in comparison with spiritual experience and the promise of eternal happiness.

The second is *death*, which to most men has been a chief object of fear, most of all since death came to be thought of as not merely putting an end to the life that we know, but as leading to another existence in which, for all who are not 'saved', punishment will be exacted for wrong-doing here. This fear, as a means of heightening the need of salvation, religions have usually done much to intensify, and in most of them belief in a future life of punishment for the wicked and happiness for the saved holds a large place. (This element in religion will have separate consideration in the following chapter.)

Thirdly, connected with this fear of punishment, but passing beyond it, is the sense of *sin* that has weighed so heavily on many of the more religious natures, not so much from fear as from a feeling of failure of response on their part to the salvation offered them, and of being through their own shortcomings outcasts from the divine love. To such as these salvation has meant, most of all, escape from the power of sin through a divine mercy that knows no limits, and a freely given grace that goes out to seek the sinners and rejoices to set them amongst the saved. This, it is plain, easily leads to a doctrine of predestination in which the saved are selected by divine grace without regard to their own deserts. A Rasputin could argue that the more sin that needs pardon the greater the satisfaction of the mercy that gives it. To finer natures it is in the sense of reconciliation with an all-comprehending and all-pardoning love, and in the devotion and strength which they draw from it, that the consciousness of salvation is attained.

Religions have differed much in the emphasis laid upon particular aspects of evil and, consequently, upon the nature of the salvation offered. It is the hope of the Buddhist, for instance, to find release at last from the burden of individual life and from the evils inevitably attendant on effort and desire. In the Hebrew Scriptures, salvation in its earlier usage meant deliverance from enemies and impending dangers; while to the later apocalyptic writers it came to mean safe passage through the approaching end of the present world-order and entrance to the restored Kingdom that was to follow. In the various 'mystery' religions, again, in which the idea of salvation and the use of the term were most prominent, it denoted assurance of a future life of happiness in another world.

There has been great difference in the means by which assurance of the attainment of salvation has been sought. Foremost throughout have been ritual observances of some kind. In the earliest religious records that have come down to us, such as those preserved in Egypt, chief emphasis is laid on the need and efficacy of prayers and spells if repeated in the proper words, and on ritual purifications. The performance, communally and individually, of ceremonial rites and the repetition of formulas enjoined by the priest are still everywhere insisted on by institutional religion; for something of the belief in magic in which much of this ritual had its origin has persisted in every age. The greatest of religious teachers have always insisted that salvation was not to be won by such means. In the path which the Buddha laid down for his followers ritual had no place. The Hebrew Prophets declared that the only worship acceptable to God is a worship of the heart that shows itself in the whole conduct of life; and this was yet more strongly insisted upon in the teaching of Jesus in his denunciations of Pharisaic formalism. Confucius and Mohammed both confined religious ceremonial to a few simple observances and laid emphasis on the performance of practical duties.

In the rejection of ritual and insistence on the greater importance of individual conduct there lies, as upholders of religious orthodoxy have been quick to see, a risk of assuming that to win salvation there is no need of divine help, but each can trust to his own merits—an assumption that is apt to lead to spiritual pride and to a formalism of another kind such as that of one type of Puritanism. While insisting, therefore, on the uselessness of mere ceremonial, religious teachers have been no less insistent that reconciliation with the divine will, constantly forsaken by human weakness, is not to be won by 'works' alone. It is to be achieved by humble acceptance of what is offered directly to the heart of man as an act of grace, 'unprevented, unimplored, unsought'. Hence the importance attached to a consciousness of 'conversion', the beginning of a new life with its sense of release from doubt and fear, and the replacement of these by faith and love.

Of all the rites held in primitive times to be essential for salvation, one of the most important and one that has continued to play a great part in shaping religious doctrine and practice was the offering of sacrifice. We are not here concerned with other ideas underlying the practice of sacrifice, such as belief in the need of blood poured upon the earth in order to ensure its fertility or as provision of sustenance for the invisible powers, but only with sacrifice regarded as a guilt-offering. Its purpose was to atone for disobedience to the divine law and to cleanse the offender from impurity by the medium of the victim's blood. A frequent feature of this kind of sacrifice was the sprinkling of blood not only upon the ground or the altar but also upon the worshipper. If the anger of an offended deity was to be averted by acceptance of the life of a victim in place of that of the offender, then to be marked with its blood was proof that the substitution had taken place. Hence the smearing of blood on doorways or on the clothes or person of the worshipper as sign that immunity had thus been bought. Furthermore, the reconciliation of the offended deity with the suppliant was symbolised by the blood sprinkled on altar and worshipper in sign of a bond of union, a blood-relationship as it were, which imposed obligations on both participants.

Blood-sacrifice as a means of atonement for sin was an important part of the religious observance of the ancient world, a practice almost universal until its hold was weakened by the general advance in civilisation that marked the epoch around the beginning of the Christian era. The heralds of this spiritual advance were the Hebrew prophets who denounced reliance upon the efficacy of sacrifice and proclaimed repentance as the true means of attaining release from sin and reconciliation with God. The offering of sacrifice as an essential part of Jewish observance was only brought to an end by the destruction of the Temple; but the change in the mode of worship made necessary by the Dispersion was in accord with a long-growing change of attitude. It was owing to this changed attitude, as well as in protest against practices in vogue in the pagan religions of the time, that Christianity rejected any form of sacrifice in its worship and took a leading part in bringing the practice to an end. But though abandoning it in practice, Christianity inherited from its parent Judaism the ideas of which blood-sacrifice was expression; and these ideas had much to do with shaping Christian theology, and have deeply coloured the doctrines of the Christian Faith.

To Christianity, as to other religions, the existence of evil and its part in the divine purpose have presented a crucial problem. Given a God of righteousness and justice, and suffering and death as the penalty of sin, how was it possible that justice should be satisfied and yet the sinner saved from the necessary result of his wrong-doing? The principle of sacrifice seemed to provide a way of escape if the burden of guilt could be laid upon a victim; still more, if it were voluntarily assumed by one whose death, accepted in substitution, could thus give redemption to others. The Hebrew custom, on the annual Day of Atonement, of laying the sins of the people on a scapegoat which was then led into the desert to die, is a humaner instance of a practice which, in more primitive times, demanded a human victim. A similar idea that the welfare of the community could be assured by vicarious sacrifice is traced by Sir James Frazer in the *Golden Bough*. A king or priest had to be killed before being overtaken by the weakness of age in order that the vigour of the community, of which he was held to be the embodiment, might be renewed in the person of his youthful successor. Both ideas were combined in the mystery religions. In these the central feature was the recurrently enacted death of a redeemer, by mystical participation in whose sufferings and return to life the worshippers also were enabled to escape from death and were freed from the burden of sin.

It is instinctive in children at any hurt or threat of danger to run to an elder for comfort and protection. So, too, human nature seeks relief from evils of any kind by reliance upon the help of some stronger power, above all a power that is felt to be divine. Men have always looked to a leader to give them a sense of protection and to tell them how to escape danger and overcome difficulty. It is by no accident of circumstance that king and priest have loomed so large in history; they have stood, however unworthily, for the satisfaction of one of the deepest needs in human nature. It is not only through pride of birth and wealth or power that they have claimed to hold their office by divine right. When men had come to believe in the existence of deities who concerned themselves with human affairs, they regarded those in authority as representatives of these deities, either by direct descent from them or as having been, by ceremonial consecration, invested with something of divine power and inspired by divine wisdom; and in the sphere of religion this tendency has operated with special force.

That some who have lived human lives, speaking and acting as men, have in their words and acts been in a special degree exponents of a divine spirit is a belief which has always found ready acceptance. Some such idea underlies the metaphor in which we speak of inspiration, deriving from times when its literal truth was taken for granted. Temporary possession by evil spirits was widely held to be the explanation of some kinds of disease and of madness. It also accounted for the utterances of false prophets; while those of the true prophet came from a divine spirit speaking through his mouth. The appearance in human form of gods who wished to take a personal part in human affairs was narrated as an event of certain (even if rare) occurrence in the myths of many races. It was easy, therefore to believe that those who had been the greatest benefactors of mankind were, in some degree, divine beings, whether or not recognised as such while they lived on earth. Ideas of this kind made it no less easy to believe that there could be one in whom the incarnation of godhead was complete, and who had taken earthly life upon himself in order to bring to men the means of salvation.

Take, for instance, the development of the Hebrew conception of a Messiah. Originally a hoped-for human ruler, a scion of the royal line who would restore the glories of the earlier kingdom, the conception came to include a prophetic figure who, as the necessary prelude to such a restoration, would recall a backsliding people to a purer worship. Then, as the political situation grew worse and it seemed evident that only by divine interposition and world-upheaval could the national restoration be brought about, it was rather as a superhuman figure that the Messiah was conceived, who would first take part in the judgment of the nations and then become ruler of the new kingdom to be established on earth for those who had throughout been found faithful to the true religion. It was this conception of one with superhuman powers though in human form, as pictured in the vision of Daniel,[1] together with that of the Servant, portrayed in the latter part of the book of Isaiah, whose sufferings were to redeem first his own people and then, through them, the whole world, that gave its form to the doctrine taught by the Apostles of the Messiah-Saviour seen by them in the person of their Master who had come, so he is recorded to have said, 'to give his life a ransom for many'.

How these words were to be interpreted, and how the death of the Saviour could bring atonement, releasing men from sin and reconciling them with God, are questions that have been endlessly discussed by Christian thinkers. By medieval theologians the word 'ransom' was taken in its literal meaning, as showing that the life of the Saviour was the price paid in abrogation of the Devil's claim to souls which, but for the payment of this price, were rightfully his as the

[1] VII. 13.

penalty of sin. In revulsion from a conception of divine justice by which—to the delight of the medieval mind that loved to make a comic figure of the enemy of mankind—the Devil was to be cheated of his due, other doctrines of the Atonement were put forward by thinkers of the eleventh and twelfth centuries. Anselm saw in the Saviour's death the supreme manifestation of vicarious sacrifice. In the Hebrew guilt-offering the life of the victim was offered in place of the penalty incurred, and by its blood the wrong-doer was purified from guilt; so also the Christ took upon himself the sin of mankind and suffered the penalty required by divine justice, and thus freed from the guilt of sin all who had faith in him.

This doctrine of expiation of sin by substitution of one victim for another is one that few today find it possible to reconcile either with their reason or their moral sense. It is a strange justice which, while it must exact its pound of flesh, allows the penalty to be taken from the innocent in place of the guilty, and is thus satisfied to annul its own law. Nor is the difficulty overcome by regarding, as some have done, the sacrifice as a symbolic payment of the required penalty, which allows the Judge to consider justice satisfied and so to follow his impulse of mercy. It is true that vicarious suffering—the sins of the fathers visited on the children and the innocent suffering for the guilty—is one of the facts of experience that have to be accepted as part of the problem of evil; but a faith that can accept the doctrine that this is the central fact on which the whole scheme of salvation has been planned can only be a faith which says *credo quia impossibile*.

Others, therefore, have been more inclined to follow Abelard in seeing in the Saviour's readiness to undergo suffering and death for the sake of mankind the supreme example of self-sacrificing love through which alone salvation can be attained. In this sacrifice the believer can continually share. He can himself experience the fulness of self-surrender and submission to the divine will, and dedicate himself anew to its service. The tendency of modern Christian thought has thus been to regard the process of salvation not as a problem of the satisfaction of justice, but as a manifestation of the love which is the fullest expression of the divine nature and the means by which evil can be overcome and turned to good. So regarded, the Christian doctrine of salvation has been of profound importance in shaping the course of spiritual evolution.

3. SALVATION IN THE PRESENT LIFE

Salvation is not only a matter of theological doctrine or of sacramental means of grace. It is also a psychological state, a spiritual experience and orientation of mind which cannot but leave profound effects upon the whole conduct of life. This is what was above called the positive aspect of salvation, beginning in the sense of relief and escape from the worst forms of evil, with the joy that this brings, and showing itself in a way of life to which it gives strength of motive and clearness of purpose.

There are, no doubt, happy natures who are seldom, if ever, conscious of such a need; who meet the inevitable troubles of life with courage and cheerfulness, and who look forward to death and whatever may lie beyond death without fear. Faults and failures, weakness or savagery of human nature give them no cause for despair or for cynical indifference, but only a stimulus to effort and a call for help. They have little need of anything that religion can offer as a means of escape from evil. But most are not so happily gifted in natural disposition and temperament. They can only reach a like serenity of mind and sureness of purpose through much suffering or as the outcome of some great spiritual experience.

In the records of those who have been regarded as prophets and saints it is remarkable in how many cases their lives have been changed by some special experience by which they have either been shaken out of absorption in worldly interests, or else freed from the misery and despair in which they were plunged by consciousness of evil in the world and in themselves. Such an experience was like emerging from darkness into daylight, bringing with it a sense of release from oppression and uncertainty, and a confidence that in sharing a divine purpose they could draw upon a strength greater than their own. To those to whom it has come, it has seemed not only to give assurance of salvation from all that could hinder and destroy the life of the spirit, but to open the gate to the true way of living.

Some such experience, bringing a consciousness of conversion, has been held by some religious teachers to be the normal and necessary way of 'finding religion' and of attaining salvation. Much mental suffering has thereby been intensified in those who neither have had, nor could persuade themselves that they had had, any such experience. In consequence they have felt themselves to be outcasts from divine grace. It is not to be expected that all natures can be equally sensitive or that those who are most sensitive will all react to experience in the same way. To demand, as the first step to a better way of life, a sudden and complete conversion is apt to encourage self-deception and cause fruitless heart-searching and discouragement; or it may convince the plain man that religion is something unreal, and the salvation that it promises only a wish-fulfilment.

While a complete change of outlook may come through some one intense experience, it can more often be a slow and gradual process, brought about by many contributory causes. It may come through the influence of religion; but it may also come through escape from a religion which has become a prison and a deadening of the spirit. It may come through a changed environment and exposure to fresh influences; or from within, through growth of thought and conscience. However it may come, it can be compared with the effect of convalescence and the relief and gladness that come with the feeling of health and strength renewed and intensified. Salvation, freed from its theological associations and from the doctrinal conditions attached to it in different religions, is but the name given, in the language of religion, to spiritual health, and the joy and sense of power that accompany it.

This joy and sense of power are the most striking characteristics of any religion in its earliest phase when it comes as a renewal of the spirit, a bringer of new hopes and communal aims, a trumpet-call to action, giving zest and purpose to life. It may be the fierce joy of the idol-breaker or, as in the early days of Islam, of the soldier-missionary spreading the true faith with the sword. It may be devoted to the service of false gods and turned to vile uses, like the reawakened spirit of hope and comradeship that we have seen exploited by 'leaders' in their quest for power—a spirit which, in the sense of salvation that it can bring to many, has in it the force of a religion. But it is not only in militancy that such a spirit can find expression. What most impressed the contemporaries of the first Christians was the gladness given by the new message of hope, with its release from the fear of death and relief from aimlessness and uncertainty and from the burdens of the Jewish Law. It inspired a courage that could cheerfully meet martyrdom and brought happiness even in the poorest conditions of life. To those who accepted the new faith salvation was of more than individual concern; it enriched all the relations of life and gave purpose to all its activities. It was consciousness of this meaning that caused the new religious outlook and its embodiment in the daily round to be first named 'the way'.

Salvation, then, in its positive aspect, is not a matter of creed or doctrine. It is not something that needs for its attainment some particular act, whether repetition of a formula or participation in a sacrament. It may, indeed, be thought of as atonement, but not in the sense of a price paid in penance or in asceticism or good works, not in that of redemption by vicarious sacrifice. In its rightful meaning it is *at-one-ment*, a coming into unison of feeling and of purpose. Such coming into unison with the supreme Reality—to be at one with God—is the object of all religion; whether it is, as regarded by the Buddhist, reunion with the undifferentiated whole of Being; or, as the West has rather felt, co-operation with a divine will in realisation of a divine purpose at work in the universe. To have reached this sense of unison, to be in communion with God and our fellow-men, with its release from doubts and fears, with the joy and strength that it brings, and the motive and meaning that it gives to all the activities of life, is to have found salvation.

4. THE PROBLEM OF EVIL

Is evil, then, to be dismissed as something merely transient or as illusory and unreal? In spite of all the efforts of theologians and philosophers to account for it in a way that can satisfy both the reason and the moral sense—that 'vain and interminable controversy', as Carlyle termed it—the presence of evil has puzzled men ever since they formed the conception of a divine Creator who was also the source and perfect exemplar of moral good.

The explanation that to primitive man, as still to the child, seemed to account for all kinds of wrong-doing, is simple enough. The difficulty of expressing any kind of mental experience otherwise than through imagery led to the dramatisation of conflict between impulse and conscience as a struggle between good and evil powers. Disobedience to the divine command embodied in the tribal or moral code could only be the work of a tempter suggesting rebellion.

Even at an advanced stage of religious development beliefs inherited from this primitive attitude of mind could continue to be held without question. To the Persian the antagonism of good and evil was as much a fact of experience as the alternation of light and darkness, and needed as little explanation. But though at present equally matched they need not always so remain. His moral sense assured him of the superiority of good and of the need to take his part in the struggle and help to bring about its final triumph. To the Hindu both good and evil are to be accepted as equally in the nature of temporal existence. Death is as necessary to the whole as life, and the divine power embodied in the form of Siva is to be worshipped in one of his aspects as destroyer no less than in another as creator. Hindu philosophy has seen in evil the inevitable outcome of the isolation of individual personality from the whole of Being; its cessation is to be found only in a final release from such isolation and a return into the undifferentiated whole.

To those, however, who came to see in goodness the essential character of Godhead it became increasingly difficult to reconcile the fact of evil with this conception, especially when belief in one God, creator and ruler of all things, replaced earlier ideas of independent or rival powers. The Hebrew, reshaping earlier myths into accord with his growing belief in a Supreme Being at once all-powerful and all-good, sought to account for the presence of evil by the disobedience of man, on whom it was thenceforth laid as punishment. Since this left unsolved the problem of why one into whom the Creator had breathed his own spirit should do wrong, the Hebrew thinker (like the Indian cosmographer who pictured the earth as supported by an elephant and had then to add a tortoise for the elephant to stand on) pushed the responsibility for evil a step further back. He attributed it to a superhuman being who had himself fallen through pride, and then through envy brought about the fall of man. It did not seem necessary to look beyond the assumption that this tempter is permitted for a time, as Prince of this world, to continue to expose man to temptation and to the evils that are the penalty of his fall. Wisdom lay in right conduct rather than in philosophic enquiry; what was certain was that evil was punishment for wrong-doing and good the reward of righteousness. This was the accepted Hebrew doctrine, of prophet as well as priest; though here and there a thinker, like the author of the book of Job, seeing clearly that this doctrine does not fit all the facts, held it to be truer that evil is a means of trial by which goodness can be perfected.

Others, more given to metaphysical speculation than was the Hebrew mind, have thought that the contradiction could be resolved by denying its reality. Oriental philosophy has tended to look upon evil as belonging to the world of appearance, an unreal world in which we are involved so long as we are living our transitory human lives detached from the unchanging spiritual reality in which our distinctions of good and evil have no place. To deny the reality of evil is to deny the reality of experience, and therefore of good also as we know it, and to make the only real good a cessation of all consciousness. This, if pushed to its logical conclusion, may seem to be the ideal good; but in that form it is the negation of religion. In practice even the Buddhist accepts the validity of experience, and for release from evil turns to means similar to those by which other religions also seek it. The Scholastic theologians also tried to avoid attribution to God of being the source of evil by denying its positive existence. It is only, so they argued, a defect, the absence of the good which is the positive existence brought about by God's fiat. Like so much of medieval philosophy, this is a question of words rather than of underlying realities. Few even of philosophers would now deny that evil is just as real a part of experience as good. Thought, therefore, has turned rather to the practical aspect of the problem: what, for us, is the meaning of evil, and how is it to be faced?

In its theological form the problem was rendered insoluble by the terms in which it was posed. If we start from the premise that the world was created by a Deity in whom absolute power is combined with absolute foreknowledge and absolute goodness, the contradictions involved by the presence of evil are intellectually irreconcilable. Moreover, this conception is itself irreconcilable with the facts of experience, from which a deity might rather be inferred who had more resemblance (as has been said) to 'a kind of experimental psychologist or the governor of a vast Borstal Institution'. But the problem is no longer the same if we look at it from the point of view of evolution, in which perfection is not to be looked for in the origin of the universe, but in an ultimate potentiality towards which it moves. If consciousness and spiritual values are thought of not as present from the first but as emergent in the process, then, while we are no nearer comprehending *why* this should be the nature of existence, there is no longer an initial contradiction between divine power and divine goodness, and we are free to consider the problem only in its practical aspect. For evil is then not something that has crept into a perfect world, but an essential condition of a world that, through seeking to overcome it, can grow nearer to perfection.

If we take this method of approach, the question that matters is what is to be our reaction to it: for if the world is still in the making, all the greater responsibility rests upon us to do our part. There is here a marked difference between the Oriental and Western outlook. To the Eastern mind it has usually seemed of most importance to escape from evil by freeing oneself from all experience of which it is a part. In the West, emphasis has rather been laid upon resistance to evil and mastery to be eventually obtained over it. While Oriental philosophy looks forward to a final merging of the particular in the universal, the conscious in the unconscious, Western thought dwells rather on an unfolding of higher from lower stages of development, the spiritual from the animal nature, the fully conscious from a lower consciousness.

It is clear that evil in its various forms is inherent in the very nature of evolution as we know it, being at once a condition of the growth of good and, in our consciousness of evil, the outcome of that growth. The very fact of development and the possibility of better adaptation imply initial imperfection and require a condition of instability. But instability which allows of development allows also of degeneracy, decay, and death. Nor is this true of biological evolution only; it holds good also in the realm of mind and spirit. Lesser forms of good become by comparison bad when greater good has been attained. Much in nature, therefore, can only seem to us cruel and wasteful; and much in ourselves, viewed from the standpoint of what we feel to be finer purposes and ideals, may be regarded as blind urges that often drag us from our chosen path. Hence the disharmony between the moral and the natural order, between 'flesh' and 'spirit', that has been so deeply felt by thinker and saint. Modes and means of life that at one stage of development have made higher good possible may become hindrances when life has outgrown them and cannot carry them with it in its advance. Primitive impulses, once the necessary agents of self-maintenance and self-expression, may now seem tempters that lead us to do what we would not. It is these that have become the devils of our imagination, powers of life now bent, so it seems, on misleading life and dragging it down; agents of evil all the darker because they are not, like hindrances from without, straightforward and acknowledged foes, but traitors within.

There are times when the sense of our weakness fills us with despair. The immense mass of pain and suffering that seem to be the inevitable lot of living things, the burden of human folly and wickedness, which go on, or break out again, as though the great teachers had never lived and we had learnt nothing from experience, weigh on us so heavily as to make life seem an evil dream from which we long to awake. With the old poet we feel, if only we had the power

To grasp this sorry scheme of things entire,
Would we not shatter it to bits—and then
Remould it nearer to the heart's desire!

But this is the very possibility that evolution offers us, as a choice either to shatter or remould. With our growing knowledge of the forms of energy at our command we can only too easily destroy our civilisation and ourselves. There are times when we seem, with our blind passions and stupidities, only too certain to do so. But if we can gain the wisdom and the will, we have the power to shape our surroundings and ourselves in accordance with whatever purpose we hold steadily before us. Whereas in the earlier stages of evolution it was the physical environment that was the shaping and selecting agent, now it is man's own mind and purpose that adapt his environment to his needs, and thus make him responsible for the direction of his own advance.

Life of any kind can only be maintained and extended by effort. By their reactions to the spur of need and the challenge of their surroundings living things have won all their powers of body and mind and spirit. As we ascend higher in the scale of life, the challenge of evil becomes more insistent; the need to master it is all the greater if we are not to slip back into the brute, and into worse than the brute since we now know better. The distribution of plant and animal on the earth's surface we can alter to suit our needs. So also can we alter the conditions of human life. If we are sufficiently in earnest about it we can put an end to war and, in great part at least, to disease and ignorance and the misery that comes from injustice and greed. It is not merely in a poet's dream that the future of the world and the shaping of human life are in our own hands, to ruin or to remould. It rests with us, with our insight, our ideals, our efforts.

Nevertheless we cannot alter things by any easy optimism. We do not annihilate evil by denying it exists, or make it less evil by asserting that if it is a means to eventual good, good and evil are one and the same thing, and so 'whatever is, is right'. We can alter what is bad only by taking it, on every level, as a warning and a call to action. *Why* the world is thus constituted and life as we know it thus conditioned is one of the ultimate questions that lie beyond the reach of human knowledge. We can imagine—as those oppressed by the weight of present evil have always loved to imagine—some other kind of world in which good would not be shadowed by evil, and in which there would be no pain or weakness, no failure—but also no advance. Of such a world we have no experience. Evolution, with its method of trial and error and its advance from lower to higher as the result of struggle, is the essential condition of the world in which we find ourselves, our training-ground and place of growth. If we so use it we may trust that from life lived to the full at this level a finer life will yet emerge.

Faced, then, with the problem of evil, we need neither adopt a defeatist attitude of acquiescence nor look to the promise of salvation by a sacrifice offered for us, an act of grace that we have only to accept by faith in its efficacy. Our religion must be one of courage in resistance to evil and of faith that it can be overcome in the strength of that greater than ourselves that makes for good. Two things above all are needed in the struggle. The one is knowledge, to trace effect and cause and show how harm is to be prevented or healed. Science has already brought us the power to do this, and will bring far more when it has explored the realm of mind as fully as the physical world. But this is not enough. Science can control and direct action towards an end; but it does not tell us what end to seek, for science knows nothing of ultimate values. For that search, to give motive and inspiration, we need religion too, the quest of the divine that is the goal of spiritual evolution. The way of spiritual advance—the way of salvation—lies not in seeking a means of escape, but in making of evil a means of good by mastery of it through knowledge used in the service of love.

CHAPTER NINE

IMMORTALITY

1. BELIEF IN SURVIVAL AFTER DEATH

In most religions a fundamental doctrine, making the strongest of appeals to the hopes and fears of believers, has been assurance of an immortality of happiness or punishment. At the present time, for various reasons to be touched on later, the force of this appeal has been greatly weakened. But even if the prevalent tendency is to treat continued existence after death as an unverified hypothesis and to transfer attention from the possibility of an after life to the needs of this one, as of more immediate importance, the question of immortality remains for religion one of deep concern.

Religion, it was said above, had one of its roots in fear. Among the fears by which it has been so largely sustained and moulded, none are stronger than those to which the fact of death has given rise. Besides natural shrinking from the physical weakness and pain that are its usual forerunners, and from cessation of all the familiar activities of life, two further grounds for fear have also been associated with death: the one, fear of continued activity and possible malignant influence of the dead upon the living; the other, fear of what may happen to the individual after the cessation of the life with which he is familiar. The former seems to have been the chief concern of primitive man in regard to death; with the growth of civilisation the second came more and more to occupy men's thoughts and to affect the forms their religions have taken.

From traces of burial customs widely practised by primitive man it seems evident that belief in some kind of survival after death was normal, if not universal. A dead body was something to put out of the way where it could neither harm nor be harmed. But a common custom of burying with the dead some of the things they had most needed in life shows that life was not thought to be completely extinguished. Their return in dreams or in waking visions could be taken as proof of their continued existence, and there was no need to question a belief strengthened alike by affection and fear. Such questioning belongs to a later stage of mental development; and even then, though a negative conclusion may be accepted as rational, it is hardly possible for anyone to *feel* that the life of which he is conscious in himself can ever come to a complete end.

But if the dead continued to exist and might still take part in the affairs of the living, here was ample ground for fears. Sir James Frazer has collected[1] many instances of such fears from accounts given by anthropologists and missionaries of the ideas and customs of peoples still to be found in various parts of the world in a primitive stage of development. These accounts make it plain that while to some tribes spirits of the dead are objects either of indifference or of affection, by most they are regarded with fear, and it is a constant preoccupation of the living to keep them from doing harm. This attitude, which is in accord with much in the old customs and traditions of civilised nations as well as with much that has been laid bare by archaeology, is in no way surprising. Anything that comes in an intangible form is uncanny; and it was inevitable that most of such spirits should be regarded as unfriendly. Precautions had therefore to be taken to lessen their power for harm. The limbs of the corpse were bound or a stake was driven through it to prevent it from moving or it was kept down by piling stones upon the grave—for there was much confusion of the disembodied spirit and the body to which it was thought to be still attached.

Another feeling, however, seems to be shown in the neolithic custom of burying the dead beneath the dwellings of the living, as still being fellow-inmates and members of the community. Such spirits must be kept in a friendly temper lest they should be offended by neglect and so become hostile. Death seemed to resemble sleep in being a temporary departure—though for a longer time—of the life-spirit that gave to the body its power of living movement. Just as in life there was need for constant care, through taboo and magical

[1] In *The Fear of the Dead in Primitive Religion* (MacMillan, 1937).

ritual, to prevent the complete withdrawal of this spirit, so equal care might ensue that the spirit of the dead should remain active for help. Hence arose practices of various kinds for maintaining the vitality and the goodwill of those whose help and protection was most to be desired. From the earliest times food and other necessaries of life, together with some of the most treasured personal possessions, were buried with the dead to help in supporting their continued existence and preserving their goodwill.

Possibly this was done in the first instance to facilitate the passage of the spirit to the other world in the hope that thus it would not remain to plague the living. Similarly the earliest purpose to be served by preservation of the corpse and by offerings subsequently made to maintain its vitality may have been to ensure to the returning spirit a body in which it would be content to remain, as in life, and so would not wander at large. But even if this may have been the original purpose, the practice came in time to have another meaning. Sir James Frazer gives instances of customs still surviving among tribes in India and elsewhere which are evidence of a desire to make the return of the spirit of the dead easier, either that they may be reincarnated in their descendants or may play a helpful part in their activities.

Various practices seem to have had this end in view. Since blood and the red hue that it gives are inseparably associated with life, the pouring of blood upon the grave or burial in red earth that would preserve some semblance of life was practised as means of ensuring to the dead power to revisit the living world and take part in its activities. This power would be still more certainly ensured if the grave could be secured by some massive superstructure against possibility of disturbance; better still if the body could be preserved by some process such as mummification and if something of the personality could be retained in an enduring likeness, as in the portrait-statues placed in or near Egyptian tombs.

Especially in the case of those, parents and leaders, kings and priests, on whom the welfare of the household or tribe or nation had depended during their lifetime, was continued maintenance of their vigour and power to help desirable. It is no wonder, therefore, that ancestor-worship has held a great part in the religion of various races of mankind, as it still does in China and Japan, as well as among some of the more primitive tribes that still remain; or that there has been so strong a tendency to look upon those who stood out above others, whether by their personality or by the power that they wielded, as differing from their fellow-men in being in some degree divine.

But while some kind of continued existence after death was thus a common matter of belief there were different ways of thought as to the nature of this after-life. Belief in survival does not necessarily imply belief in immortality, or in an existence fuller than that of the present life. From the practice of burial beneath the ground arose, naturally enough, the idea of a dwelling-place of the dead in a gloomy underworld, such as that described by Homer or the Hebrew *Sheol*, from which they might occasionally revisit the upper earth. In such an underworld the spirits of the dead could only be thought to have a poor ghostly kind of existence. From it they could be summoned by necromantic arts, but of themselves could only return in hours of darkness, to haunt the living as spectres, unless by due offerings some more vital kind of existence could be given them.

Not all peoples, however, buried their dead. Some disposed of corpses by burning them: possibly, it has been suggested,[1] forced to do so in times of invasion or migration when burial would have left the corpse exposed to the malice of enemies and beyond the reach of customary rites, whereas ashes would be safer from ill-treatment or could be carried to a new home. It is tempting to think that this practice may have given rise to a different idea as to the dwelling-place of the dead. The destruction of the body by flames that leap upwards may have suggested that the spirit also, instead of passing down into a gloomy underworld, could rise into an upper world of light where the sky-deities were thought to dwell. On the other hand it seems certain that from an early stage of civilisation this belief was not incompatible with the practice of burial. From the abundance of material preserved in Egypt we have fuller evidence there than elsewhere of the development of ideas concerning existence after death. This was evidently the chief preoccupation of Egyptian religion. It is possible to trace two main lines along which Egyptian belief developed before they eventually coalesced. The one was associated with the official worship of the sun-god, Ra, who was thought to reign in an upper sky-world of light and happiness, just as his representative, the Pharaoh, reigned on earth. To this sky-world the Pharaoh and his

[1] E.g. by Gilbert Murray in *The Rise of the Greek Epic*.

court would ascend after death, their continued existence, on which also the continued welfare of the State was held to depend, being ensured by the preservation of their bodies in massive tombs and the perpetual performance of the necessary rites by priesthoods established for this purpose. This was, naturally, the court religion, immortality being the privilege of rank and needing wealth to ensure it.

The other line of belief belonged rather to the religion of the peasantry. This, as in all agricultural communities, was profoundly affected by the recurrent miracle of germination. The seed, laid in the ground as a dead body is laid in the grave, in due time comes to life with youth renewed and fertility increased; might not what was laid in the earth as a corpse also rise again to a renewed and enhanced existence? This hope found its chief nourishment and assurance in the rites by which the death and resurrection of Osiris, the vegetation spirit, were presented, and by which the annual miracle was to be furthered. To all who joined in the cult of Osiris—and, whatever the official worship, these included the great majority of the Egyptian people—immortality depended on the due performance of this ritual, and was to be ensured by religious observance instead of being the privilege of rank and wealth. This was the belief that ultimately prevailed. Of the records of Egyptian religion that have been preserved the greater part is occupied with observances to win divine favour and spells to avert dangers both before and after death. But we can see also the growth of a conviction that in the life to come after death the well-being of the individual would depend not merely upon the performance of observances but most of all on a general conduct of life of which the gods approved. Thus the hope of future happiness, which earlier had been limited to those who had played the most prominent part in the community, came in time to include even the humbler, provided that their actions in the life on earth had merited this approval. As corollary to this hope grew also a belief in the inevitable punishment that would be the doom of those who in this life had forfeited the favour of the gods by neglect of religious observance and by any kind of wrong-doing. The development that can thus be traced in Egyptian religion serves well to show a trend that is characteristic of religious evolution in general.

2. HEAVEN AND HELL

While some kind of continued existence after death has been commonly taken as certain both among primitive peoples and in the historical religions, this future life has been regarded with very different feelings. To those, for instance, who thought of the spirits of the dead as leading a shadowy existence, deprived of vigour and vitality, in some dim underworld allowing only faint resemblance to life on earth, such a prospect held little to desire. It was something to be endured, like the disabilities of age, and made as tolerable as possible by taking into the spirit-world such possessions as could be placed in the grave; but even so it could only be viewed with shrinking and dread. The picture given in the 11th book of the Odyssey of the crowd of unsubstantial ghosts, jostling one another in their eagerness to taste the blood that for a few moments would bring back some feeling of corporeal reality and enable them to express their longing for earthly life and its lost joys, presents a state of being that no one could contemplate with pleasure. No wonder that Achilles could declare it was better to be the meanest churl on earth than a king among the dead.

Even when men began to imagine the kind of existence that would be theirs after death as something more than a mere shadow of life on earth, it was more often associated with a feeling of fear than of hope. For one thing, whatever might await them was strange and uncertain; and there are few to whom the unknown does not inspire dread. Better even familiar ills than something of which we have no certain knowledge. And if future happiness or unhappiness depends on the balance of right and wrong-doing here, who could be sure that the scale would turn in his favour? The growth of belief that death will bring to each a judgment passed upon his life on earth has in all ages intensified the dread of a future existence. For although it was a main function of religion to give assurance to the believer, and to show how salvation was to be obtained, this might at any time be forfeited by neglect or transgression of its injunctions.

There has always been a tendency on the part of official guardians and exponents of religion to exploit these fears and to paint the punishments awaiting wrong-doers and unbelievers in the most lurid colours. Of the terrors thus exploited, with the hypocrisies and cruelties to which they gave rise, the records of even the humanest of religions furnish abundant evidence. Christianity is not yet wholly free from the medieval doctrines of a Hell of unending torment, based, paradoxical as it seems, on words[1] recorded as spoken by one who taught that God is the loving Father of mankind. An allusion to constantly burnish rubbish heaps, in illustration of the fitting end for what is worthless, was taken as a literal statement of eternal torment awaiting all who were not 'saved', and thus became a belief that for centuries haunted the thought and darkened the lives of even the best of Christians. It was in mitigation of such terrors that the Catholic Church elaborated the doctrine of Purgatory, with the possibility of expiation through suffering. This conception, even if repudiated as a dogma, is more in accord with the spirit of Christianity than belief in a doom of unending punishment which most Christians find impossible to reconcile with belief in a God of justice and still more in a God of love.

There has also been at all stages of religious evolution a counter-tendency to find in anticipation of survival after death a source of hope. All living things, at least when in normal health and vigour, are actuated by an inherent urge to maintain and extend their life. When the level of self-consciousness has been reached, this innate urge becomes, for most, a conscious desire for unending existence, a desire which is reinforced by certain states of common experience. There can be few who do not wish that the moments of happiness which come to them, however rarely, should be more lasting, or who would not welcome an existence that promised a continuance of such moments if assured that they would not be outweighed by others of painful experience. This assurance religion holds out. It has also brought to many the hope of compensation for suffering here, which so often seems to be unjust, as being either wholly undeserved or at least excessive. The stronger the faith that human life is not the plaything of indifferent or malicious spirits and that the Power that has made men what they are cannot be less just or loving than themselves, the stronger becomes the conviction that the present life with so much

[1] '. . . to be cast into hell where their worm dieth not and their fire is not quenched' (Mark IX. 40). The word translated 'hell' is in the Greek *Gehenna*—the valley of Hinnom outside Jerusalem, where refuse from the city was burnt and, it is said, corpses of outcasts were left unburied.

inevitable suffering cannot be the whole of the divine purpose; and the desire for a further life in which wrongs will be righted, and the contradiction between divine power and divine love will no longer exist when all is made plain.

Still more if death puts an end to life in its prime or in youth, cutting off its activities before they can reach fulfilment, is there, in the resulting sense of frustration, a further factor making for desire of a future life to redress the failures of the present. Common to thinker and saint, craftsman and lover is the longing for a perfection that always eludes us here, the vision of something that lies beyond our present reach, an absolute truth and beauty and love which experience here can only foreshadow. The will-to-live is inherent in all life. When it has evolved consciousness as an instrument of self-preservation it becomes a will to continually fuller life, which can hope to find fulfilment only if death is not to bring its final frustration. Thus belief in a future life seems to be necessary for a full satisfaction of our moral sense, as well as of the kindred aesthetic sense, with its demand for harmony and completeness: and in this very necessity it finds confirmation of its hope.

It is, of course, easy to label this as 'wishful thinking' and to regard it as thereby disproved. Wishful in one sense it is, like most of our thinking, which has been evolved in the service of instinctive desires and is based on intuitions that we accept as self-evident. While it is the function of the critical judgment to question these intuitions and desires and to test conclusions based upon them, it is no less the function of religion to ensure that this shall be no merely negative process leading to a scepticism that inhibits action. It is for religion to bring its faith and devotion to reinforce effort and enlarge experience. To it man turns to find assurance for his instinctive sense of continuing life. Some few of the great religions, like the teaching of Confucius and the Mosaic Law, are so fully occupied with the conduct of the present life that they have little thought to spare for its continuance after death. In others this has been a main object of concern. Some, as already said, have exploited the fears with which they have surrounded it in order to secure a fuller obedience to their requirements; and in so doing they have made religion of this kind one of the burdens and curses of humanity.

Yet even these have done so in order to heighten by contrast the hopes held out to the obedient. One might well take as touchstone of the spiritual quality of a religion how far it has made its main appeal not to fear but to feelings associated with hope. In some, as in ancient Egypt, the chief preoccupation would seem to have been with overcoming fear by the use of all kinds of magic and ceremonial observance. It was no small advance when the hope of future happiness was no longer the privilege of power and wealth, but open to all who embraced the means of salvation offered to them. Here lay the strength of the appeal of the 'mystery' religions, in which salvation was to be attained through the efficacy of a sacramental act whereby the death and renewal of life of a divine figure were symbolised, and a like renewal of life after death and attainment of an immortality of happiness was promised to those who shared in the mysteries.

It was assurance of continued existence, with the promise of eternal happiness through participation in the life of the risen Saviour, that was the central theme in the 'good news' proclaimed by the Apostles after the death of their Master—the conclusive proof which they gave of the truth of their message being his reappearance among them in living form. A like bodily resurrection for all his followers would take place, they declared, at the second coming of one in whom they now recognised the Messiah of Hebrew prophecy. This second coming the first generation of Christians regarded as imminent, to bring judgment on the nations and to establish on earth a kingdom into which all would enter who believed in the redeeming power of the Christ and who followed the way that he had shown. On the passing of that generation with the hope unrealised, another interpretation was put on the Apostles' message. The earthly kingdom had already been established in the growing company of Christian believers. The second coming had either already taken place in an outpouring of the Holy Spirit, or else (as most came to believe) was to take place at some future day of judgment. Individual souls would then awake from the sleep of death, and sincere believers would thenceforward live a life of eternal happiness in some heavenly sphere, freed from all earthly troubles and the vicissitudes of temporal things. Throughout eighteen centuries it has remained the hope of those holding the Christian faith that an immortality of spiritual existence awaits them after the death of the body has ended their earthly life.

To primitive man, as we have seen, an after-life seemed only, at best, a faint imitation of that of substantial beings. Without bodily organs and senses it could be but a poor and shadowy being that survived, though one that could to some extent still take part in mundane affairs. But now what had seemed to be a loss came to be seen as a gain. In being parted from the body the spirit could be regarded as freed from its constraints rather than deprived of its powers. Life beyond the grave came to be looked on as being the fulfilment of what had necessarily here been only a partial experience, with enrichment of its joys and with compensation for its sufferings.

So far, indeed, was it held to transcend earthly existence that it has not infrequently tended to make this seem, in comparison, utterly worthless. In all ages prophets and saints have been ready to abandon family ties and to sacrifice all other interests in order to devote their whole lives to what they felt to be the service of God. But there is an 'other-worldliness' which is rather a means of escape from the present, refusing to face the demands of life and shrinking from its responsibilities; or prompting extremes of asceticism in the hope of ultimate reward and in gratification of spiritual pride. The anchorite and pillar-saint of the early centuries of the Christian era and the fakir of today are only extreme instances of a tendency fostered by any religion that points away from the present to the future.

There have always been some to whom assurance of future happiness would not be complete if it had not its dark side. To them a justice that is to bring compensation for injustice here must include punishment for wrong-doing and compensatory suffering to make up for ill-gotten gains in a life lived only for pleasure and self-seeking. To some even of the saints, as well as to ordinary human nature, the contemplation of such a reversal of fortune has seemed to be a necessary background for the happiness of the saved. When imagination has tried to picture future existence there has been little difficulty in portraying tortures, in which human ingenuity has always been fertile. The cruelty that is so strong an element in human natures has thereby been gratified. To the pleasure that most derive from the merited misfortunes of others has been added the thrill felt by one who looks with horror over the extreme verge of danger, but is conscious that for him the plunge is not inevitable. It is not surprising, therefore, that Dante's Inferno and Milton's Hell are more vividly presented to the reader's imagination than their visions of Paradise. Descriptions of

Heaven, like all the utopias in which a better state of existence has been pictured, fail to carry conviction. Whereas cruelty changes but little, an ideal of happiness—whether it be the Elysian Fields of classical mythology, the Valhalla of the northern sagas, Mohammed's Paradise of the sensual satisfactions valued by denizens of the desert, or a Christian Heaven, depicted at one time as a perpetual church service, at another as a lecture-room for theological exposition—has little meaning or attraction for another age. Even if the conditions they show could ensure happiness (and how is this possible for all varieties of human nature?), yet none of them can escape from the ultimate fate of monotony and boredom.

All such attempts have for most of us today only a literary or historical interest. Even to those who regard some kind of personal immortality as beyond question, doctrines of Heaven and Hell shaped by the hopes and fears of past ages have little meaning, and make little appeal to a moral sense that rejects bribes and threats alike. We recognise how often promise of compensation in another world has been employed as a drug to deaden consciousness of injustice and economic servitude in this one, and refuse to accept promissory notes as payment for present wrong. Few, moreover, can now fit into any conception of divine justice a sentence of endless punishment for wrongdoings and shortcomings that are the inevitable outcome of ignorance and of weakness inherent in human nature. Nor can most of us feel interest in a state of being in which there would be no need for further effort. Those who look forward to continued existence, therefore, tend rather, if they try to picture it to themselves in accordance with their sense of values, to think of it as a continued spiritual development, however much the conditions under which it is to continue may differ from those now imposed by bodily life. Some accept the Oriental doctrine of successive earthly lives as the most rational way in which further development can be conceived as taking place. Others think of it as continuing no longer on earth but in some other dimension of being, or in a succession of such modes of experience, in which each one, however poor the use to which he may have been able to put his earthly life, can find fresh possibilities of spiritual growth and thereby make contribution to the spiritual evolution of the whole.

3. SCIENCE AND A FUTURE LIFE

Few changes in the modern attitude towards religion are more striking than the small part which belief in a future life of happiness or punishment now holds either as source of interest or motive of conduct. This is due principally to the influence of science and the scientific attitude of mind, which is now the subconscious mould for all our working beliefs. Science, with its gaze fixed upon matters of sense-perception subject to exact measurement and experimental treatment, tends to ignore or deny the existence of anything beyond its methods of proof. It has seemed to give warrant for a purely materialist philosophy; and to the materialist life is a product of physical conditions and necessarily ceases when these conditions are radically changed. To him, therefore, a continuation of life after death is not possible and immortality is merely a groundless hope. For this position based on the physical sciences further support is adduced from psychology. Mental processes, it is argued, are the product of bodily needs and subserve the struggle for existence. As part of the struggle, the mind is prone to drug itself with dream-fantasies, waking as well as sleeping, in satisfaction of its desires, and to create defence mechanisms as protection against unpleasant realities. The heaven of religion is thus to be regarded as a wish-fulfilment giving assurance of the complete and continuing happiness that we never find in life as it is: as the outcome, that is, of a biological need to comfort ourselves with the hope of immortality in order to prevent the paralysis of activity that might otherwise result from despair and fear of death.

If this conclusion is accepted as final, the response will vary with the spiritual development of the individual. To some it will be: 'Let us eat and drink, for tomorrow we die,' an attitude which at least holds more promise of human fellowship and happiness than that of the sour-faced Puritan or self-centred ascetic. To the more generous nature it is: 'I expect to pass through this world but once. Any good, therefore, that I can do or any kindness that I can show to any fellow-creature, let me do it now'; in which there is a spirit of religion all the finer if it has no hope of eventual reward. It is possible, indeed, to look forward to extinction not merely with resignation but with relief; the prospect of a cessation of all consciousness at death may be no less welcome than sleep at the end of a tiring day. Others, however, even if they would themselves regard the end of personal existence as a release to be desired, cannot accept as conclusive a view which minimises the spiritual element in life and treats potentialities that lie, for the present at any rate, outside the range of science as being for this reason mere illusions. The negation of survival is no less dogmatic than its assertion. They are content, therefore, while seeing in the present life a sufficient field for our activities and aims, to accept in a spirit of trust whatever is to follow, whether the dreamless sleep of entire cessation of consciousness or some further stage of living effort in conditions as yet beyond our knowledge.

In challenge to the negative attitude of science, experimental proofs of survival after death have been offered in the experience of persons susceptible to abnormal happenings which they attribute to spiritual agency. Both by the mediums themselves and by many who witness the phenomena associated with them it is believed that in this way communications are received from those who have already entered upon another stage of life. The evidence, however, for such communications is in dispute. The phenomena, even when accepted as genuine, are capable of another interpretation; and orthodox science, therefore, remains for the most part adverse to the claim. It admits the presence, in certain individuals, of psychic powers that are as yet abnormal but not therefore to be dismissed as fictitious or merely fraudulent; and it inclines to think that any assumed transmission through a medium of messages from the dead is to be regarded as an unconscious use of powers such as telepathy and thought-transference. The somewhat unwilling recognition hitherto accorded to enquiry into the subject, as to a poor relation suspected of shady practices, must sooner or later give place to a serious investigation of the spiritualist claims, with a view either to establishing on a scientific basis the fact of survival and the possibility of communication, or to showing beyond a doubt how the phenomena on which the assumption rests are to be accounted for. Till this is done the verdict can only be 'not proven'.

The influence of science, then, has usually encouraged disbelief in survival after death, or at least a suspension of judgment on the matter, which in practice amounts to much the same thing by making it of little practical importance. There is, however, one line of scientific thought which has had a more positive influence. In establishing the principle of organic evolution, Darwin opened up a still wider field of study. The principle is one that can be extended in both directions: on the one side to inorganic matter (if, indeed, even this should not be regarded as showing some degree of organisation), and on the other to the mental and spiritual powers that have emerged in the course of organic evolution. This emergence gives at least a presumption that besides the bodily life there is something more for which a further evolution is possible. And since evolution is a time-process, there is here an intelligible meaning in an immortality of endless life.

The promise of immortality has usually been understood as an assurance that, in spite of the death of the body, life goes on 'for ever and ever, world without end'. Both in Eastern and Western religions life on earth is regarded as a period of probation, a single stage in a spiritual development in which, through association with a particular body, an individual soul becomes a centre of separate life. To the Buddhist this is not endless. He holds that, after the lessons of experience have been fully learnt in a succession of earthly lives, the final goal to be attained is release from the limitations of individuality by reabsorption in the world-soul. The Christian, on the other hand, looks forward to a personal immortality which implies continued differentiation from others and continued individual experience. Such a continued existence, if we attempt to picture it, is necessarily subject to conditions of time and change; for though it may be possible in thought to treat these as non-essential conditions of reality, any state of being that we can imagine must retain some fundamental resemblance to the world of experience.

Thus the thought of individual existence continued after death tends to take the form of a further evolution towards a spiritual perfection to which, though not fully attainable in any conditions into which time enters, we can hope more and more nearly to approximate. If our present life is a stage in this evolution—a stage at best brief, even if not prematurely cut short, and for most, through adverse circumstances, unable to be used to the full—whatever is to come after death would then be a further stage in which, we may hope, further powers could be developed; a continuation of life as known to us, but rising, through wisdom brought by suffering and effort, to higher levels of experience.

Such a conception of immortality is in accord with the modern tendency of science and philosophy to regard all being as process, and to see its essence in an urge towards greater fulness rather than in any static condition. To the potentialities inherent in such a process arbitrary limits cannot be set. In the course of evolution hitherto there has been a successive emergence of higher kinds of existence, organic from the so-called inorganic, mental and spiritual from material. How, then, can it be laid down for certain that the possibilities of evolution are exhausted or that there cannot be further levels of existence under conditions beyond knowledge at our present level? Though such knowledge is not yet possible, faith cannot be debarred from its assurance of further advance, whether for life as a whole or for the individual consciousness. This conviction philosophy as well as religion has upheld as an intuition of reality. When Spinoza affirmed 'we know and feel that we are immortal' he was speaking not merely as an inspired seer, but as an exponent of rational thought. It was the affirmation of one fully assured that the universe is rational and that, as part of its rationality, it is also not indifferent to moral issues. If our human values are in accord with the nature of things, there is here an assurance of immortality: for a universe in which personality is evolved only to perish is not one in which the highest values are achieved.

4. 'LIFE ETERNAL'

But, it may be said, while a prospect of continued spiritual evolution through further modes of experience is more in accord with the trend of modern thought than the old ideas of Heaven and Hell, there is one respect in which it fails to satisfy either thought or feeling. To philosophy, as to religion, immortality has meant something more than life without end in endless time. There is an intellectual as well as an emotional craving for perfection which to many has seemed a sufficient guarantee that perfection is not unattainable. But time implies change—the only means by which it can be apprehended—and change implies imperfection, since any change from perfection must be for the worse. Philosophy has, therefore, tended to regard time as unreal, or as a condition attached to a passing phase of existence from which it seeks to free itself. For this reason philosophers have been chiefly concerned with absolutes and abstractions, as being independent of any time-element and freed from the contingency of actual experience. Science also, in its search for an absolute truth, disregards time whenever possible. Those sciences are regarded as the 'purest' which approximate most nearly to mathematics and logic—the two which in their structure and methods (as distinct from any subject-matter with which they may deal) are wholly abstract and timeless. An unending time-process of continued evolution which, though ever drawing nearer to perfection, could never fully reach it, does not satisfy the intellectual and aesthetic demand for the attainment, in actual experience, of what can be conceived as an object of thought and feeling. If this demand is to be justified, the problem must find its final solution, the drama must reach its fully satisfying end, or perfection will not be attained.

Since perfection is completeness—a state of being to which nothing could be added unless there is first a diminishing of its perfection—fulfilment of this demand is compatible with cessation of consciousness at the moment of its attainment, and this to some minds has seemed a truer interpretation of perfection than any eternity of consciousness apart from change. To austerer Buddhists such an end of conscious endeavour is the goal to which they look forward as the crowning completion of experience, a merging of the individual in the universal, of the personal in an impersonal; and it is only by the cessation of personal consciousness that the ideal of perfection is attained. Mystics of other religions also find this ideal in the final merging of the human in the Divine, but with a heightened consciousness in a henceforward unchanging apprehension of the Divine Reality with which they will then be in full instead of, as at present, only partial communion.

To most, however, for the full satisfaction of feeling such a state of being, with whatever degree of consciousness, is not enough unless there is also continuance of personality and communion of each with others as well as with the whole, since to them there can be no perfect state of being that does not allow of the fulfilment of human love.

It is here that imagination comes to a stand. In any conception of 'each' and 'others' and of personal relations between them, there are necessarily limiting distinctions and means of intercourse, and we are back once more in a world of space and time such as we know here. Abstractions have little to offer to human feeling. Like Nirvana, 'eternity' as a philosophic conception has in it too little of the warmth of living reality to afford spiritual sustenance or motive. Hence the lack of interest in all such speculation. Alike in religion and in philosophy, the present tendency is away from conceptions, wholly remote from experience, of absolute and unchanging perfection, to concern with life as a process advancing from a mainly material to an increasingly spiritual mode of activity. To this stage of existence belong time and change and the other conditions of life as we know it. What final stage may lie beyond the reach of imagination we cannot know; all that we can picture of a life that does not end with the dissolution of the body is, not an eternity of perfection, but a continuation of the evolutionary process, with fuller possibilities of spiritual growth.

There is, however, another possible interpretation of eternity. We are already, at least at moments, aware of a kind of life that is eternal in the sense in which we speak of eternal values—as being, that is, beyond time and chance and unaffected by changing events. In the fourth Gospel 'life eternal' is declared to be knowledge of 'the only true God' and of the Christ who had come to reveal this true God to men. The words are put by the writer into the mouth of Jesus himself; as expression, that is, of what to 'the disciple whom Jesus loved' seemed to sum up the teaching of one in whom he saw the incarnation, in human personality at its highest reach, of those supreme values which are to us divine. In this interpretation immortality is not so much escape from death or from time and change as escape from the narrow limitations of self—not by merging it (which is only a mode of enlargement) in a greater self or party or the State, but by rising above it into a life of fuller comprehension and fuller love. It is not to be thought of as life renewed and perfected only after the death of the body, but rather as life on a spiritual level that is possible in at least some degree of attainment even here and now.

Such a life of the spirit in communion with the eternal values can be entered by many doors. Even if only at intervals and for a season (this is one of the limitations imposed by mortality), it may be entered by poet and musician, by thinker and discoverer, by friend and lover, by mystic and saint; by all, in short, who know the joy of transcendence of self. Nor is it open only to the greatly gifted. There are those also in the simplest circumstances who are possessed of a serenity of wisdom and a comprehensiveness of love that mark them out as having found the secret of admission. In all these we get glimpses of a life above and beyond the limitations of self in which we are bound—life of the spirit that is the true object of man's unending quest, whether here only or in any further spheres of experience that may await us.

If the thought of future rewards or punishment has little practical influence on the actions of most today, there is in this nothing to deplore. It is part of an attitude of mind that sees in morality something more than self-interest, and that no longer attaches high value to punishment as a deterrent. And so too, if but little energy is spent in contemplation, whether coloured by hope or fear, of a future life, it is all to the good that more should be given to the solution of present problems and the bettering of relations and conditions on which the present life depends. A religion which would set present needs aside as of small value in comparison with dreams of another world is not a religion that can now win widespread allegiance or that deserves to do so.

But that is not to say that all thought of 'eternal' life has no place in religion today. For all who realise how little even the longest life on earth can accomplish and who are saddened by the setbacks and disappointments of which they are conscious in themselves and in the world about them, the faith that this is but a part of experience, to be renewed and enlarged in other kinds of life, may well be a source from which to draw strength and encouragement. And even for those who put aside this assurance as at best no more than an object of hope, there is a source of strength in the faith that, in a world of experience which is subject to time and change and to evil in all its forms, there are eternal values in which, by fuller apprehension and by responsive love, we can even here have a part. This is the essence of religion, whether or not it looks forward to an immortality, either in time or beyond time, of further life.

It is much as with the old question of divine immanence or transcendence. Truth, beauty, love, are eternal values just because they transcend changing experience and give assurance of a realm beyond the reach of death. Yet it is possible, as Blake knew—it is the experience of all mystics—to

hold infinity in the palm of your hand
and eternity in an hour.

It matters little whether we look forward to an endless sleep, or to an unending process of further growth, or to some unimaginable state of unchanging perfection. It matters much that we should have before our eyes and in our hearts an eternal order of being in which life here, whatever death may bring, can find its inspiration and direction.

CHAPTER TEN

RELIGION AND MORALITY

1. THE SOCIAL ASPECT OF MORALITY

THROUGHOUT the history of man's development as a civilised being there has been an increasingly close connection between the moral code accepted in any community and its religious beliefs. In order to strengthen observance of social custom and an ordered system of human relationships, lawgivers and moralists have commonly claimed divine sanction for the rules of conduct they have wished to enforce; and religious teachers on their side have claimed that the source of morality is to be found in the will of God, whether revealed in some divinely given law or in the promptings of conscience to the individual soul. Morality has thus come to be commonly regarded as derived from religion and dependent upon it for validity and direction. But this view can only be maintained if we overlook their separate origin and development. They may rather be compared to two rivers having different sources, but drawing nearer to each other until they flow together, though still, as at the junction of the Saone and Rhone, they may do so without fully mingling.

In all communities there is some generally accepted standard of morality which is the outcome of tradition and experience. This common standard of conduct, with its variations for different individuals or classes, is determined mainly by the way of life, circumstances, and upbringing of each, and for the most part is but little affected by the practice or disregard of any religious observance. There have been attempts in historical times—the Jewish theocracy, for instance, and Islam on a national scale, and those of Savonarola and Calvin in smaller communities—to base the whole of government and all social relationships upon religion, and thus to do away with any distinction between religion and morality. But such attempts have served to show how difficult, if not impossible, it is to maintain that identity in practical affairs. The increasing tendency of modern times has been to draw a sharp distinction between the civil and religious aspects of conduct. The one is confined to the social morality of action in relation to one's fellows, and this mostly on its negative side of avoidance of injury or disregard of their rights; the other is more concerned with the morality of personal conduct and motive. In the one aspect wrongdoing is *crime*: injury, that is, looked upon as done not only to one or more individuals but to the community as a whole in disregarding its accepted standards of social conduct. In the other it is *sin*: conduct looked upon as disregard of a divine command made known either through the voice of conscience or in a moral code inspired by religion—as a wrong that is not only against our fellows but against our own better knowledge and that which we recognise as divine. There may thus be at times not only little agreement but even actual opposition between the two ways of regarding conduct. What is enjoined by religion may be to the civil law a crime for which an Antigone must be immured in a living tomb and martyrs thrown into the arena or sent to a concentration camp. And so, too, what is enjoined by the civil law may to religion be a sin. In all ages there have been those who for conscience' sake have refused to obey the law of the State and have chosen rather to suffer its worst penalties. If morality and religion, so far from being inseparable, can thus at times be in direct antagonism, the connection which has been claimed, and which by many is instinctively felt to exist between them, must be sought in the lines along which they have each evolved.

Morality at its lowest level is customary observance of laws and injunctions imposed by the community on the individual. There can be no sort of common life, whether in a family, a tribe, a group associated for some special purpose, or in larger communities in which there is any kind of intercourse and co-operation without some common understanding, accepted by the various members, in accordance with which they are to regulate their conduct instead of merely trying to satisfy their own needs regardless of those of others. In this common understanding, either accepted as part of the instinctive and traditional ordering of life or imposed by authority on those who do not so accept it, all further development of morality has its roots.

The essence of morality is expressed in the word 'ought'. The moral man is one who does what he ought to do. In its social aspect, morality is what is recognised as due from the individual to the community as a whole and to its various members. Thus in the simplest form of community, the family, it has everywhere been recognised as the duty of children to be obedient and helpful to their parents, from whom they receive care, protection, and teaching. The 'ought' is taken for granted as a natural obligation on both sides, rooted in experience that goes back to a pre-human stage of evolution and includes instinctive affections as well as necessary submission to the will of the stronger. So too there is an admitted 'ought' of loyalty and service on the part of its members towards the tribe and its leaders. As in the family, this is accepted as a natural right, strengthened by ties of blood-relationship, old tradition and ingrained habit. And so also with the expansion of tribe into nation and the crystallisation of tradition into law. Behind the organisation of State and society is the weight of immemorial custom and the sense of decent and orderly conduct that it has established. Traditional rules of conduct thus grew into established systems of social morality. This is morality in its objective aspect; its subjective and personal aspect is a sense of 'ought' fostered by observance of these rules, but in its fuller development passing beyond them.

Morality has thus, in the main, developed independently of religion. But while it is possible, both in the ordinary conduct of life and in philosophic theory, to keep them entirely distinct, in the evolution of each there has been a tendency to find points of contact and common interest. Religion has come to see in social as well as in personal morality aspects of life with which it is deeply concerned; and on their side exponents of morality have looked to religion to reinforce its claims. For with every extension of the community the instinctive element of family relationship, with its personal contacts and sense of interdependence, was necessarily lessened. Some other basis, therefore, had to be found for the sense of social obligation and for acceptance of the recognised code of conduct by which any social structure is maintained. One means of ensuring such conduct is compulsion by force. But force alone has never proved a permanent basis of government, and rulers have found it wise to appeal to some kind of right other than mere might. If there is to be any stable society there must be a large measure of willing acceptance of its codes. To the philosopher enlightened self-interest may be sufficient ground for this; but philosophers are few and self-interest is apt to be very far from enlightened. There has therefore been a tendency on the part of those in authority to appeal to religion as furnishing a strong and readily accepted basis for the 'ought' on which all social organisation rests.

This religious basis for social obligation was all the stronger and more readily accepted since religion also had its 'ought', in what was due to the unseen Powers whose approval or anger could affect the welfare of the community and of its several members. Though religion is ultimately a personal matter—the response of the individual to that which he feels to lie beyond the material environment and its immediate claims—yet in its primitive modes of expression it was mainly a communal concern. Since the life of the individual was so closely dependent on the activities of the group to which he belonged, it was long before he could think of himself as separate from it or as having needs of any kind distinct from those of the group as a whole. His fears and hopes and his attempts to influence the unseen Powers found their fullest expression in communal activities such as ritual song and dance, in which feeling was heightened by sympathy and mass-suggestion. These observances took rank with the strongest of customary obligations as a necessary part of normal social morality. And since the welfare of the community, to which an orderly social life is essential, was held to depend on the favour of the gods and only to be secured by obedience to their requirements, it could be claimed by those in authority that conformity to the social code was a religious obligation, with the sanction not merely of traditional usage or the will of the stronger but also of a divine command.

The sense of social obligation has undoubtedly been strengthened by this connection with religion. For the prevention of anti-social actions it is often not enough to appeal to custom or expediency. There is bound to come a time when the value of any custom is challenged, and it is not always immediately obvious or readily admitted that a particular line of conduct is harmful to the community. But if it could be presented as divinely forbidden and displeasing to the Power on whose favour the life and welfare of all depended, a motive was thus found more likely to ensure willing obedience.[1] Thus in the evolution of civilised life religion, though often indifferent or even at times opposed to the customary requirements of social morality, has also been its powerful ally. It was largely through belief in the divine origin of social institutions, and in the sanctity of laws as divine commands, that social morality was established on a basis of something more than traditional observance of taboos and social conventions or obedience to the will of the stronger.

2. THE PERSONAL ASPECT

'Ought' implies admission of a claim on the part of someone or something beyond oneself, a claim to which self-impulses, so far as they tend to resist it, must be subordinated. The claim once admitted —*felt*, that is, to be valid, though there may be no understanding of the ground for it—there is a sense of failure, a lessening of self-respect, if it is disregarded. This is conscience, the inward aspect of morality, with an 'ought' that is felt at first in response to the claims of other persons, and then to something deeper-lying which gives to a line of conduct the character of right or wrong.

The sense of 'ought' is at first no more than acceptance of an external standard through sensitivity to the feeling of others; but in the satisfaction brought by this response to the external claim, and in the sense of failure and disloyalty if the response is withheld, it comes to be felt not merely as a matter of external compulsion but as a personal need, an inner claim that carries its own authority. Thus from the social conscience of loyalty to the group has developed a personal conscience of loyalty to an inner 'ought' which it cannot disregard without disloyalty to what is best in us. In following the dictates of this claim from within we have become aware of a morality which seems to have a sanction even stronger than that arising from the needs of social life. External codes of morality are shaped by the

[1] A single instance may be taken from the Mosaic Law, in the injunction (Deuteronomy XXIII. 12–14) that excrement should at once be covered with earth. Anyone who has been in the Near East can recognise the need not only of the injunction but of some sanction carrying a strong appeal if it is to be effective. Hence the addition: 'For the Lord thy God walketh in the midst of thy camp, to deliver thee; therefore shall thy camp be holy; that He see no unclean thing in thee, and turn away from thee.'

needs and adapted to the capabilities of those who form the main body of the community. The standard required is necessarily, therefore, that of the average of its members rather than of its finer natures. For this reason the claims of personal morality are, by these finer natures, felt to be of a higher kind, not to be satisfied merely by following the accepted code. Occasions inevitably arise when the two claims are in opposition and a choice has to be made between them. In such cases the community, as something greater than any of its members, demands that the individual conscience must give way. Most of us find it easier to submit, even though in so doing we may have a sense of disloyalty to a higher claim. But in all ages there have been those who put conscience first and shaped their conduct by its inner light; and in the world's judgment these have followed the nobler course.

This growth of the moral sense has at once influenced and been informed by the development of religion. For religion, though it has its social aspect, is ultimately a personal matter. The morality enjoined by religion—the 'ought' that man feels to be due from him to the Divine Power that he worships, in distinction from what he feels to be due to his fellows—inevitably changed with the development of his conception of godhead. So long as this appeared to him to be revealed in the capricious exercise of superhuman powers, his chief concern was strict observance of the rites and taboos enjoined by those who possessed traditional knowledge of what was necessary to win divine favour and avert divine displeasure. Right and wrong were thus, at first, what was commanded or forbidden by the priest. In all ages much has been accepted as right because enjoined by religion—human sacrifice, for instance, in one age; persecution and torture in others—even though increasingly repugnant to the better feeling of the time. And with a more spiritual conception of godhead—itself brought about by the development of the moral sense—came also a new conception of what was required by the divine will. The worship that was due from man to God was no longer to be regarded as fully paid by ceremonial observance and the offering of gifts, but demanded a 'righteousness' that extended to the whole conduct of life.

A morality which found its ultimate sanction in the divine nature made demands stricter than those of the ordinary codes of social conduct, and thus tended to make conscience more sensitive. In most of the affairs of life the accepted standard of right conduct is that which is laid down by tradition and backed by authority. Where the accepted code ends, or does not satisfy the moral sense, religion has offered something more on which to lean. And with the spiritual growth that has taken place within religion itself, this something more has been less concerned with conformity to an external standard than with the springs of conduct and the inward apprehension of the spirit. So long as the whole duty of man was held to lie in obedience to a divine will transmitted and interpreted by the guardians of religion, all was as simple as in childhood, when right and wrong are determined by the approval and disapproval of elders. But just as with growing children this standard comes to be questioned, and is eventually replaced by one shaped in part by external requirements and in part by individual judgment and conscience, so also has spiritual growth brought a questioning of traditional interpretations of divine commands and reference to a personal morality of will and motive. The tendency of religious evolution has thus been to find in the individual conscience a revelation of the divine will, and thereby not only to give to the claims of conscience a validity stronger than that of any social code but, paradoxically, to set them above claims made in the name of religion itself.

If religion has owed much to the development of the moral sense, this in its turn has gained, through its association with religion, a clearer apprehension of the ultimate foundation on which its 'ought' rests. Beginning with recognition of claims made by society, it has advanced to that of claims made by the inner law of conscience—felt, that is, to be valid independently of any external claim. Of these the strongest is that made by values that we regard as ultimate; so that finally morality becomes recognition not merely of a social or personal but of a cosmic 'ought'. Viewed in this light, morality, as a writer on ethics[1] has suggested, may be regarded as 'practical necessity endowed with religious feeling'. If we must reject the claim of any particular form of religion to speak with full divine authority or to find in a divinely issued fiat the ultimate sanction of right and wrong, no more can we be satisfied with a view of morality as merely enlightened self-interest or consideration of what on the whole seems most likely to be productive of general well-being. This certainly it is;

[1] I. Levine in *Reason and Morals*.

and it is imperative to endeavour, in any given case, to discover by use of our reason what course of action can be so regarded. But when we have done this we still have not reached the deepest source of the 'ought' that we feel. Beneath all such considerations lie sympathies that are more fundamental than reason, and an apprehension of values as intuitions of reality. That there is something 'in the nature of things' which makes for the apprehension of an ultimate good in what seems to us *right*, no less than in what seems beautiful or true, is just as much a matter of faith as any religious doctrine. In this sense, therefore, as resting upon faith and not merely on experience, morality may be said to find its ultimate sanction in what is also the fundamental reality of religion, call it God or what you will.

3. INTERACTION OF RELIGION AND MORALITY

When in the course of religious evolution the highest object of men's worship was conceived as a universal God of righteousness, who required from worshippers as their chief service that they should deal righteously with their fellows, religion brought to morality not only a heightened sensitivity of conscience but also an enlargement of its scope. Social morality is the code of conduct recognised as desirable between members of a community. Being the embodiment of established custom, it bears the impress of the ordinary conditions of life in the community in question. It has always, therefore, tended to differential treatment as between those who are social equals and those regarded as inferiors—between the sexes, for example, between different classes, and towards those of another country or race. In these respects religion has helped to extend the sense of moral obligation by insistence upon the brotherhood of all as children of one divine Father, who for this reason owe to each other an equal measure of justice and brotherly love. Thus, for example, Christianity has unquestionably done much to promote growth of the moral sense in regard to slavery, by furnishing an added motive for natural impulses of kindness and for curbing ill-treatment and injustice; and by giving the force of religious fervour to denial of the right to enslave others on the ground that they have an inferior moral claim.

So also in regard to the status of women. Religion, it is true, throughout the greater part of history accepted and even intensified the prevalent male attitude towards women as means of use and pleasure, inferiors not posessed of the potentialities inherent in men or of the rights that these conferred. It has usually confined them, in all forms of religious practice, to the lower kinds of service. It has upheld as a religious duty acts and ideas—the Hindu practice of *suttee*, for example—which, apart from its sanction, the moral sense would condemn. But, in spite of all this, religion has also helped to raise the general standard in regard to the treatment of women. By giving sanctity to marriage, for instance, it has done something to assure for them greater protection and security. As with slavery, the Christian doctrine of the equality of all human souls in the eyes of God has tended, however slowly, wherever Christian influences have penetrated, to lessen inequality of treatment and to establish a juster relationship between the sexes. Moreover, in most of the widely extended world-religions amongst objects of worship to whom the highest honour is given are female figures. These are not merely, as in more primitive religions, symbols of fertility and representations of powers of nature or consorts of male deities, endowed by the fancy of myth-makers with terrible or lovely shapes to heighten the romance of their stories; but rather embodiments of maternal love and of qualities in which it is recognised that, in Goethe's words: 'Das Ewig-Weibliche zieht uns hinan.' This is in itself a proof of a development of the moral sense which the higher religions, with their gospel of pity and love, have helped to foster.

All the great religions have given to help of the less fortunate a foremost place in the conduct they enjoin. In the relief of poverty and the care of the sick and helpless, in the provision of almshouses and hospitals, in the spread of education to all classes of the community, votaries of religion have usually led the way. The growth, so marked throughout the Christian era, of sensitivity to needs of this kind has been in no small measure due to the efforts of those who have been inspired by religion and have looked upon service to their fellows as service done to God.

In such ways religion has helped to widen the scope of social morality and to spiritualise and strengthen the sense of justice. It is, however, no less possible to point to ways in which the influence of religion has been a hindrance to the growth of the moral sense rather than a gain. The sanctity of religious tradition, for instance, has often continued to uphold a standard of morality belonging to an earlier age. Unseen powers that were objects of fear and worship to primitive man were conceived by him as beings superhuman in power but often sub-human in morality, since they were free from human limitations and could act as human beings would like to act if not subject to any kind of restraint upon their passions. In primitive myths these beings were shown as doing things that later came to be repugnant to the moral sense and were forbidden in the normal life of the community. But though actions attributed to the gods might be condemned in the accepted moral code, such myths were still regarded by religious conservatism as sacred, and thereby could not but have a detrimental influence on moral growth. Rejection of such teaching has in all ages been one of the objects of religious reform.

So also with practices enjoined by religion. Much of primitive religious ritual had for its object the promotion of fertility of plants and animals on which the community depended for subsistence. To primitive man the surest way to bring about what he desired was the employment of sympathetic magic. When once he had realised the connection between sexual intercourse and the propagation of life, this was the way, he thought, by which the progenitive power of nature could be aroused and its fertility assured. Sexual orgies, therefore, were a part of the religious rites directed to this end. Even when primitive ideas of magic were outgrown and a social code had been established in which sexual promiscuity was discouraged, festivals were kept up at which normal morality was set aside; and in some cults prostitution was long invested with the sanctity of religious service.

Amongst all peoples the strongest of taboos has been that against the shedding of human blood amongst members of the same community, except as a religious rite or in expiation of crime. While the latter exception is still allowed throughout a great part of the civilised world, though with growing doubts as to its justification, the former has long been condemned by the moral sense of mankind. It had originally a similar motive in securing the safety of the community by removal of a source of danger. The sacrifice of priest or king, or of someone embodying the vegetation spirit, was requisite from time to time since the welfare of the community depended on him and he must not be allowed to become old or weak. In the *Golden Bough* Sir James Frazer has traced such ideas and practices in many parts of the world, and their gradual modification as a growing moral sense brought a humanising of traditional custom.[1] But even when this softening process had, in normal times, replaced human sacrifice by other offerings, in a time of special danger the official guardians of religion might declare that the anger of the gods could only be averted and their favour won by an offering of human life, and this, it might be, the life of one whom the worshipper held dearest. Throughout history there have been, even among civilised peoples, occasions when human lives, children most of all, have been offered up in sacrifice although, apart from the sanction of religion, such an action was abhorrent to the moral feeling not only of the more sensitive but of the whole community.

In the treatment of enemies, again, religion has given sanction and added intensity to the inhumanity of war. Complete destruction of men, women, and children could be enjoined as a religious duty, and failure to carry it out denounced as opposition to the divine will.[2] Nor was such savagery at the behest of religion confined to ancient times. Later history also is stained with crimes which religion has countenanced or incited by its fanaticism, such as the destruction by fire and sword of the peaceful community of the Albigenses in the name of religious orthodoxy, and the torture and burning of those accused of heretical doctrines or held to have dealings with evil spirits. It is not difficult to find justification for an indictment of religion as a foremost agency, by claiming divine sanction for the baser human passions, and by giving its support to the crimes and follies of princes and the pride and greed of dignitaries of the church, in retarding moral progress and blunting the moral sense.

It may also be said that the influence of social morality in humanising religion, as concerned not alone with an unseen world but with the relations of ordinary life, has brought certain dangers to religion itself. In this association with mundane affairs there is always a tendency to identify religion with a traditional code of conduct, to claim its support for established distinctions of caste and 'rights' of power

[1] In ancient literature—in the Old Testament, for example, and in the Homeric poems—we can see how earlier records have been worked over at a later time in order to remove mention of human sacrifice and other practices which in a later age could no longer be tolerated.

[2] E.g. the Story of Saul and the Amalekites in 1 Samuel xv.

and property, and thus help to perpetuate, in the name of religion, conditions in which there may be much injustice. Where it has become associated, as it so commonly is, with vested interests and maintenance of the status quo, there is little wonder that in many countries the established church should be identified with oppression, and the feeling towards it, expressed in Voltaire's cry, 'Ecrasez l'infame', translated into action at times when revolt is possible.

Yet another danger lies in the association of religion with a merely negative aspect of morality. There is always a tendency, in reaction against the relaxation of moral restraint that accompanies the growth of wealth and luxury, to exalt asceticism as the highest form of morality. In setting its face against ways of life which tend to degrade humanity, religion is only too apt to insist on the need of repression of the lower impulses rather than on a liberation of the higher. Much of its fervour has, therefore, in all the great religions been diverted to the practice of extreme forms of asceticism. They have had their hermits and saints who have carried this practice to lengths that might well seem beyond the limit of human endurance; and through association, in the minds of those who marvelled at their achievement, of spiritual sanctity with abstention from every kind of pleasure, they have helped to establish an ideal of repressive morality as a necessary part of religion. The Puritanism which regards a great deal of normal life and a wide range of human interests as inconsistent with morality has been intensified by a belief, which religion has fostered, that there is an inherent corruption in human nature, and therefore a virtue in repression for its own sake, which sets the 'thou shalt not' of law above the spontaneity of love. There can be no greater disservice done to either than such an association of religion that is self-centred and lacking in human fellowship with a morality that lessens the sum of human happiness and lowers the level alike of bodily, mental, and spiritual health. Against this there is bound, sooner or later, to be a reaction in which both the religion and the morality associated with it are thrown aside.

4. A MUTUAL NEED

No form that has been taken either by morality or religion can be held to be final. They must continually find modes of expression shaped not merely by tradition, however venerable, but by the need and conditions of each age, with its powers and possibilities, its knowledge and outlook, different from those of the past. And in so doing each can strengthen and enrich the other, for both are modes of the urge to fuller spiritual life. At the same time the union may have its dangers if it means a subordination of either so complete that its claims are sacrificed to those put forward by the other. In all religions reverence for tradition, together with the assumption made by each that to it alone absolute truth and right have been revealed, tends to rigidity and intolerance. Nor is this true only of the creeds of the Churches. In our own time we see how conformity to a particular ideology can be invested with the sanction and fervour of a religion and ruthlessly enforced without regard to claims of the individual conscience.

But the dangers that have been so often exemplified in history are not necessarily inherent in any and every connection between religion and morality. They arise from the narrow and partial forms in which both have found expression. If religion is chiefly concerned with external rites or with an other-world mysticism and if morality is mainly negative or confined to the observance of some traditional code of duties, the union of the two can only make them yet narrower and more rigid. But if they are to be more than this, each has a contribution of value to make. For their full development, indeed, each is in some degree dependent on the other: religion turns to morality for enlargement of its scope and for direction of its practical activities; morality to religion for warmth and intensity of devotion to the highest that we know. No religion can now command assent or retain its hold unless it is concerned with all the relations of human life. And our morality is inevitably the expression of some kind of faith. In the spirit in which we act and in the values that underlie our judgments and are the motive-springs of conduct is shown the faith by which we live; and this, though it may not be formulated in religious terms, is for each of us the essence of religion.

That morality and religion should be in this close relation with one another is no merely pragmatic alliance for mutual support, but has a deeper lying cause in the fact that both have a common principle and a common aim. Each in its own way is a means of giving to life a greater fulness by escape from the limitations of self. Morality begins in recognition of the claims of others and in subordination of self-impulses to those that prompt social conduct and bring satisfaction of social needs. By such conduct the content and interest of experience are immeasurably enlarged. Through participation in the life of others is opened a way of passing beyond the limits of the individual, and in the growth of the moral sense we gain a continually richer apprehension of values in which life is more fully experienced. This is true also of religion, with its recognition of something beyond the immediate world of the senses and the needs of the bodily life. It opens a way of escape from self into the greater reality that it apprehends, a spiritual world in which each individual is one with other selves and with the whole, a world of eternal values towards which life in the material world, blindly at first but by degrees with clearer vision, seeks to move.

Religion is the quest for God and service of the God that it apprehends. In all the great religions an ideal of righteousness has been an integral part of their conception of Godhead, and in obedience to moral law they have found a means of approach to this ideal. They have, that is, first given a definition of the divine in terms of a particular conception of morality, and then have taught that this morality is binding as being an expression of the divine will. By thus subordinating morality to religion they have given it the added force of a religious sanction, but they have also brought to it an element of weakness. For in being made a part of religion it has been made to rest upon a particular system of theology; and then, if that is shaken, the morality based on it falls in ruins. But this does not mean that there can be no helpful connection between them. Morality has its own realm of values into which religion may not enter as dictator to over-rule or repress. But coming as a powerful ally religion can bring added strength and inspiration. For its highest fulfilment morality needs something of the religious spirit and a faith that gives the breath of life to what we do and what we are. Morality is more than an 'ought'. It is not to be satisfied merely by doing one's duty or by doing justice. These may in themselves be cold and of little moral value apart from the spirit in which duty is performed and justice interpreted. An action is not in the full sense moral if done merely as a duty, but only when it is the spontaneous outcome of free will. Morality begins in a sense of 'ought'; but to reach its full development it must pass beyond the constraint of 'ought' into the freedom of love.

There are (we see it more clearly than ever today) two main ways in which escape from the limitations of self can be sought, two contrasted faiths, each with the moral code that it inspires. The one is the 'will to power': enlargement of self, no matter at what cost, having as its aim mastery of every hindrance and every means of power, with knowledge and force as the instruments by which this mastery is to be achieved. But along this way there is no escape: with each expansion self becomes more conscious of limitations and avid of further enlargements. The other is the way of love: transcending self by merging it in other selves and in a larger whole, finding its fulfilment in a common good to be attained by common effort freely given. Both are necessary elements in life as it is. In human institutions at all times there has been some admixture of the two. The will to power has usually been predominant; but it is in the way of love that the great teachers and, dimly and uncertainly, the general consensus of mankind, have seen the main line of spiritual advance.

Of this faith the great religions have for the most part been the standard bearers, and it may seem that any abandonment of their creeds and forms of worship must involve its loss as well. There are those, no doubt, of whom this is true. In giving up dogmas they can no longer hold they turn away also from all that has been associated with them, and thenceforward find the only criterion of morality and the only outlet for an unsatisfied religious sense in the service of the will to power. To what this can lead, when it has no aim beyond itself to direct its energies and decide the means to be employed, we see only too clearly in the world around us. Should it prevail, it would check and turn back the course that can be traced in spiritual evolution hitherto. To meet it there is need of two things: a clear-sighted morality, social and personal, in which power is an aim only for use in the service of love; and a strength of purpose invigorated and maintained by the faith that has inspired all that is best in religion. Moral insight and religious fervour are not to be found only in association with the forms and dogmas of institutional religion; it is only when intellectual integrity is satisfied that they can give expression to our deepest intuitions.

CHAPTER ELEVEN

WORSHIP

1. VISION

IN Chapter VI some account was given of the use, in the liturgies of various religions, of certain common forms of worship—sacrifice, prayer, song, the reading of sacred scriptures, and the performance of sacramental rites—through which man has sought to establish safe and helpful contacts with the unseen world, and to give expression to the responsive feelings and impulses that such contacts have evoked. If worship, as was said at the outset, is an essential element in religion, it is in these feelings and impulses rather than in particular modes of ritual observance that its significance is to be found.

In all worship the basic element is apprehension of something that is not merely greater but is felt to be 'higher' than oneself. Since language was developed in the first place in service of the bodily life, as a means to the satisfaction of bodily needs, it was inevitable that its terms should be representations of objects and events in the external world and of their inter-relations as perceived by our external senses. With growing awareness of an inner life of feeling and thought, a life of the spirit and its needs for which also some expression in language must be found, the simplest way of doing this was to use the same terms and turns of speech to denote, in what may be called the 'picture-language' of metaphor, spiritual experience and inter-relations apprehended by 'inner' senses. For this reason in speaking of the life of the spirit we have to use spatial terms such as 'inner' and 'higher', but with so little trace of the literal meaning that we are hardly conscious of the metaphor.

WORSHIP

Amongst the 'inner' senses in which different modes of spiritual apprehension can be conveniently distinguished—the sense of beauty and the moral sense, for instance—is that which has been called the sense of the 'numinous' or, in a later stage of spiritual evolution, of the 'holy'. At its simplest and as a term to include all its manifestations this sense of a world of spiritual reality has here been called apprehension of the 'Unseen'. This, it must be remembered, includes two meanings, distinguishing, in the first place, another kind of reality from that apprehended through the external senses, and, in the second, what is not yet actual, but only possible, from what exists here and now. In the one meaning it is spiritual reality, in the other, potential or ideal reality. Wherever there is apprehension of a reality of either kind as an element of experience awaking reverence and aspiration and profoundly affecting human life, there is worship in its inner aspect; and in so far as such spiritual apprehension seeks to embody itself in act and purpose, there is worship in its outward aspect.

To speak of the reality thus apprehended as the 'Unseen' is to use a convenient metaphor that allows a growing awareness of its presence to be described as the growth of a faculty of inner spiritual vision, one that has been no less instrumental in the development of man's religious nature than the sense of sight in furthering his physical and mental evolution. The analogy has also a further fitness in the fact that, just as the bodily senses vary in different individuals in their degree of sensitivity, so also is there an immense range of difference in spiritual sensitivity, from a state in which there may seem to be a complete lack of it up to its highest manifestations in those whom mankind reveres as the greatest of artists and saints and the religious leaders in whom their followers have come to see the fullest incarnation of all that they feel to be divine.

Wherever and in whatever degree there is spiritual vision, there is also worship. For, read rightly, the poet's assertion is profoundly true that 'we needs must love the highest when we see it'—if, that is, it is *seen* in its reality, not merely as perceived by the bodily eye but revealed to the inner vision. It is this sense of revelation—the apprehension of a 'higher'—and the complex of feeling (summed in the poet's 'love') which it calls forth that unite in worship, whether it be that of a lover in presence or in thought of the beloved or that of the painter aware of some glory called forth by the play of light, or, at its fullest, the adoration of the mystic lost in his beatific vision. In whatever way it comes, it opens to the inner sense a vision, as in Jacob's dream, of a stairway between earth and heaven, 'and behold the angels of God ascending and descending on it'. In the Old Testament picture-language of myth and legend thoughts, intuitions, impulses, seeming to come from elsewhere and to have a separate being of their own, were thus imaged as messengers from the Unseen; and since, by what is a necessity of language, we still speak of the unseen world as a heaven 'above', there is nothing strange to us in this vision of a stairway by which, though we no longer give them winged forms, such visitants can come and go—thoughts, emotions, volitions, climbing to lose themselves in adoration and thanksgiving, or bringing to us rich blessing of keener spiritual insight, with renewal of hope and courage and strengthening of purpose for whatever service we can give.

To some any such experience is associated with appointed times and places and a customary ritual of worship, as being of divine appointment and alone offering a sure and permitted approach to the Unseen. But the vision is not given only to those who seek it by such means. Some glimpses of it may come at any moment, in a sense of wonder that deepens into awe or leaps into exultation, a heightened sense of values that finds in the moment's experience a worth far beyond itself and makes of it, as in the old legend, 'the gate of heaven'. It can come in ways that may seem far removed from any form of religious experience: in the song of a bird, perhaps, which may just then awaken more responsive feeling than the finest of church music; or when we merely 'stand and stare', and a spray of blackthorn in the hedge may be as much of a marvel as the starry immensities of space; in a sudden solution of some problem in thought or conduct; or in quickened heartbeat at sight or tale of some act of heroism or self-forgetting love—anything that, for what seems a moment of eternity, can enlarge awareness both of sense and spirit may be a porch through which to enter the House of God.

For religion is not concerned with another world separate from ours to which there is but a single authorised way of admission. Though unseen to the bodily eye the world revealed to our inner vision is no less real than the one that, like the air around us without which we cannot live, it surrounds and inter-penetrates. In this 'unseen' world also we live and move and have our being in so far as we have risen from lower evolutionary levels to that of man with his powers and potentialities of fuller life and awareness of values that draw feeling, will, and thought towards a 'higher' than himself. But it is in the world of sense and action that we find the means through which the Unseen is revealed and through which we can take part in the work of spiritual evolution by giving to the spiritual some embodiment in the actual. And this is worship in its widest sense, not confined to any peculiarly 'sacred' setting, but all the nearer to the heart of religion when it does not need initiation into holy mysteries but is the outcome of our common humanity in the daily commerce of life.

But even if thus inherent in human nature, not every kind of worship, any more than every form taken by religion, is necessarily good, either in itself or as a means of good. Worship may be given to an unworthy object or may find its expression in ways that degrade rather than bring enrichment of life, whether through mistaken choice or overmastering circumstances. We know in our own experience how from age to age—if not from hour to hour—our values change with growing clarity or dimming of the inner vision. We know how pressure from without or within can obscure and mislead, making some impulses of the moment stronger than the 'higher' that is seen, or presenting as worthy of our worship what at another time can be recognised for the idol that it is. Such errors warn us how dense are the mists that can change common objects into shapes of wonder whose meaning and value are hard to tell and easy to mistake. It is not some particular manner of its use or certain conditions of attendant circumstance, but spiritual insight that makes worship true. Our prayer must ever be that of the blind men at Jericho, 'that our eyes may be opened'.[1]

2. SERVICE

Worship, then, begins in vision, and on this, clear or obscured and distorted, depends its quality. But in worship, as part of our common experience, there is something more. To some, it may be, that inner vision at its fullest is all in all, satisfying every sense and concentrating every responsive impulse in an adoration that neither needs nor allows

[1] Mat. xx. 33.

any form of outward expression. The Indian Yogi can, it is said, by the practice of his discipline withdraw his inner self from all normal functions of life and attain this height of adoring contemplation; and in the history of religious mysticism there have been, in all ages, those to whom some such supreme and ineffable experience has been granted. But even if this is worship in its purest form, lifting the worshipper, as those who have experienced it aver, out of time into eternity, for the great majority it is not possible (or only, perhaps, at some rare moments) to live at such a height and breathe so rarefied an atmosphere. While we live in a world of time and change which, for better or worse, is affected by what we do, it is not in escape from the needs and conditions of such a world that our worship finds its fullest expression, but rather in seeking to shape these conditions and to embody in the actual something of the higher that it sees.

This is worship in its creative aspect. On its stairway between earth and heaven up which feeling, will, thought, ascend in adoration there are descending angels also, impulses to give expression, in some responsive form of word and action, to the glory to which the eyes of the spirit have been opened, and thus, in however imperfect embodiment, bring something of heaven to earth. Outlet for an urge that is no less instinctive than the adoration evoked in presence of a 'higher' is provided by every religious cult in the rites of worship required of its adherents. Such rites have a double purpose: to do homage to the Unseen Power and thus establish a mutual relationship of what is due, and at the same time to give, in these acts of service, the outward expression of which the worshipper feels need. Liturgy is thus (as the word means) a public form of service, in which homage is paid to the Deity and expression given to the responsive emotions of those who at such times, it is felt, are brought directly into the divine presence.

As a means of such expression it would hardly be possible to overrate the influence on religious evolution of the forms given to worship by association with it of the various arts; or, in return, what a great part religion has had in the development of the arts—dance, song, instrumental music, architecture, sculpture, painting, dramatic and lyric poetry, and epic story in both poetry and prose: all have been pressed into service to give expression to its worship. And rightly, in so far as these are wholehearted responses of the spirit of man to something beyond the immediate satisfaction of material needs, a reaching out to the 'higher' of his inner vision, and not used merely as a drug-intoxication of the senses, or, as so often, for the display of pride and pomp, or become only a matter of routine, empty of feeling, to which no more is given than lip-service or passive assent.

A main purpose of the ritual enjoined by all religions upon the worshipper on such occasions is to deepen the sense of awe on their coming into the divine presence, and to symbolise a fitting attitude of reverent humility, of willing obedience to divinely given law and penitence for past errors and shortcomings. But in all such ritual there is a constant danger that its value may seem to inhere in the outward form apart from what it is intended to express; and it can thus become a bar rather than an aid to spiritual vision. For observance that is only formal is not merely empty of value but a breeder of false values. In the history of all religions it has been shown again and again how easily what is held to give immunity from past wrongdoing can offer a cloak for its continuance; and how strong is the tendency of careful adherence to the letter of the law to become a 'righteousness' of pride and censorious condemnation of other standards of conduct.

But if there is little need to press the point that all forms of worship are of religious value only if prompted or accompanied by a spiritual experience to which they are meant to give expression, the need of regular practice of such forms is insisted upon all the more for this very reason. To go through prescribed acts of worship is the surest way, it is urged, to bring about the desired spiritual response. This is in line with a psychology that sees in emotion an outcome rather than a precondition of instinctive response: we do not, according to this view, resort to violence or evasive action because of anger or fear felt in presence of opposition or danger, but experience these feelings as part of the action taken; and we know how much, at such times, it can help to overcome them if we force ourselves to adopt a kindly tone and a quiet demeanour. And so too with worship. Places and postures associated with devout feeling, familiar cadences of words and music, can contribute to this end and create an environment favourable to spiritual response. But strongly as some may feel such influences on each occasion, more often they tend to be dulled and weakened by repetition; and where the response evoked is merely a reflex without spontaneity of feeling there can be little reality of worship but only, it may be, satisfaction in custom complied with or a duty done.

There is in all organised and formal worship a tendency to become an end in itself, as a due paid to the Deity in whose honour the 'divine service' is performed, and, when thus paid, completed. Against this narrow conception of worship, prophet and reformer have inveighed, declaring all service which expends itself in ceremonial to be of little value in comparison with that which is shown not in acts of formal worship but in the actions of daily life. For this wider conception of worship traditional observances are not to be regarded as a form of service complete in itself, but rather as a means of opening the eyes of the spirit and evoking feeling and will that, besides these immediate outlets given to them, may seek to embody and make actual in the doings and relations of life something of the aspirations thus aroused.

Worship, then, in the full sense of the word—that which is felt to be of greatest *worth*—is not only the vision of the Unseen in which the spirit is lifted in adoration of the higher that it sees, but also the longing to give outward expression to that vision in some creative service, some furtherance of those ultimate values of the spirit which to religion are divine attributes, adumbrations of the transcendent object of its worship. Whatever form this may take, it is no less a 'divine service' (and more truly to be so named) than that associated with special times and places and rites singled out as 'sacred'. If it is given to few to do great creative work in the sphere of thought and knowledge, in the art, or in shaping human relationships, yet there are matters in which all can have some part, however humble. Wherever there is sincerity of word or act, wherever there is a sense of order or an added touch of grace in what is done, there is an act of worship, though it has no 'sacred' setting or intention.

For the 'beauty of holiness' in which the psalmist would have us worship needs no 'holy array' (as was no doubt his meaning) of priests and worshippers in some gorgeous temple ceremonial. It can be seen in the inner integrity and spiritual health that can give to the homeliest features a beauty of expression and stamp of character. To Keats truth and beauty were one; so also to the Greek 'the beautiful' and 'the good' were two ways of naming a quality that was essentially the same. And both were right; for in these modes of spiritual apprehension we see different facets of the same reality, and in whichever way it is revealed to us our response is worship. All the great religions are at one in regarding holiness as the highest attribute of the divine Being to whom worship is offered, and as that which is required of the worshipper, not only in a ritual holiness of approach but, beyond this, in the springs of conduct and the manner of life. Such service of the heart, finding expression not merely in a prescribed ritual but in the daily round of opportunities and challenges, great or small, that life brings to each of us, the greatest of religious teachers have declared to be the truest and most acceptable that man can offer to God. And it is not in a special department of experience, labelled religious, that this service can be given, but most of all in

> *that best portion of a good man's life,*
> *His little, nameless, unremembered acts*
> *Of kindness and of love*

which, in sum, make the greatest contribution both to human happiness and to the life of the spirit.

3. COMMUNION

Besides the adoration which is called forth by vision of a higher and its outward expression in some form of service, there is yet a third aspect of worship in the sense of communion—the 'keyword' of religion, as it has been well called—that it brings, both with the Unseen Reality that is the source of all spiritual value and with one's fellows. As with religion, while the essential character of worship is to be found in a personal relationship with the Unseen, it was in its communal character and as a social agency that it took shape in so wide a variety of cults.

In the most primitive of these, still to be found in communities that have not advanced beyond the tribal stage of social evolution, the sense of dependence upon unseen Powers finds expression in some kind of communal dance giving dramatic presentation to the ends for which their intervention is desired and the means by which their renewed activity is thought to be promoted. Such a ritual performance, having for object the preservation and welfare of the whole community and requiring the fullest participation of all its members, is a potent agency in arousing and maintaining a sense of union so close that the individuality of each was merged in the needs and welfare of the whole; and this sense of unity with one's fellows and subordination of self to its claims has been from the first one of the strongest elements in religion and an essential part of its expression in worship. But with the growth of communities to a size in which a common activity of the whole was no longer possible, it was inevitable that this sense of fellowship should be weakened, or at least narrowed in range, and associated less with acts of worship than with a patriotic response to national danger or with some local or party interest.

For the ritual of worship also enlargement of the community has had a similar disintegrating effect. From some kind of dramatic dance in which all alike took part were developed, under differing conditions, different forms of ritual practised in various cults, but with common characteristics since they arose from similar needs and similar instinctive modes of response. Since all must be done duly, in such a way as to give no offence to the Power approached, such forms would necessarily come to follow a fixed routine; and since this routine was a traditional lore safeguarded by those who, through their special knowledge and the sanctity it gave, alone could conduct it rightly and speak as mouthpiece of the people, what had once been an act of worship in which the community as a whole took part has tended more and more to be something offered on its behalf by officiating priests. Thus today, even in those parts of the ritual in which the whole congregation is required to take part, this is usually done for them by a special choir; thereby, no doubt, enhancing the formal beauty of the service, but making of it less a communal act of worship than an operatic performance in which most of those present become little more than passive spectators.

There is beyond question something more than a merely aesthetic gain in associating with public worship all the dignity and beauty that can be given by the surroundings in which it takes place and by the manner in which it is conducted. But however much the effect of the whole may thus be heightened and a deeper impression made on the individual worshipper, there is inevitably some loss of that sense of communion with fellow-worshippers which is most fully given by participation in a common activity. In so far as it is no longer itself the expression of such a sense of communion and does not in turn help to heighten and extend it, any form of public worship has lost a great part of its value; and this is one reason why the instinctive need for its satisfaction now turns to other kinds of experience in which that satisfaction can be found.

However much deplored by those who see in this a weakening in the hold of religion, it must not be overlooked that the loss of interest in public worship is due also to another reason, and is not merely a sign of indifference but itself an outcome, even if largely unconscious, of religious development from a communal to a more personal response to the claims of the Unseen: from an observance, that is, of ritual acts on which the safety and welfare of the community were held to depend to a recognition that these have little to do with the reality of religion. From the days of the great Hebrew prophets onward reformers have insisted that religion is not a matter of forms and ceremonies, and that worship has little value unless it is a personal response, showing itself not in what may be only empty observances but in the whole manner of life. While recognition of this truth has marked a great advance in spiritual evolution, the very fact that in every age it has been necessary to repeat such a warning has tended to bring also a weakening of belief in any kind of formal worship and in any religion that makes such worship binding on its adherents.

Insistence on the personal nature of worship may seem, in making it a matter of purely individual rather than of communal concern, to see in it a means of bringing man into closer communion with God, but without effect, either outward or inward, on his relationship with his fellow men. In all worship that comes from the heart the central experience is the sense of being in presence of a 'higher', whether this 'higher' is thought of as some glimpse of spiritual Reality or—all such terms are attempts to put into words a conception that transcends the limitations of language—is felt to be a divine Being, with whom the worshipper enters into communion when the individual will is, as it were, caught up into a higher will with which it is felt to be at one.

Such communion of will, with the release from all anxiety and doubt, and the strength to meet whatever may come, that are given by the sense of oneness with a divine purpose, is a height of spiritual experience to which most of us can only rarely attain. Only those most fully endowed with religious genius have been able to live constantly at this height, drawing from it a spiritual power which all who come under its influence felt to be a manifestation of God in human form and act. But even to those to whom living at this height is not possible there are two ways in which, at times and in some degree, such sense of communion may come. One is the way of resignation. At an hour when one is face to face with defeat and what seems an end of all one's hopes; or standing beside the grave of one deeply loved, lost, perhaps, before a richly opening promise could reach fulfilment; or in imagination beside one's own, made conscious of how much has been unfinished, how little even begun; at such moments one can only bow the head—and trust. The other way can be found in participation, in which the sense of oneness with a higher will comes not through surrender of self but when all one's powers are gathered and devoted to some aim felt to give part in the unending work of creation by which life, material and spiritual, is enriched and raised to higher levels.

In such participation we are not only coming, as we feel, into closer communion with God but are also in closer communion with our fellows. The adoration of the mystic, like the withdrawal from all the distractions of existence that is the goal of the Buddhistic endeavour, is an experience that, however intense and satisfying, may tend rather to separate him from his fellows than to unite him more closely with them. But if, as those have held whom we look upon as greatest of religious and ethical teachers, the highest of spiritual gifts and the chief factor in spiritual evolution is love, it is not only in rising to greater heights of adoring love of God that this finds its fulfilment but in the realisation in our human life of loving-kindness and human fellowship. Here, then, communion with the Unseen and with our fellows is at one, in a worship showing itself not in acts of homage to a Heavenly King but in all that can help to establish a Kingdom of Heaven upon earth.

CHAPTER TWELVE

'THESE THREE'

1. RETURN OR RENEWAL?

IN earlier chapters we have seen something of the origins of religion and of the influences, geographical, economic, and historical, that helped to shape its various developments. We have also traced in outline the rise and general character of the chief world-religions, and have seen that, with their individual differences, they have certain features in common and have followed a similar course of development. In all there is a mingling of primitive ideas and the highest spiritual experience. Crude beliefs and practices have lingered on as superstitions or have been maintained as traditionally sacred long after they had become unacceptable to later thought and feeling. And in all a tendency to rigidity and formalism has overlaid with dogma and ritual the spiritual insight of their founders. In none is it possible to see, at any stage of its development, something to be accepted as final in its presentation of truth or in its forms of worship.

What then—to return to our starting-point—are we to do at a time when there is so widespread a weakening of religious belief and abandonment of religious observance? Are we to regard this as a sign that spiritual evolution has come to a dead end and that religion has ceased to have, for all but a minority, any vital meaning and vital need? Or are we to see in this present tendency a temporary warping of human nature, a disease that may be made to yield to treatment, an aberration from which recall is possible to the old ways that alone can bring spiritual health? Or may it be that it is not so much a decadence of religion that we are witnessing as a turning-point when it has to find expression in ways more closely in touch with modern needs and new conditions?

To the present writer there seems to be little room for doubt as to the answer to such questions. It is not that religion has ceased to be a permanent element in human nature, or that this has suffered a sudden deterioration making it insensitive to a spiritual need; but rather that beliefs and observances upheld by the Churches as essentials of religion no longer command the assent or satisfy the requirements of an age very different from ages in which these beliefs and observances could be accepted as divinely given truth and as bringing to the worshipper assurance of salvation. It would be as easy to restore feudal ideas and institutions in a present-day democracy as to return to what is still largely a medieval presentation of religion, with its attitude of mind that looked back rather than forward, and its claim that only in unquestioning acceptance of its traditional rites and doctrines could the true meaning and true use of life be found. Such an attitude inevitably provokes the counter-feeling that, if that is religion, it is a worn-out mummery which, except as an occasional matter of social obligation or display, can be treated with indifference.

Yet in an age of social upheaval and moral confusion like the present, when long-established guides of conduct are discredited and old ideals apt to be dismissed as illusions; an age in which so much of what seemed permanently fixed in the ordering of life and in fundamental beliefs and values now lies in ruins, leaving a waste land where the spirit of man, looking for what may offer shelter and security, sees little, except perhaps some 'ideology' of revolutionary change, to awaken faith and hope—in such an age there is, more than ever, need of religion to give conscious and—of still greater moment—subconscious motive and direction to aim and effort in our life today. If, then, as presented by the Churches, it has lost its hold, and much in the beliefs and ritual which they declare to be its true embodiment has, in our modern world, as little meaning and as little likelihood of revival as the Ptolemaic astronomy and the pretensions of astrologers and alchemists, is it possible to see in what form religion can now find renewal?

Put in this way, the question is one that only a dogmatist could answer with assurance, since what is needed is release, not further imprisonment of the spirit in some fixed form of creed and observance. But there are at least certain postulates required for making a practical approach to the problem.

'THESE THREE'

1. If religion is to be a living force, moving all sorts and conditions of men, the faith that underlies and inspires it is not to be thought of as concerned with matters of theological and metaphysical disputation, to be accepted on authority because beyond the reach of ordinary intelligence, but with values of the spirit that can, in some degree be felt by all. And it will find expression not in any narrow ecclesiasticism but in the whole field of human activity, as a humanism that recognises both the material and spiritual needs and potentialities of man's nature, and has for its aim that he 'may have life, and may have it more abundantly'.

2. The main line of religious evolution has been from a communal obligation, to be satisfied by the performance of certain external rites, to recognition of the personal and inward aspect of religion as apprehension of spiritual values that call forth a response of the spirit not merely in acts of formal worship but in the deeper springs of motion and conduct. In such response thought, feeling, and will all have part, and only when all give full assent, and can give it freely, is religion more than an empty profession or a blind fanaticism.

3. Though it is not to insistence on acceptance of this or that form of words or on conformity to this or that set of observances that we must look for the renewal of religion, that does not mean that there is nothing we can do to further this end. In any community—home, school, nation, whatever it may be—there are an accepted way of life and principles, implicit in its various relationships, which are instilled by training and subconsciously absorbed in the give-and-take of daily experience. All who feel the need of religion as a motive-force and guide in life must wish to see it included in the training that is given, but rather —if it is something other than doctrinal and ritual obligation that we have in mind—by example and experience than by professedly 'religious' instruction. As with primitive man, so also with each of us, it is in social relationships and as matter of social concern that religion has its earliest development. In the home, if it is a good one, is its surest beginning, for there is the source of the deepest and most lasting impressions. Next to the influence of such a home (and, for many, having to make up for what was there lacking) is that of school. This, however, is to be taken in no narrow sense but to include all means of training; for it is not by class-teaching of

'divinity' that religion is instilled but by the spirit that pervades the whole of the school life, in the teaching of every subject, in the relationship established, in the values it upholds and the outlook that it gives. There, rather than in the Churches, we may look for the renascence of a religion which is not a matter of external forms but a growth from within.

4. Refurbishing of old rites and a more vivid presentation of old doctrines cannot restore to them the old sanctity and credence. Yet those who advocate religious continuity by such means are so far right that, to be a living growth, our religion must have roots in established habits of thought and feeling. For us of the Western world the greater part of our mental and spiritual background and our highest ideals are derived from a millennium and a half of Christian tradition, and it is from this soil that any fresh growth must come. To allow of such growth there must be much cutting away of what is dead in the tradition and in the forms in which it has clothed itself. It is not in a theology compounded of Hebrew myth, Jewish eschatology, and Greek metaphysic, or in observances derived from Mosaic ritual and 'mystery' cults, that we can hope to find what our time needs, but in the Christian ethic and in the spirit that has inspired all that is best in a Christian way of life; not, that is, by starting from the outside, with insistence upon the necessity of particular rites and formulations of belief (serving, with most, only to choke and hinder growth from within), but if, not only at times and in ways kept separate from other concerns of life, something of that spirit finds expression in the whole social environment as well as in our teaching.

To those to whom religion implies a hierarchic structure, with its orthodoxies of doctrine and observance, such an indirect approach must seem, in its omission of what is to them of so much importance, to be merely the negation of religion. Yet is it not nearer than any pomp of gorgeous ceremonial and thunders of an Athanasian creed to the meaning of religion as taught by one to whom the form mattered little, the in-dwelling spirit was all in all, and worship of the God who 'is spirit' was to be (so he is recorded to have said to the woman of Samaria[1]) 'neither in this mountain nor in Jerusalem, but in spirit and truth'?

To the greatest of missionaries who spread his teaching, three

[1] John IV. 21, 24.

things—faith, hope, and love—were the essential characteristics, both as outcome and as sustainment, of the Christian spirit and way of life. And these are what, more than ever, is needed in our world today.

2. 'PROVING OF THINGS NOT SEEN'

When, at his trial, Jesus said that his mission was to 'bear witness unto the truth', Pilate dismissed the subject with the contemptuous retort 'What is truth?' To the harassed man of affairs it was not a question of ultimate realities but of expediency. Yet, as the event showed, the question can never be so dismissed. Each age and each individual has to find, even if subconsciously, some answer; and the answer that is found, whether formulated in a creed or not, gives to the life of each its religious basis.

To philosophers truth may be something abstract and universal: but as such it has no meaning to the seeker for truth as a guide in actual life. To him it is always something tentative in answer to questions that he puts to himself and to his surroundings, something to be brought to the test of actual experience.

In its narrowest meaning truth is accuracy of some particular statement. A statement is true when its words and their meaning correspond with objective fact. There is a truth, that is, of observation and interpretation—the truth of everyday experience and of experimental science—resting on the evidence of the senses. But it must also contain no contradiction with itself or with other accepted facts and with the whole body of knowledge obtained by sense-experience or inferred from it by reasoning. There is also, that is, a truth of logic, imposed on sense-experience by the mind—the truth that is the concern of abstract science.

Both kinds of truth rest upon certain assumptions that we cannot prove but take for granted. There could be no certain knowledge of the external world unless we assume the continuity and rationality of its processes: that events, for instance, occur in fixed sequences, that like causes produce like results, and that the laws of nature are in some accord with the laws of thought. And we could have no coherent experience at all if we do not also assume the continuity and rationality of our own existence and its psychological processes.

Thus truth and all possibility of attaining it rest upon intuitions, confirmed by experience but otherwise incapable of verification—in other words on faith.

If this is true even of our knowledge of the external world with its material supplied by the evidence of the bodily senses, so also it is true of the apprehension, through an inner sense of values, of another kind of reality which is the fundamental experience in religion. In their intuitions of reality both science and religion rest upon faith; but whereas science, once its premises are assumed, can then ignore them and proceed 'by sight', religion, being concerned with the Unseen, must continue to 'walk by faith'. Thus religion has always seemed to be more of a revelation than other modes of apprehension, and its intuitions have claimed the authority of 'thus saith the Lord'. But like all our modes of apprehension they need the confirmation of experience. Intuition is, in itself, no more infallible than sense-experience or reason. Even if we could put complete trust in the findings, so far as they go, of any of these means of reaching truth, there is no warrant for supposing that the human mind, for all its marvellous achievements, is capable of comprehending the full answer to the questions it seeks to put as to the nature of the universe, the meaning of existence and the goal of spiritual evolution.

We may believe that in the intuitions of religious genius we find the nearest approach that man has yet made to an answer to such questions; but, as in the findings of science so also here, it is mere presumption to assert that we have a complete and final solution of the mysteries with which we are surrounded, or that, if we believe religion to bear witness to the truth, every assertion made in its name is to be accepted as true. There are conditions with which a religious belief must comply. If it is to continue to be accepted and to be a living force in the lives of those who hold it, it must not only be felt to be true in all its implications but must not contain anything irreconcilable either with reason or experience. It must conform, that is, like other convictions on which action is to be based, to the normal criteria of truth: it must be in accordance with facts, so far as these are known to us; it must be coherent with the rest of our knowledge and beliefs; and it must prove itself valid in actual experience, in supporting and enlarging life on its higher levels.

'"Faith," as Dr. Inge has often said, "begins in an experiment and ends in an experience."'[1] We must dare, that is, to stake action on our intuitions of value, and thus bring them to the test of experience. If we do not do so, what we may call our faith is only acceptance of convention or an emotional attitude caught by sympathy. Not that we can get away from the influence of our social environment, or from our racial inheritance and the 'second nature' shaped by our upbringing. But while these all help to determine our beliefs, there is something more fundamental in the sincerity with which we hold them. This we cannot take ready-made whether from any person or religious body or sacred book. We may feel the need of external support to give assurance of certainty; but spiritual fulfilment is not to be had by jettisoning free will. We cannot escape the need to judge for ourselves where help is to be found, and by whom it can best be given.

Faith, then, is for each of us ultimately a personal matter. It is our intuitive certainty—the clearer in proportion as it is accepted with the concurrence of all our powers of judgment and strengthened by our own experience and that of those in whom we feel most trust—of a spiritual reality apprehended in our highest values; the sense of a world which lies beyond the actual, not as a mirage of the imagination but as a potentiality calling us to take our part in its actualisation. Vision, conviction, courage, these are the characteristics of faith. Except to its vision the world of spiritual reality, here and hereafter, is unseen. We can only go forward, like those moving in darkness, trusting to our ultimate values as fixed stars to guide us and to the narrow circle of light thrown on our way by the torch of knowledge. To doubts and warnings that the quest is hopeless and the goal too remote for creatures so weak, stumbling, and selfish, to attain—even if mankind is not destined to be cut off by the inevitable end that must some day come to our planet—faith opposes its conviction that such immensities of power as have gone to the making of humanity, and such potentialities of love as its spiritual evolution has revealed, cannot have been all for nothing; whatever the fate of our earth and of ourselves, that real world remains. Meanwhile, here and now, the quest is ours and must not fail because, like that object of the poet's scorn 'chi fece per viltate il gran rifiuto', we have not the courage to play our part.

Faith is deeper and more central in human nature and experience

[1] Canon Bezzant in *Aspects of Belief*.

than the intellectual acceptance of any creed in which it can be formulated. An organised system of belief is the product of the intellect, and can therefore be submitted to the critical examination of reason: but faith springs from that deeper region of the mind where thought and feeling are not differentiated. In its essential quality it is one with the sense of values which underlies all experience; it becomes the fundamental characteristic of religion when there is apprehension of a spiritual reality as the source and sum of our highest values. Such a faith holds to the assurance, in spite of all that seems to deny or cast doubt upon it, that beauty and truth, justice and love are the very soul of things, the living core of reality; and that it is for these and towards these that the universal process moves. Yet not as a preordained and inevitable process in which we have no part. Far as it passes beyond our comprehension, we cannot believe that we are only spectators of the stupendous drama of existence, or no more than motes drifting blindly and to no purpose at the mercy of each chance current. Faith holds that in the vast web of interrelated workings our participation not only forms a part of the pattern but has some power of shaping the pattern as we will. It is for us, therefore, so far as is in our power, to shape it in accord with our faith. Thus, in the language of religion, we can help to bring nearer the Kingdom of God.

Whatever the Power that works in the universe may be, one thing is certain—it is creative. We feel ourselves most in accord with it, sharing most fully in its work, when what we do is itself constructive, as attempt to make an ideal actual. When faith is most living it is no merely emotional attitude towards the mystery of the universe, but a forward leap of the spirit, an urge to express, in terms of human life, the values that we recognise as highest. Wherever there is this living faith, there, in any form it may take, will be religion. At one time it may be enfeebled with doubts and disappointments; at another it will burn with vigour of life renewed, gaining (as we may hope) with the growth of knowledge clearer vision of the purpose it sets before itself, and greater mastery of the means by which this purpose may be realised.

3. 'ASSURANCE OF THINGS HOPED FOR'

It will not have escaped the reader that, in what has been said of faith, something more than faith has been assumed. As the Apostle saw, faith alone is not all that is needed for a religion that is to be not merely submission to a divine will but also the fullest and most vigorous human fellowship. There can be a faith that is merely negative, that apprehends the ultimate reality as something so vast and so remote as to be indifferent to our values, or so bound and determined by unalterable law as to be unaffected by our strivings. Such a faith may have for outcome an attitude of fatalism, accepting all that comes in a spirit of resignation or stoical endurance, since effort either to escape or alter it is alike useless. Or its attitude may be one of pessimism, in which action, if not wholly inhibited by despair, is weakened by being undertaken without hope. For in all activity the strongest of agents for bringing about the purposed end is belief in the possibility of its attainment; doubt of such possibility reinforces all that tends to bring the expected failure. For a faith that is to be creative of good as yet unachieved there is need of hope as well.

All our instinctive desires carry with them what may be termed a biological confidence—we take for granted that they can, given suitable conditions, obtain their natural satisfaction. Were it not so they could not have been established and become instinctive. Something of this same confidence we carry over into the realm of spiritual desires. If not, like our instincts, necessary for physical survival, they are, in fact, no less so for the fuller life of which we have become conscious; they have been developed in us as the outcome of living on this spiritual level. That is the basis of hope in relation to the whole realm of experience in which we walk by faith rather than by sight.

It is from lack of such hope that the present age is suffering. Having lost the old comforting assurance of religious certainty, and with it the codes of conduct that had a religious sanction, the modern spirit is at a loss; it does not know in what it can put its trust or where it shall turn for guidance. The hopefulness of the Victorian age, with its liberal ideals and belief in the innate goodness and perfectibility of human nature, and in the inevitability of moral advance as the accompaniment of economic and political progress and the spread of education, has foundered in the shocks of war and outbreaks of ruthless savagery that have given the lie (or so it may appear) to all its easy assumptions. Ideals that were not realised have come to seem not merely useless but deceptions, the outcome only of empty hopes; after their loss, so it seemed, it would be folly to form any ideal or to let any hope be a guide to purpose. And so for many there is little, beyond satisfaction of the moment's impulses, that seems worth attempting. The spirit wanders in a desert in which distinctions of right and wrong are blurred and the old virtues no more than a mirage; and with conviction and hope much also of the joy of life is lost.

That there is any meaning in life beyond the transient satisfaction, so far as a callous environment will allow, of our immediate needs; that good—what we feel and what we seek as such—has any function or any value in the universe beyond ourselves; that there is in evolution, organic and psychological, anything more than a blind mechanical process, or any spiritual end towards which it moves—these and the like are matters, not of knowledge such as we can have of the external world, but of faith. Of faith and of hope; for where a better and a worse are alike possible of acceptance, and where our choice between them is a factor, as it seems, in helping to realise the one or the other in actual experience, it is gratuitous folly to accept the worse. It is true that our hopes, like our beliefs, must be brought to the test of reason and experience, for only so can they become serviceable for practical ends. But that is not to say that hope, any more than faith, is an illusion which cannot be trusted; or that a faith which dares to affirm and trust its hopes is thereby of necessity less true than one which doubts and denies.

To each of us his own experience is real. With Descartes he can say, 'Cogito ergo sum'—I can think and feel, and in that awareness I exist. Since in our own experience there is not anything more real than our apprehension of values, why should we doubt its certainty that they are part of a reality beyond ourselves? To the faith that, besides the world revealed by the senses, there is an 'unseen' spiritual reality, hope brings its added assurance that at the core of this reality is good. In both the seen and the unseen, we feel, is something that is responsive to our needs. The universe, for all its vastness, is not utterly indifferent, and for all its incomprehensibility, not wholly unintelligible. Since, like our outward sense, our powers of inner apprehension have developed as a part of its processes and in response to its challenge, it cannot be wholly irrational or exempt from moral law. Why not dare then, hope adds, to trust that evolution is itself no meaningless process in its successive emergences of organic life and mind and spiritual values, but points the way to something higher still? For us, at least, experience has a meaning; this life of ours, as Keats put it, 'a vale of soul-making', if by soul we mean human personality in quest of its highest values. What other ends this stupendous scheme of things may serve, we cannot guess. We can hardly in our conceit suppose that it exists solely for us any more than that we exist for the sake of the germs we harbour. But since we have been brought thus far, hope bids us trust that in spiritual evolution we have a clue to the mystery and a guide for effort.

Of the unseen reality that gives meaning to life we cannot have the kind of certainty given by knowledge, fallible enough at best, which is based on our limited powers of sense-experience and intellect. But we have the deeper-lying certainty of faith; and faith is strongest and fullest of inspiration in its working when it is bright with hope. In the greatest things of life we must dare to act—as we do in the practical affairs of every day—not only *as if* life has a meaning, but as if that meaning is in accord with our values, with the highest values of the spirit no less than the values of the senses.

But if we do, it may be said, is not this to make of religion what some hold it to be, no more than a wish-fulfilment? Is it not to cheat ourselves with an illusion that things are not so bad as they appear, and that, in the end at least if not now, all will be well and we shall 'live happily ever after'? If the appeal is to reason, we must admit that it may be so. It may be that in this, as in our youthful dreams and ambitions, Nature for her own purposes sees to it that the stimulus of hope is ever renewed, so that we may be willing to keep on and undertake the tasks required of us. Yet why should we suppose that in this perpetual renewal of hope there is no other meaning, and that Nature's purpose is all a cheat? While it is foolish to act on assumptions that have no ground except our wishes, it is still more foolish not to act, where alternatives are possible, upon the one that better satisfies our sense of values, that makes more demand upon creative effort, and gives to life more meaning and more worth. Even if there can be no other certainty, if all the earlier aids to faith are stripped away, and if hope is left, as in the Victorian picture, blindfold and listening to the one string that remains, it is none the less wise

> *to hope till hope creates*
> *From its own wreck the thing it contemplates.*

Just as in our sense-impressions we have, in practical matters, sufficient guarantee of the existence of a sensible world that is in relation with our physical needs, so also in our intuitions of value we have assurance of a spiritual reality that is good. If we seek a guarantee that this is not merely a wish-illusion, but that the fundamental nature of things and the ultimate meaning of life are good, is it not there for all to see—philosopher as well as artist, the man in the street no less than the Saint—in the beauty that is, so to speak, thrown in as a free gift, over and above the ordinary traffic of utility, in the whole range of nature from the starry heavens to the tiniest flower or diatom, and in the art of man's creation? In a world in which the urge of being must find expression in beauty, faith is not without warrant for its hope.

It is right, then, that hope and with it joy should be a characteristic of religion. Like beauty joy is a sign of full and vigorous life, the outcome and accompaniment of health in the exercise of natural function, in the satisfaction of needs and in meeting the challenges that life brings. This is no less true of spiritual than of physical activity, and of spiritual than of bodily and mental health. There is something at fault with a religion that does not bring joy; still more at fault if it turns a sour face on the gladness of life, or imagines that good can be done in a grudging or bitter spirit. Not that joy is dependent on what is pleasant, any more than beauty is the same as prettiness. There is a stern and terrible beauty, and a beauty of tragedy that touches the utmost heights and depths of experience; so too there can be joy in hardships and danger, a joy even of the martyr at the stake. One of the surest marks of religion is its power to reveal the spiritual beauty in experience and transfigure the actual with the radiance of the spirit.

Joy is, in essence, active, the emotional tone of the creative urge. Hope and joy have little in common with the passive endurance and resignation which have sometimes been upheld as the aim of religion. There are times when endurance is the only course, and resignation the wisest frame of mind. But it is a narrow conception of religion that would make of these the crown of human endeavour. Stoicism, it is true, like the Buddhist longing to escape from the wheel of active existence and the Christian or Mohammedan resignation that is content to say 'Thy will be done', has been associated in deeply religious natures with nobility of character and with splendid achievement; but what they achieved was due rather to a passion for truth or justice or to pity and love than to a philosophy which enjoined passive acceptance as the wisest attitude towards experience. In the early days of Christianity what struck their contemporaries as the most distinctive mark of those who followed the new Way was the joyousness of their attitude towards life and all that it might bring. This joyousness was the outcome of a sense of new life giving vigour to all they did, and of a fellowship with others that must find expression in every kind of active helpfulness. So it is always. Love and creative activity are the springs of joy; a religion that does not show itself in these has little of the fulness of life. Religion will have most motive-force and inspiration when its faith is glad with the hope that seeks to create a heaven upon earth.

4. 'THE GREATEST OF THESE'

With faith and hope Paul included love as third essential in the three-fold response of our nature to the apprehension of spiritual reality. In love he saw the very core of the religion which he had come to know in his own experience and burned to make known to the whole world. And he was right. Faith and hope alone are not enough; a religion may have these and yet be a curse. Faith fired by assurance of victory may be no more than the fierce zeal of the fanatic who subordinates every consideration, not only of expediency and well-being but of justice and humanity also, to the triumph of his cause. And the joy that springs from creative effort can accompany all output of evergy that satisfies the desire for mastery and gives a sense of power. A zeal that turns to persecution and finds delight in cruelty has in all ages been one of the ways in which religious emotion has found outlet. We see it at work in the service of the ideologies which, in so much of the world today, take the place of religious creeds. Religion with all its possibilities of good has possibilities of evil too, all the greater the more passionate its faith, if together with faith and hope there is not also love as its main motive and guide.

Does this condition attached to it seem, perhaps, to narrow and weaken religion? If we think only of love in its commonest usage as expressing some kind of sex-emotion, a religion of love might seem to be no more than one in which an emotional state, sexual in origin, found some form of orgiastic or mystic satisfaction. But an emotional state of this kind is only one aspect of love. In its full meaning is included every kind of impulse that is not self-regarding, every relationship in which self-interest is merged in a sense of something greater and more satisfying—between parents and children, between friend and friend, between fellow-workers, between the individual consciousness and all in which it finds its highest values. It is sympathy, compassion, protection, trust, reverence, admiration, the reaching out of the human spirit to all that is felt to be lovely, in our fellow-beings, in the world of events and potentialities by which we are surrounded, and in whatever spiritual reality we apprehend beyond them. So far from narrowing religion, in love alone can it find its full meaning and means of expression. There is in the New Testament no more comprehensive statement of the meaning of religion than the saying that God is love; nor could faith and worship be summed in wider terms than as love of God and of our fellow-men.

There are those who hold, with Nietzsche, that to insist on love as its essential quality is to emasculate religion, to make of it only a refuge for the weak and spiritless and a consolation for the unhappy, rather than an inspiration for the strong and masterful to take control of their destiny and shape human life into something grander than it has yet attained, no matter at what cost to those who cannot rise to such heights. There is here a counter-ideal of religion, having for its main object and the means through which it works not love but power. The pursuit of power may take many forms. It may disguise itself in an outward garment of ecclesiasticism, as doing honour to God in magnifying an office or a cult; or of humanitarianism, in promoting the well-being of mankind; or it may be nakedly directed to personal or national aggrandisement and imperial domination. Whatever its professed aims may be, there is in the exercise of unrestricted power, as all history has shown—and never more clearly than today—a corrupting influence that brings spiritual deterioration to those who can no longer be on terms of equality with others, and who have lost the human fellowship without which religion is no more than a cancer in the life of the spirit.

There is indeed an aspect of the pursuit of power which is of immense value to mankind—the quest of knowledge, and of skill in its use, which gives continually growing mastery over our surroundings and over ourselves. But the knowledge and mastery thus to be obtained are not in themselves an end, even if scientists and practical men may so regard them, but only a means to the spiritual ends in which the fullest life is to be found. And so an age which seeks its spiritual sustenance and realisation of its values in science and in the mechanisation of life is inevitably dissatisfied. It is aware, at least subconsciously, of a lack of purpose and direction, and the more ready, therefore, to try any nostrum or to follow any cause that seems to offer the spiritual satisfaction for which it longs.

This is a reason why so many of the young and ardent turn to Communism as offering a faith freed from the outworn trappings of religion, and a way of life that promises equality of opportunity to all and gladness of common effort for a common end, and thus giving to it an appeal that is essentially religious. The summing up of its basic principle as 'from each according to his ability, to each according to his need',[1] was that of practical Christianity in its early Apostolic stage. But whatever its ideal, it is in actual working that the claims of any faith, religious or social, must be judged; and one that is rigidly set about with dogmas to be accepted without question, and that demands, with service, subordination not only of intellectual judgment but of conscience, is perpetuating the worst evils of religion in the past.

Whatever form religion may now take, into whatever channel its fervour may be directed, there are two needs that it must satisfy: the one (of which the challenge of Communism is itself a proof) that it must neglect none of the activities and needs of life as lying outside its sphere; and the other (of which, in its methods of government, Communism in practice is the negation) that all individual potentialities are of like spiritual worth. Differences of ability and experience, and therefore differences of function, there must always be; but in such differences there is no ground for inequality of treatment or for

[1] The true form, though in the present 'intermediate' stage 'to each according to his work', is substituted.

denying to any the opportunity for the fullest development and use of his powers of which he may be capable. A religion of which fellowship is an essential principle will make for equality of social and economic opportunity and treatment, to take the place of competing interests between individuals and classes and nations. If it looks to the future rather than to the past, it will seek to do away with conditions that are a bar to the further ascent of humanity. Religion is only stultifying itself and betraying its trust if it does not make the conscience of the community more sensitive to all exploitations of the labour and lives of others, and to any assumption of a right to secure well-being and happiness at the cost of their degradation; and if it does not turn against war, and against the causes, economic and psychological, that lead to war, the passionate enthusiasm that inspired religious wars in the past.

But equality of opportunity and due observance of the rights of others are not all. Justice, with its weighing of claims and care for what is due, is a prime requisite in social relationships; but alone it lacks the crowning grace of human fellowship. As with morality, the 'thou shalt not' of law, while it can prevent hindrances to freedom and equality, in itself takes us nowhere. Justice, like the 'ought' of duty, is a cold and narrow rule of life apart from the generosity and warmth of love. While duty looks back to some established right, love leaps forward to greet possibilities descried by the spirit in its moments of clearest vision. In its fulness of apprehension and in its spontaneity of impulse love, as those who have reached the greatest height of spiritual development have taught, at once fulfils and replaces moral law.

It is in this spontaneity of feeling, in which utility and reward have no conscious place, that the religious sense has so close an affinity with the sense of beauty. Just as beauty, in so far as we are aware of it in any of its manifestations, makes instant appeal to us in proportion to the depth and range of our apprehension, so also does religion in its twofold aspect of love of God and love of man. 'We needs must love the highest when we see it.' It is in the seeing that we differ, and so to each of us 'God' has a different meaning. As with a sense of beauty that is only contemplative and does not seek some creative embodiment in the daily needs and surroundings, so also love of God may have but little substance and actuality if it is merely mystical and other-worldly, and does not find expression in an active love of our fellows.

Those are the true religious teachers who in their own lives have manifested the certainty of their faith in an unseen spiritual reality, and the depth and fulness of their love for their fellow men. 'Founders and reformers of religions, mystics and saints,' as Bergson says,[1] 'obscure heroes of moral life whom we have met on our way and who are in our eyes the equal of the greatest, they are all there: inspired by their example we follow them as if we were joining an army of conquerors: they have . . . raised humanity to a new destiny.' To tune our spirit to something of that certainty of faith and that intensity of feeling is the function of religion. To some it is given to have direct apprehension of new spiritual truth, and to embody it for others in their lives and in their teaching. For most it is only possible to reach, through them, a lower height, to catch something of the truth they saw and of the love with which they were filled. Not that we are bound to think in all ways as they thought, or to act as they acted; still less to accept the legends that surround them or the doctrines and practices that have been promulgated in their names. But in their example and in the spirit of their teaching we see something of the meaning of religion; and however different the ways in which, in a changing world, it may find expression, mankind will not cease to honour them or to draw inspiration from their teaching and example.

And most of all from those in whose teaching and example love was shown to be the supreme motive and fulfilment of religion, at once the end it seeks and the means by which its purpose is to be attained. It is because, in the teaching of its Founder and in the lives of its truest adherents, love—the love of God and of one's fellows—is its central principle, that Christianity, from its humble beginnings as the faith of a despised and persecuted sect, has proved itself the strongest and the most universal of religions. In this way it has done more than any to leaven civilisation, permeating with its influence the outlook and conscience of mankind, and not only among those that have been its professed adherents. Theological doctrines and ecclesiastical institutions lose their meaning and their hold; but it is the spirit, not the form, that gives life, and has still its chief work to do in the fuller realisation, in all the concerns of life, of its message of faith and hope and love.

[1] In *The Two Sources of Morality and Religion.*

INDEX

(Names of supernatural and mythical beings and titles of books and literary collections are given in italic type)

16

INDEX

INDEX

Printed in the United States
by Baker & Taylor Publisher Services